Wings *over the* Western Front

The First World War Diaries of Collingwood Ingram

Wings *over the* Western Front

The First World War Diaries of Collingwood Ingram

Edited by Ernest Pollard and Hazel Strouts

DAY BOOKS
OXFORDSHIRE

ISBN 978 0953 22139 4

A catalogue record for this book is available from the British Library

First published by Day Books, 2014

Printed in the United Kingdom by the Information Press, Eynsham, Oxfordshire

Day Books, Orchard Piece, Crawborough, Charlbury, OX7 3TX, UK
www.day-books.com

Contents

'In those dark days I found some support in the steady progress unchanged of the beauty of the seasons. Every year, as spring came back unfailing and unfaltering, the leaves came out with the same tender green, the birds sang, the flowers came up and opened, and I felt that a great power of Nature for beauty was not affected by the War. It was like a great sanctuary into which we could go and find refuge.'

Sir Edward Grey

Introduction

COLLINGWOOD INGRAM, PERHAPS THE FINEST FIELD ORNITHOLOGIST of his generation, was born on 30 October 1880 at 65 Cromwell Road, South Kensington, nearly opposite the newly built Natural History Museum.[1] He was the youngest son of William Ingram, and a grandson of Herbert Ingram, founder of *The Illustrated London News.*

Family and early life
Collingwood's mother, Mary Eliza Collingwood Stirling, had grown up in Australia. Her father Edward Stirling – the son of a Scottish plantation owner in Jamaica and an African slave – had emigrated to Australia in 1839, and made a fortune in copper-mining before returning to England to educate his children.[2]

It was in London that Mary Stirling met and married William Ingram, a university friend of her brothers. In due course William succeeded his father both as proprietor of *The Illustrated London News*[3] and as member of Parliament for Boston, and in 1893 he was created baronet.

Both Collingwood's parents were interested in the natural world. In Australia his mother had lived in a household full of pets, and in England she kept Japanese dogs (as many as thirty-five at one time) and pet birds. While William kept aviaries of exotic species – and, at Westgate-on-Sea, a small private zoo – many of Mary's birds enjoyed the freedom of the house. Jackdaws

1

and blackbirds strutted with their young across carpeted floors, or over the dinner table; at dusk sparrows slept in the sleeves of her nightgown; at dawn fledglings were checked for warmth and fed with mealworms. For their nests, Mary gave them locks of her own hair, fur from her sable cape, or ribbons from her dress. She ignored convention and the risks to the grand piano and her expensive silk curtains.[4]

In these circumstances it would be an understatement to say that Mary was fortunate in her marriage. 'I married,' she wrote, 'a husband as fond of birds and animals as myself.' And William's concern for birds can be seen in his own account of how he once rescued two fledglings:

> I picked up … the new arrivals lying on the floor apparently dead; but seeing there was a flicker of life in them, I brought them into the kitchen where with the aid of a warm flannel, they soon revived, and within two hours afterwards my man placed them under another bird.[5]

The parents' love of birds would be fully matched by that of their youngest son.

Collingwood was a frail child. Unlike his brothers Herbert and Bruce, who both went to Winchester and Oxford, Collingwood was educated at home by tutors. Much of his boyhood was spent on the Isle of Thanet, where his parents owned a house called The Bungalow[6] at the newly fashionable resort of Westgate-on-Sea. The Bungalow was near Quex Park, home of the explorer and collector Percy Powell-Cotton, and there Collingwood could watch birds to his heart's content.

In old age he recalled this idyllic childhood, writing that from the age of ten he had spent his days in search of birds. On one outing he met Jenner Weir, an elderly ornithologist who befriended him and encouraged his interest in birds. 'For that encouragement,' Ingram wrote, 'I owe his memory a deep and lasting debt of gratitude.'[7] He was also encouraged to develop his sketching skills by a family friend, Louis Wain, the popular artist who specialised in drawing cats (for *The Illustrated London News*, among others).[8] So Collingwood

Collingwood's earliest surviving sketch, drawn when he was eleven or twelve years old

Drawings made at the Natural History Museum and the London Zoo

Ringed plovers on coastal marshes, Thanet

Ingram became an avid and sensitive wildlife artist. His sketchbooks and diaries show his particular fascination with birds and his excitement at discovering nests. By the age of fifteen he had produced and illustrated a hand-written book on the birds of Britain.

It was not only in the English countryside that Collingwood indulged his passion. In London he could visit the zoo at Regent's Park and the Natural History Museum; and since his family wintered in warm places, he was able to study birds in Egypt and on the Riviera.[9]

A sporting life

By the time he was eleven Collingwood's life in the country also embraced the local hunt. The flat farmland of Thanet was ideal for hunting, and the quarry was the hare. Pangs of compassion for the hare, he tells us, would alternate in his heart with the thrill of the chase, but it was the thrill that proved the stronger. He idolised a local farmer called Ambrose Collard, Master of the Thanet Harriers. On Collard's retirement Collingwood himself became Master, thanks to his father's wealth; but this new career did not last long. He was still only seventeen, and while the hunt committee was pleased to accept the father's money, it was less pleased to accept the son's control. Confronting them, Collingwood showed the arrogance of youth: 'I bluntly told them that if I were not old enough to call the tune, I was certainly not old enough to pay the piper, and with that I tendered my resignation.'[10] But this encounter in no way dampened his love for the hunt.

The Thanet Harriers

Sir William Ingram's horse Comfrey won the Cambridgeshire Handicap at Newmarket in 1897 (painting by Collingwood Ingram)

Ingram's diaries find him participating in most of the social pursuits of the day. He attended the theatre and concert hall; he watched cricket at Lords, and boat races at Henley; he sailed in his father's yacht, shot deer in Scotland and went to the races. But his love of birds pervaded everything:

> Today I went to the Derby, run at Epsom. What a crowd! What a din! '4 to 1 Galtee More'[11] sounding from every direction and other cries coming from the mass, but even above it all I heard the music of the lark.

The fixed points in his year were fox-hunting in winter, bird-watching in spring, grouse-shooting in August and deer-stalking in November. In his early twenties he also travelled extensively, with long trips to South America and Australia, where he shot and hunted and also added to his experience of the natural world. In Australia he stayed with his uncle, Edward Charles Stirling. Stirling was not only Professor of Physiology at the University of Adelaide, but also a surgeon, explorer, anthropologist, artist, and director of the South Australian Museum.

The ornithologist

In 1905 Sir William Ingram commissioned the naturalist Wilfred Stalker to collect bird specimens in Australia. The skins were sent to Collingwood at the Natural History Museum, and here he got to know many of the foremost ornithologists of his day.[12] Sir William's most dramatic venture was his bid to rescue the Greater Bird of Paradise, found on the islands of Aru and New Guinea, but (since its feathers adorned many a fashionable hat) then thought to be in danger of extinction. Sir William bought Little Tobago, a 400-acre uninhabited island off Tobago, and hired a naturalist to collect live specimens from their native habitats. Then he shipped them off to breed in the protection of their new island home.[13]

At this time scientific ornithology was still largely restricted to taxonomy (the identification and classification of species) and to the study of anatomy and geographical distribution. These were based mainly on the examination of dead birds shot by professional collectors. Collecting was then essential, since much of the world's fauna was still unknown; and London, being at the heart of a great empire, was an ideal centre for research. Collingwood Ingram's roots were firmly in this collecting tradition, but he was also deeply interested in birds in their natural habitats. His field skills were outstanding. Lacking modern optics, comprehensive field guides, distribution atlases and recordings of bird song, he relied on keen observation, acute hearing and fieldcraft, all skills he had developed during his boyhood on the Isle of Thanet.

Ingram's passion for birds was never more apparent than after he married Florence Laing in 1906. Although his bride shared his enthusiasm for hunting, she had no interest in birds; she was also a bad sailor. Nevertheless it was the bridegroom's wishes that prevailed, and on their honeymoon[14] they went by sea to Japan, where Ingram hoped to locate the nest and eggs of White's Thrush. Returning to England via the trans-Siberian railway, Ingram looked out over the great Manchurian plain and conceived his next project: to study the birds of Manchuria.

While in Japan Ingram had met the animal dealer Alan Owston, who employed his own Japanese collectors. A letter from

Owston shows not only the harsh reality of collecting, but also his admiration for Ingram's field skills:

> I am sending you by parcel post a box containing nest, three eggs and one parent bird of *E. yessoensis*.[15] ... It is most extraordinary, seeing the enormous amount of egg collecting done during a number of years by my men in the Fuji district, that they never came across the eggs of *yessoensis*, till you discovered the exact locality.[16]

The years between his marriage and the outbreak of war were productive ones for Ingram, both as family man and as ornithologist: his three sons were born, and he published many ornithological papers. In 1913, his last full year of research, these included *Birds of Paradise in the West Indies*[17] and *On the Marsh and Willow Tits of France*; another was on the birds of South Central Asia. Research for a more ambitious work – *The Birds of France* – took him across the Channel many times before the War, but the book was never completed.

Kent Cyclists exercising on the coast near Romney Marsh in 1915 (photograph by Collingwood Ingram)

Outbreak of war

Shortly after the outbreak of war in August 1914, Ingram was commissioned in the Kent Cyclist Battalion, and later attained the rank of temporary captain.[18] Britain's home defences in the First

Studies of Kentish plovers

World War depended to some extent on bicycles. This amused people even at the time; but the KCB, which eventually attained the strength of three battalions, did useful work. Its members watched the coast for signs of enemy incursions, and reported sightings of planes and zeppelins.

When his detachment was posted to Romney Marsh, Ingram found himself in an ornithologist's heaven. There had been an RSPB presence at Dungeness since 1905: it was an area where migrant species made landfall in the spring, and which was home to a wide variety of breeding birds. Ingram spent many off-duty hours studying, sketching and mapping the distribution of the Kentish plover, which nested on the shingle. [19]

These halcyon days were short-lived. By October 1914 the enemy had already captured Zeebrugge and Ostend, threatening not only Kent but the whole of the Thames Estuary as far as London. In December a single bomb dropped on Dover showed the dangers that might lie ahead. The Thames Estuary was the site of the important naval bases of Chatham and Sheerness, and the task of defending it fell not to the Royal Flying Corps but to the Royal Naval Air Service, a separate entity with its own planes and pilots.

Even before the war the RNAS had considered establishing a base at Westgate, and in 1913 had sent an officer to reconnoitre.

Seaplanes of the RNAS at Westgate attracting attention in 1914 (photograph by Collingwood Ingram)

Westgate's destinies, reported the officer, 'are ruled over by Sir William Ingram, who owns most of the town and endeavours to keep it quiet and exclusive'.[20]

But once the RNAS had expressed an interest in a base, the Ingrams became closely involved, and when war broke out the base was already in operation. Later the family helped to find a new and larger airfield inland, known today as Manston Airport. When Collingwood was taken on his first flight, he wrote in his diary that he was entranced to get 'a real bird's eye view of Thanet'.

In the course of 1916 the KCB underwent major redeployments,[21] and that autumn Ingram was seconded to the Admiralty at Deptford to learn the art of compass adjusting. No doubt the move owed something to his contacts with the RNAS; yet it could not have happened had he lacked native ability or a proper grounding in mathematics from his early tutors. Soon his temporary captaincy was made substantive, and he was seconded to the Royal Flying Corps.

The Royal Flying Corps
The RFC, formed in 1912 as a branch of the army, comprised at the start of the war some 150 men and fewer than a hundred

Collingwood Ingram in
uniform

planes. By the end of the war the new Royal Air Force[22] comprised
some 290,000 men and over 22,000 planes, more than half of
them in France.

In 1914 aeroplanes were primitive machines, made of wood,
wire and canvas, and still regarded as playthings for the rich; in
the early months of the war they were used almost exclusively for
observation. The pilot sat in an open cockpit, clad in sheepskin,
silk or fur, and anything else that might help to keep him warm.
Next to the cold his biggest problem was navigation, and for this
he carried five vital aids: an air speed indicator, an altimeter, a
map, a torch, and – Ingram's speciality – a compass. But a pilot's
best guides were still his eyes. Flying at night or in cloud was
dangerous. Direction-finding was particularly important to the
British, since their pilots were ordered to attack behind enemy
lines, whereas the German air force fought a defensive war, largely
staying behind their own lines. Getting lost was obviously more
dangerous over enemy territory.

It was as an adjuster of compasses that, on 7 December 1916,
Ingram arrived in France.

RFC officers were generally well billeted, sometimes in tents, sometimes in prefabricated Nissen or Armstrong huts, sometimes even in a local château. In any of these they might enjoy wine and champagne, gramophone records, newspapers and magazines such as *The Field* (relished by Ingram for its articles on the countryside and birds) – and, in the châteaux at least, creature comforts to offset the horrors and dangers of war. For the RFC, these dangers were to reach a peak shortly after Ingram's arrival.

In northern France there were many RFC aerodromes scattered behind British lines, and Ingram would travel to most of them. They could sprout up virtually overnight on farmers' fields, and often disappear just as quickly. Generally a couple of squadrons were based at each aerodrome, although the relationship between squadron and aerodrome was liable to change. The largest aerodrome on the Western Front, and the RFC's main logistics centre, was at St-Omer, which until March 1916 was also RFC headquarters. [23]

The technicians' main bases were the No. 1 Aircraft Depot at St-Omer, which serviced the numerous aerodromes west of Ypres; and the No. 2 Aircraft Depot near Candas, which serviced the aerodromes supporting the British armies in the Somme valley. Each depot had attached to it an Aircraft Park, or mobile repair unit, able to move at two hours' notice. Each Aircraft Park was a gigantic technical factory and emporium, repairing anything from aircraft to wireless equipment.

A compass required frequent adjustment, and return visits to aerodromes could be painful: at the worst period of the war the life expectancy of a pilot was a matter of days. [24] 'The place awakens sad memories,' wrote Ingram after one such return:

for how many of the old crowd are still alive? Lubbock, Bransby Williams, Truscott, Griffiths and a dozen others have been killed … in fact I should say that not more than four or five are still alive. And what good fellows they were too!

Whenever he could, Ingram sought refuge in the countryside. He explored the woods and rivers, the valleys and farmlands, and whatever he saw on his travels – landscapes, wildlife, buildings, people – he noted and sketched. Against the sombre backcloth of war we are enabled to glimpse through his eyes a happier world: a world in which spring always returns, and where birds still sing.

Notes

[1]The Natural History Museum first opened its doors to the public on Easter Monday, 18 April 1881.

[2]She may have been a freed slave. Information about the Stirling family has been provided by Jude Skurray of Melbourne, a descendant of Edward Stirling.

[3]Herbert Ingram founded *The Illustrated London News* in 1842. In 1860 Ingram, together with his eldest son Herbert, was drowned in a paddle-steamer accident on Lake Michigan: he was forty-nine. The magazine continued to be associated with the Ingram family – Collingwood's brother Bruce was its editor for over sixty years – until 1963.

[4]The information on Mary Ingram's life and pets comes from her own article in *The Windsor Magazine*, 'My friends in feather and fur' (November 1905), and oral recollections of an Australian collateral descendant, Edward Stirling Booth (transcribed in 1995 by his granddaughter, Anna Pope of Adelaide).

[5]See Sir William Ingram, 'Breeding Gray's Bare-Throated Francolins' (*Avicultural Magazine*, 1905).

[6]The Bungalow, built in 1869 by a London doctor and unique at the time, was nothing like the seaside bungalows of today. It was a grand affair modelled on those built in India to house the servants of the Raj.

[7]See Collingwood Ingram's *Random Thoughts on Bird Life* (undated, but c. 1978).

[8]Collingwood Ingram drew several portraits of Louis Wain. One was published in Rodney Dale's *Louis Wain: The Man Who Drew Cats* (William Kimber, 1968).

[9]In 1897 Sir William Ingram bought some land on the coast near Monte Carlo: here he built La Vigie, a substantial house completed in 1902.

[10]The quotation is from a typescript found amongst Ingram's papers.

[11]This was the 'Jubilee Derby' of 2 June 1897. In the same year the three-year-old Galtee More won the 2000 Guineas at Newmarket and the St Leger at Doncaster, thus gaining the English Triple Crown.

[12]At this time many ornithologists were amateurs, rich men who belonged to the British Ornithologists' Club and who often paid professionals to collect on their behalf. Members of the club would meet in London restaurants and lay out on the table their latest specimens for comment. Ingram was a member from 1901 until his death.

[13]The colony survived on Bird of Paradise Island (as Little Tobago came to be called) at least until 1968, but is now extinct there. See J.J. Dinsmore: *History and*

Natural History of Paradisaea apoda *on Little Tobago* (from the *Journal of Caribbean Science* **10**: 93–100).

[14]The trip to Japan in fact took place in 1907, six months after the wedding: according to family tradition it was a delayed honeymoon.

[15]*Emberiza yessoensis*, the Japanese reed bunting.

[16]Alan Owston (whose father was for forty years vicar of Pirbright in Surrey) died in 1916, and was buried in the foreigners' cemetery in Yokohama.

[17]Ingram had gone to the West Indies to observe the progress of his father's colony of birds of paradise.

[18]Ingram was later seconded to the RFC, but he remained on the staff of the Kent Cyclists throughout the war. Most of the information on the KCB is from Cyril Bristow: *The Kent Cyclists' Battalion: A Short History* (1996 revision).

[19]Romney Marsh was once the English stronghold of the Kentish plover, a bird that no longer breeds in the British Isles. Ingram's Dungeness diary of 1915 is filled with sketches of this and other coastal species.

[20]See Geoffrey Williams: *Wings over Westgate* (Kent County Library, 1985).

[21]In February 1916 a KCB battalion was sent to India to release regular troops for redeployment in the main theatres of war. The remaining battalions continued to perform their duties at home.

[22]The RAF was formed on 1 April 1918 by amalgamating the RFC with the RNAS. The numbers of planes and airmen here quoted are taken from Ralph Barker: *The Royal Flying Corps in World War I* (Robinson 2002, p. 468).

[23]In March 1916 RFC headquarters moved from St-Omer to the Château of St-André-au-Bois, near Hesdin, returning to St-Omer in 1917.

[24]In an unpublished script written after the war, Collingwood Ingram wrote that the life expectancy of aircrew during the period of German predominance was fifty-four flying hours, which (assuming a daily average of three to four such hours) translates into about fifteen days. Ralph Barker in his estimate of life expectancy for newly arrived pilots during 'Bloody April' reaches a comparable figure of seventeen days (*The Royal Flying Corps in World War I*, p. 278).

THE WESTERN FRONT
1916

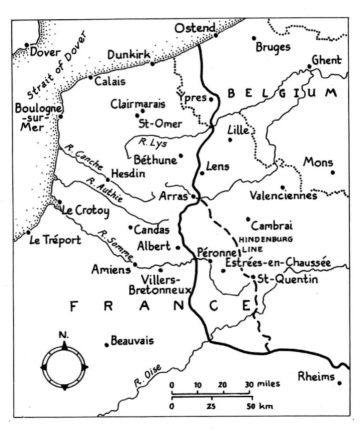

1.
Setting off for War
(7 Dec. 1916–21 Feb. 1917)

In December 1916 *Collingwood Ingram, a newly qualified compass officer of thirty-six, set off for the war. In appearance he was small, wiry, and thin-featured, with blue eyes and dark unruly hair; by temperament he was robust, uncomplicated and outspoken – sometimes outrageously so – and with a zest for life that charmed his friends. That he was also a gifted ornithologist would not have seemed important to anyone, least of all himself. Sailing in an officers' boat escorted by two destroyers, he was arriving in France at the start of one of the coldest winters on record. The date was 7 December: the very day on which David Lloyd George replaced Herbert Asquith as Prime Minister.*

On land the war had reached stalemate. Early in February the Germans would begin their secret retreat from the Arras–Péronne–Soissons front, preparatory to making a stand on the Hindenburg (or Siegfried) line in March. Meanwhile they were pinning their hopes of victory on the power of their submarines to cut off sea-borne supplies to England and starve her into submission.

For his first few months in France Ingram was based mainly at St-Omer, whence in his capacity as adjuster of compasses he travelled to the surrounding aerodromes.

Thursday 7 December 1916, St-Omer
When last I crossed the Channel in the summer of 1914 I never dreamt that the next occasion would be under such very different circumstances. Today a troopship and an officers' boat (both packed with khaki-clad men wearing life-belts) were escorted over by two watchful destroyers, who wallowed in a cross-sea, one on our port and the other on our starboard beam.

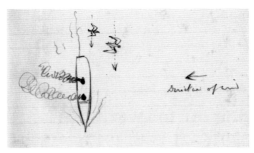

A fresh wind was blowing from the east. It was very interesting to note how the eight or ten herring gulls that followed us across managed to keep pace with the vessel without any apparent effort for minutes together. As their heads were turned towards the wind they were actually progressing sideways and practically at right-angles to its force, and were doing so with only a very occasional wing-beat.

Although there were a great number of black-headed gulls in Folkestone harbour, none attempted to follow us over and we did not see any again until we arrived at Boulogne. Just before entering this latter harbour, two or three lesser black-backed gulls flew past and I also noticed three hoodies.[1]

We had orders to report to the Railway Transport Officer at 8 p.m., but our train did not get away until 2 a.m. and it was 7.50 a.m. before we reached St-Omer – a long and very cold journey. I am billeted in a fine château about two kilometres to the south of St-Omer. It stands back from the high road and is surrounded by tall trees, which appear to form a quiet sanctuary for birds. The number of jays that frequent these grounds is rather surprising – I have just seen four hopping about among the fallen leaves on the lawn in front of the house. They are possibly winter migrants. Jackdaws and rooks are also about in goodly numbers. House sparrows are plentiful and have already gained confidence near the busy aerodrome. Blackbirds and starlings have also been noted. A party of a dozen long-tailed tits passed through the upper tracery of leafless boughs; robins, chaffinches and goldcrests were all denizens of the garden and are as friendly as in England.

Monday 11 December, St-Omer
My official address is:

> Aircraft Repair Section
> No. 1 Aircraft Depot
> British Expeditionary Force.

The Censor does not approve of full addresses and I suppose he will not like my saying that the Aircraft Repair Section of No. 1 Aircraft Depot is on the old St-Omer racecourse beside the main road to Boulogne! St-Omer itself is still the same sleepy city despite its many incongruous sights – British 'Tommies' mouching about, English notices and the great army tenders and lorries splashing through the streets. The shops are not behindhand and sell all manner of things that are so typically English that a few years ago the average Frenchman would probably never even have heard of them – English tobaccos, newspapers, games, clothes, drinks, etc. etc. – while all the shop-people are to be found poring over English dictionaries and school primers!

Crested larks are very fond of the aerodrome and are remarkably tame, strutting about in pairs between the aeroplane sheds and around the mess and canteen tents. I think there can be little doubt that these birds pair for life, for the individuals of each couple appear to be very attached to one another.[2]

In a little roadside bosky – clumps of birch and pine interspaced with grassy glades – I noticed an assortment of birds, great, blue and marsh (?) tits, blackbirds, hedge sparrows, goldcrests, magpies, chaffinches and two bullfinches. The latter, a pair, were in the birch trees and were no doubt feeding on the buds of these trees.

Rooks ply back and forth overhead, usually with an attendant sprinkling of talkative daws. Meadow pipits and yellowhammers have also been noted and a wagtail which, from a distance, certainly appears to be *Motacilla baorula*.[3]

Tuesday 12 December
The 'churry' alarm note of a wren was heard by the roadside and again in the château gardens – this bird is probably common enough hereabouts.

Friday/Saturday 15/16 December, St-Omer

Today being warmer, a thrush was singing softly to itself from an ivy-clad tree. Song thrushes are nothing like so plentiful as blackbirds, which abound wherever there are gardens or shrubberies. I saw a mistle thrush today and several hoodies in the ploughed fields between the château and St-Omer. In the blue haze of a winter's day the town of St-Omer appears to rise imposingly from the surrounding country. From the south, the cathedral and other public buildings are picturesquely outlined against the grey sky and they stand a good head and shoulders above the neighbouring buildings.

I visited the private collection of an aged bird-stuffer – one M. Dezand by name – being in his 92nd year and of feeble health I could not see him personally, but 'Mademoiselle' – herself an old white-haired woman – showed me the atrociously stuffed assembly of dusty specimens.

Although the good lady assured me that they were all '*du payee*' there was no inscription to show their provenance. However it is fair to assume that the majority of birds were killed locally.

Saturday 16 December, St-Omer

I saw a hawfinch in the garden today; as it flew out of a yew bush its white markings on the wing served to distinguish it. Quite a number of wood-pigeons have been about here lately – at least I have seen two or three fair-sized flocks in the distance. Today one of these birds passed me within easy gunshot, flying with head held high and heavy crop. I am pretty certain that I heard a tree-creeper[4] today, but failed to spot him among the tall trees. The gardener tells me two or three pheasants have been about the grounds for some time.

Sunday 17 December, St-Omer

After a frosty night it turned into a glorious day with gratefully warm sunshine. Being Sunday I managed to get an afternoon off and motored out a few miles along the Boulogne road. Dismissing the tender I strolled along the river bank and found my way into a little copse. This yielded quite a number of observations. A party of siskins and goldfinches were busily engaged in some alder trees feeding on the pendant clusters of seeds. The siskins were delightfully tame and it was very pretty to see the tit-like attitudes in which they placed themselves in order to search the under surface of the small cones. The goldfinches did not attempt these acrobatic feats but looked the seeds over in a more matter of fact manner.

A tree-creeper was jerking its way up the sunny side of the bole of an oak, occasionally uttering its characteristic call-note. It shuffled about in the sunshine taking evident pleasure in the warmth. A solitary redwing, alert and nervous, pitched into a tree close to me, unaware of my presence. I have heard the thin wintry cry of this bird several times since I have been in St-Omer.

Magpies were aggressively plentiful, chattering loudly whenever they had anything to say. At one time I saw nine close together and five more a few hundred yards further on. There were also a fair number of jays about – they are much tamer than in England, which suggests that they are not molested here as they are by our gamekeepers at home.

The bird that pleased me most was a little owl. He was sitting on the crown of a pollarded willow – rather hunched up and not fully awake. I managed to make a sketch of him before he tumbled – it was a very clumsy performance – into the crevice below him and which was evidently his home. I heard him calling for a few minutes before – although the note was familiar I could not place it until I saw this little owl silhouetted against the sky. In the water meadows I saw several moorhens, one or two meadow pipits and a grey wagtail.

On leaving the valley I climbed on to the light cultivated lands above. Here I found large numbers of grey partridges and flocks of skylarks rose with their purring notes at my feet. The former were surprisingly plentiful and judging by the size of the coveys could not have been shot at this year. Although, owing to 'La Guerre' there is supposed to be no shooting, I met a gunman and heard several distant reports. This man told me he had shot two small wild pigeons – evidently stock doves. The partridges however were on preserved territory. I saw huge flocks of rooks. These birds appear to make their way north-eastwards at night, towards some favourite roosting place. Earlier in the day as a flock passed overhead I noticed that all the birds had their feet clogged with a ball of the clinging clayey soil.

Towards dusk, it being a still, saffron twilight, the partridges commenced calling on all sides and rose in coveys with a hurried silky swish of the wings as I plodded across the plough and stubble.

Sunday 23 December, Abeele

I am now temporarily attached to the 41st Squadron to attend to their compasses. They sent a tender yesterday afternoon to fetch me from St-Omer. During the morning I had returned from Boulogne where I had stayed the night in order to see Bruce[5] who was passing through on his way to England for ten days' leave.

On leaving Boulogne the car I was in met with a nasty accident, which was scarcely surprising, considering the reckless speed at which we were travelling. A lorry appearing suddenly from a side road caused the driver to swerve into the curb against which we collided violently, bursting the front tyre with a loud bang. This caused us to swing across to the opposite and right side of the road. We finally fetched up on the left side-walk, the machine badly crippled with a bent axle, a smashed wheel and a burst tyre. As I had promised to be back in St-Omer during the course of the morning this accident put me in rather a quandary, while a heavy downpour of rain added to my discomfort. Luckily however, another eastbound car passed very shortly afterwards and gave me a lift into St-Omer.

The cobbled road from St-Omer led through a flattish country, the highways all avenued while the landscape was fairly sprinkled with trees, these being occasionally grouped into dark woods and spinneys. Presently, however, we came to a strange hill, rising unnaturally out of the cultivated plain. Upon its shoulder stood five delightful old windmills, all beckoning a welcome to us with hurriedly revolving arms. As we came nearer it could be seen that a town of some importance was built upon the summit and outlying cottages and villas straggled down the slope to meet us. This was Cassel. The incongruity of this typically foreign and strangely sited town was greatly enhanced by the presence of English troops. Nor was it lessened by the long lines of ammunition wagons drawn up by the side of the road, and the thinly disguised London motor buses that occasionally came rattling over the *pavé*.

On looking back into a stormy sunset one obtained a view over an immense stretch of country, a harmony in browns and greens, melting into the transparent blue of distance. In my opinion a view from some steep acclivity is infinitely preferable to that obtained from space; the eye is led by easy stages into the vistas of the unknown, whereas from an aeroplane the landscape lies below one with map-like severity, much of it crudely patched and streaked, with little or no perspective.

By the way, when I went up over St-Omer the other day* I was struck by the 'brownness' of the landscape. There seemed to be practically no green fields within sight, but only endless arable with dark clumps of woodland and still darker, almost black, patches of gorse intersected by long straight roads lined with trees on either side.

After leaving Cassel we descended again into the flat country beyond and were soon over the Belgian frontier, which was crossed without any formalities, and at dusk we reached the aerodrome close to Abeele.

The wind has been blowing a gale since the morning, threatening the sheds, breaking windows and dismembering trees of some of their largest boughs. Work on aeroplanes in these conditions was of course impossible, so I took a walk in the afternoon into Abeele. It was too stormy even for birds and besides a large flock of starlings, tacking as they rose and fell against the wind in their efforts to make their roosting sites, I saw nothing of interest.

Added later: Captain Lowery took me up on this occasion. About the end of March he was reported missing.[6]

Tuesday 25 December, Abeele

Yesterday the weather was perfect – a clean bright atmosphere with a light westerly breeze blowing out of a cloudless sky. This was an ideal day for flying and quite a number of machines from both sides were up in the air. Two fellows from this Squadron returned after having had a lively encounter with Huns; one of them, Jackson, with half a dozen shot-holes in his machine. It appears he was so busy fighting, and struggling to get his spare ammunition drums out of their boxes, that he found himself about 600 feet over the enemy trenches looking down on their upturned faces before he realised where he was. Needless to say he was soon reminded of this by a fusillade – rifles and machine guns pooping off as fast as they could. One shot passed through the nose of his FE8 and missed his feet by about two inches.

Today I had my first experience of 'Archie' fire.* A warning bell announces the approach of a Hun machine and soon afterwards the sky will be punctuated with little puffs of white smoke, dotting a pattern in the sky around the tiny glittering speck that represents the Hun 'plane. These are British shrapnel; the German Archies usually cough up HEs[7] which leave behind them a dirty blackish ball of smoke when they burst, an ugly black spot in the blue heavens.

Archies were constantly at work during the morning and several little groups of twenty and thirty balls of smoke could be seen hanging in the sky at the same time. In stillish weather they take quite a while to disperse.

Xmas morning broke with another gale roaring through the trees, a pleasant sound for the pilots as it means a day of peace for them. Major Lawson very kindly lent me his car to visit Ypres, or all that was left of Ypres. As we proceeded eastward the signs of warfare became increasingly apparent; troops patently fresh from the trenches passed us on the road. Ammunition dumps, camps, parks and gun emplacements were wayside objects, while the civilian population became fewer and fewer.

In Poperinge a large notice-board bore the words 'Wind Safe'. The outskirts of this town already showed the scars of shell-fire. The country was now flat and ugly – a dreary water-logged landscape, stricken and pitted with shell holes. Ypres itself, even in broad daylight, was a nightmare of a town, hopelessly ruined and entirely deserted. It was this desertion, this empty silence of the streets that struck one more than anything else. A few, a very few, soldiers were living like rats among the tumbled piles of bricks but otherwise the once populous streets were lifeless. The famous Cloth Hall and Cathedral were a pitiable sight – battered almost beyond recognition, the lead-work hung in ribbons across the blind windows, the masonry was gashed and splashed with shell marks and beautiful carved stonework lay shattered among other debris in the grass-grown court. The Huns were even now shelling the northern extremity of the town – with a whistling shriek they passed overhead bursting with a splitting report some half a mile away. Two unexploded shells were lying in the ruins of the Cathedral and one of these my companion carried away as a souvenir.

Starlings, wrens, sparrows and robins were all noted in Ypres, several mobbing a cat that was prowling about in search of rats. Hoodies were common in the fields – also rooks and jackdaws.

Added later: Anti-aircraft guns are called 'Archie'.

Friday 28 December, Abeele

The last two days have been frosty and this morning the ground was iron hard. I have not been beyond the aerodrome so I have not seen many birds – a few crested and common larks, a couple of blue tits, a redwing and a meadow pipit are about all besides the ever-present sparrow, chaffinch and starling. The latter, by the way, have passed over the northern end of the aerodrome each evening in an immense flock numbering many thousands. They tell me these birds journey east every morning and cross the front lines, returning again at sundown. Porter, one of the pilots here, tells me he shot a starling the other day with a kind of bridle attached to its body; unfortunately he did not keep it.*

Cody[8] had a narrow escape yesterday – a shot struck the cap of his petrol tank, narrowly missing his head. Porter flushed a snipe from the rank sodden meadow at the end of the aerodrome.

Added later: Starling subsequently found – alongside is a rough sketch of the bridle referred to.

Tuesday 2 January 1917, Ste-Marie-Cappel

Two days ago, I joined 45 Squadron

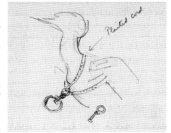

to attend to their compasses – and a sorry condition some of them were in.

Ste-Marie-Cappel lies on the lowlands a few miles south of Cassel – the latter town being seen prettily perched upon its hill top.

Eric Lubbock* – one of the Flight Commanders here – took me up for 25 minutes yesterday morning in his machine – a two-seater Sopwith, this type being one of the fastest two-seaters that flies, doing over 100 mph. It was the most glorious experience. The sky was wonderfully diversified with heavy banks of clouds, and these trailed off into fleecy islands to the northwards and dappled the brown earth with moving shadows of purple. In the very far distance these colours melted into a hazy pearl-grey – occasionally relieved by the sparkling glitter of water – and in turn this shaded into the blue sky beyond the invisible horizon. The cloud from above shone dazzlingly white in the sunlight, but in their even folds they held shades of a deep leaden grey. In between the open spaces immediately below one, the dark, sunless earth could be seen – and a huddled mass of roofs with infinitely small dots for carts etc. – representing Hazebrouck. The country hereabouts appears to be very evenly sprinkled with homesteads, around which are grass fields darkly outlined with hedges and trees. These green fields look like oases in a world of brown plough-lands.

A small flock of tree sparrows keep about the aerodrome and are usually to be found perched on a hedgerow near some corn stacks – being unmolested, they are friendly little birds and mixed with common sparrows compare very favourably with their coarser cousins. The same hedgerow is also a resort for yellowhammers. Blackbirds, robins, rooks, grey wagtails and a goldfinch have all been noted in the immediate vicinity of the aerodrome.

*Added later. Poor Lubbock was killed in an aerial fight on 11 March. I understand his longeron was shot through and when this ultimately gave way the tail of his machine broke and he came crashing to the ground. A short time previously (10.2.17) Lubbock had had a miraculous escape. He wrote me as follows, 'My own beautiful machine was destroyed in a fight yesterday. She was badly shot about and to get the Hun off my tail I had to loop. My tail plane broke, I fell vertically for 1,000 ft and I then managed to glide home. Nasty.' There have been few finer characters than Lubbock – a man of more than ordinary intelligence, he devoted all his mental and physical energy to his work and during my stay with 45 Squadron no pilot was so frequently in air. Absolutely unaffected, he was as courteous as he was kind, and from the very first moment I saw him he treated me with a natural politeness that set me entirely at my ease and made me feel as though I had known him for years. This sincerity was unquestionable. With Lubbock's death the Flying Corps has lost a valuable officer and England a gallant pure-minded gentleman that will be difficult to replace.[9]

Friday 5 January, Ste-Marie-Cappel
I had my seventh flight today – Griffin being the pilot. Although interesting, the effects were not so charming as the other day for the atmosphere was heavy with moisture and visibility was poor.

In the evening the sky cleared and twilight fell with a crisp, frosty sunset, which was followed by bright moonlight. In this I walked to Cassel, climbing the steep cobbled roadway that led into the old-fashioned town. The streets were strangely deserted and the unlit windows looked blindly down upon the silent, moon-flooded pavements.

As I passed beyond the limits of the town an owl called with a mewing cry from the tall trees and, save for the distant click-clack of a peasant's heels upon the cobbles, this was the only sound to fall upon my ears. I heard this cry also at Abeele and believe it is uttered by the little owl, in which case this species must be fairly common in this Flemish part of France.

At dusk I noticed a broad phalanx of rooks – black specks stretching far across the orange sky – winging their way in a westerly direction. As the birds near St-Omer fly at night in a north-easterly direction, it is more than probable that all concentrate at night in the Clairmarais Forest. Once or twice I have heard grey partridge calling at daybreak, but these birds are not so plentiful as near St-Omer. Other species seen: greenfinches – three or four; wrens – a few; great tit – one or two.

I have questioned several pilots as to the highest elevation at which they have met birds and all agree that it is unusual to encounter them at great heights. Lubbock was told by a friend of geese being seen at 3,000 ft and another fellow says he has noticed swifts at 2,500 ft – this latter observation agrees with my own experience in the Auvergne and elsewhere.

Saturday 6 January
Major Read took me over to St-Omer in a Sopwith two-seater this morning and flew me back for lunch.

Sunday 7 January
Having received a wire last night announcing the arrival of a baby girl, I decided to take the bull by the horns and ask the GOC commanding the 2nd Brigade, to which I am temporarily attached (General Webb-Bowen) if I could have a couple of days leave to see Flo and the infant.[10] Much to everybody's surprise this was granted and as luck would have it Major Read (OC No. 45 Squadron) happened to be flying over to England this morning.

I was delighted at the prospect of the cross-Channel flight (which meant a gain of many hours at home) and, in my eagerness for a fine day, kept waking in the early hours to see if the moon was still shining and the heavens clear. At first there was some doubt as the day broke with heavy banks of grey clouds north and west of Ste-Marie-Cappel. However at nine exactly the chocks were pulled away and we glided out of St-Omer aerodrome, rose in a wide sweeping turn and climbed into the northern sky. Rising on a steady incline with ever widening horizon, the world below us appeared to slip slowly backwards, while the cold upper air – as cold and crisp as though it blew from off some snowy peak – roared with a noisy rush in our ears.

The chocolate earth, a spreading patchwork of purplish brown, grew more and more remote. Inconceivably small trains puffed along tiny lines and little bunches of red and grey roofs clustered round certain roadways like nests of insects about a stalk. These were the habitations of man, himself too far distant to be seen by the naked eye. Presently, Calais slid towards us with its docks and its roads, its squares and its railways clearly mapped against the land's edge. One could now see the coast bending southward by Cap Gris-Nez, beyond which it gradually melted into the filmy ground mist. Presently a long tapering streamer of clouds, white and dense, completely shut out a portion of the landscape. When this was passed we found ourselves over a rippled green sea, which seemed to curl upwards towards an invisible horizon.

And where was England? Could it be that dark smudge floating high up in the sky? I never looked for it there – I could hardly believe my eyes and I had to wait until the familiar chalk cliffs assured me that this dark stain was actually substantial and moreover the land of my birth. Given good visibility and a fair knowledge of the country, it is astonishingly easy to find one's way by maps – there is Dungeness, the white buttress of Dover cliffs, Deal and the sweeping coast of Thanet nosing into the North Sea – all lying within the arc of one's vision.

When within a few miles of the shore, looking down into the funnels of the steamers that crept under the South Foreland, we lowered to about 2,000 ft, turned more northward and flew over the old familiar golf courses of Deal, St George's, Ebbsfleet and finally spiralled down and landed, with the gentleness that denoted a master hand, on Manston Aerodrome – one hour and twenty minutes after leaving St-Omer. Half an hour later I walked into Flo's room and was introduced to a very minute infant – I need hardly say my unexpected arrival was a very complete surprise for everyone.

Wednesday 10 January, Ste-Marie-Cappel
My luck followed me on my return journey – I was given a lift in a motor from Calais to St-Omer – where by a happy chance I found a tender of No. 45 Squadron waiting in the Square: so in this way I was able to reach my destination comfortably and in time for dinner, a contrast to the ineffable tediousness of my first journey to St-Omer.

Thursday 11 January, Abeele
After reporting at Wing HQ at Eecke I went on to No. 6 Squadron, which shares with No. 41 the Abeele aerodrome. Having to visit

five squadrons in as many days, I shall have little time to do justice to my work – for one cannot do much by merely *looking* at a compass – and still less for making notes.

The whole afternoon there has been an angry roar of artillery from the direction of Ypres – the air vibrating with a dull, heavy, thunderous sound which rose and fell with varying intensity, and at night their flashes flickered in the sky for all the world like summer lightning. At dusk too, against a background of dark, grey clouds, I could see the 'Archies' bursting round some poor devil in an aeroplane – at this distance these showed like little sparks of yellow light. During the afternoon one of our observation balloons – several of these long, sausage-shaped bodies may be seen any fine day from Abeele – was brought down in flames. I am glad to say both occupants escaped by means of their parachute. I am told there has not been such a big 'strafe' in this part of the line during the last eight or nine months.

Sunday 14 January, Bailleul

Having visited No. 46 Squadron at Droglandt, I came on here in the evening of the 12th. Bailleul is even more under the influence of British troops than St-Omer – or, perhaps I should say, has more wholeheartedly laid itself out to net in the sheckels of the unwary soldier. The number of houses that sell 'English Beer' and take in washing is perfectly amazing! The weather has been vile all day – a clammy wet snow making the ground abominably slushy. I visited Nos 42, 53 and No. 1 during my stay in this Flemish town.

Monday 15 January, Auchel

Last night I slept at 2nd Brigade HQ – in a comfortable château between Lillers and Chocques and had the rather unusual luxury of a bath. This morning was fresh and sunny – a pleasant change from the windy type of weather that has prevailed in the last week or so. Quite a lot of bird-life was to be noticed in and about the château parkland.

Grey wagtails appear to be fairly common winter visitors to this part of France as I have noticed them in quite a number of localities.

Later in the morning I came on here to be temporarily attached to No. 25 Squadron.

Tuesday 16 January, Auchel
A cold night left a sprinkling of snow on the ground. I had a short ride during the afternoon and noticed a fair show of grey partridges. Skylarks were seen in flocks and one or two crested larks were also observed besides the usual common species. One of the pilots in this squadron says he has seen geese at a considerable height, while another declares he saw three birds 'about the size of pigeons' at nearly 10,000 ft.

What strikes me as an interesting fact is the different 'feeling' in each squadron. Each one has an impress of its own, intangible but yet apparent to the casual visitor. It may be in the trend of conversation, it may be in their pastimes, or it may even show itself in the number and kind of drinks they take. One squadron will be keener on their job than another – keener on their machines or possibly more anxious for a scrap. Whatever it is, to an outsider spending a few days in their midst the difference makes itself felt. They are nearly all nice fellows – a leaven of English gentlemen and rough Colonials – Australian or Canadian.

The following locally killed birds are stuffed in the billet I am staying in – trophies of the *chasse*: curlew/black-headed gull (winter plumage)/water rail/hawfinch. Tree sparrows have been noted near Auchel on two or three occasions.

Saturday 20 January, Aire
Yesterday afternoon I left No. 25 Squadron and came into No. 40, whose aerodrome is about two miles from Aire. On the way I noted quite a number of birds – all somewhat subdued and tamed by the frost and snow. In some practically submerged fields I saw a fair-sized flock of fieldfares (the first I have seen) among which were a few redwings. Crested larks, looking more cobby and chubby than ever, were common roadside birds all the way from Auchel.[11] The sub-soil appears to be chalk in the latter district and sandstone near Aire – both light enough to suit the tastes of this lark.

A flock of linnets were feeding tamely on the bare patches

near the aerodrome, evidently gathering infinitesimal grass seeds – at any rate a casual scrutiny failed to detect any visible form of sustenance – sparrows, meadow pipits, yellowhammers, chaffinches and four or five white wagtails were also foraging round the sheds and buildings.

This afternoon I went for a ride, passing through Lambres and thence across a cultivated plain onto a wooded hill. From here I obtained a wide view over the white country. It was indeed a wintry scene. Under a drab sky, the trees and woods stood out stark and cold in the frost-bound air – the distant villages pearly grey and the nearer trees a dark, purplish brown. The whole aspect was one of silence and death – the plain stretched away into the haze without as much as a ploughman, not even a beast, to relieve the monotony of this drear waste of snow. The crinkled leaves rustled crisply on their stalks as a chill breath moved up the slope, but otherwise the only sound was the faraway rumbling thunder of artillery and an occasional croak of a hoodie. The birds were all puffed out and heavy with cold. Rooks scarcely deigned to get out of my way – hoodies, jackdaws and magpies were hardly more alert, while the crested larks only fluttered out of the road under my horse's hoofs.

Just beyond Lambres, a solitary curlew rose almost within shot and circled round before making off. A great grey-backed shrike came skimming over the ground with scintillating wings, followed by a couple of white wagtails. He surprised a flock of linnets and these rose with a noisy twittering chorus and made a feeble attempt to mob him. The shrike settled on a plant stem in an open field. Crested larks are very common – also common larks, but these latter are in flocks while the former are scattered conspicuously along the roads in couples. They occasionally utter their fluty call-note.

In a wood of spruce and pine – where the rabbits had made a pretty tracery of foot-prints in the snow – I found a few goldcrests and heard the harsh cry of a jay.

In a copy of *The Field* a correspondent states he has kept a captive red-legged partridge in Spain for eleven months without water – the bird would not drink when offered it. He suggests that they do not drink in the wild state.

The Flying Corps have evolved a slang vocabulary of their own – this is a sample of it:

'The Bosche *Archie* were busy today and the fellow at *Plug Street* coughed up a lot of stuff at me during my morning *offensive* and my old buss was fairly plastered. Rather bad luck – I nearly got a *Blighty*, one piece missing my toe by an inch or two. I can tell you I properly got the *gust up* when I found a Bosche sitting on my tail – that's the worst of these *Fee-birds*, you can't see 'em coming up behind you. I think he must have *jambed* for he didn't fire more than a dozen rounds or so. I turned vertically, side-slipped and *zoomed* off to the right. Although he had the legs of me he wasn't taking any when I wanted to tackle him. He nose-dived through the clouds and was soon lost. W. was *stunting* at about 500 this morning with S. I wouldn't loop a Sopwith myself with two up – her tail will fall off one of these days. W. is a topping pilot, but he crashed a buss only last week and has now *hot-stuffed* J's.'

Archie – anti-aircraft gun.[12]
Plug Street – the nickname of a wood near our front line.
Offensive – Offensive Patrol, viz. when the patrol crosses the line and enters enemy territory.
Blighty – home, i.e. England, the reference here is to a wound that would necessitate returning to England.
Gust up – or wind up, fright.
Fee-birds – FE, types of aeroplanes, 'pusher' machines.
Jambed – jambed his machine gun.
Zoomed – is a kind of switch-back manœuvre.
Stunting – doing tricks in the air.
Hot-stuffed – appropriated.

Tuesday 23 January, Bruay
I am now attached to No. 16 Squadron, which is quartered in this squalid colliery town. Two officers – Lieutenant Fernihough from No. 2 and Captain Lomer from No. 10 – are also attached to this squadron to learn compass adjustment under me.

The cold weather persists, but the drab, snow-laden sky has cleared and the sun rises and sets with the coppery glory that is peculiar to a hard frost. The poor birds are feeling it severely. The rooks crowd around the small stacks and tear at the thatching in the hopes of finding grain. By the way, although I have kept my eyes open for any signs of a rookery – which would surely be conspicuous enough at this leafless season – I have seen none, so have come to the conclusion that these birds do not nest in the districts I have lately visited. Crested larks have been noted on the outskirts of the town, where they seem to be more at home than on the open fields.

I have heard this evening that Hay[13] – one of the nicest fellows in No. 41 – has just been brought down in flames. When I think of all his little kindnesses and courtesies – his unbounded good nature at bridge – I feel that I have lost a friend although I only knew him for the week that I was at Abeele.

Friday 26 January, Hesdigneul

I was not sorry to be quit of Bruay and its sooted surroundings. Although I am only a few miles away, this place is fairly 'countryfied' and not overshadowed by tall chimneys, belching clouds of blackened smoke all day long. I am now with No. 2 Squadron, billeted in the schoolhouse overlooking the pleasant village green. Despite the presence of a small stove – a miserable substitute for a fire to be sure – the cold is so intense that the water in my jug was frozen when I got up this morning.

In a small straggling copse I saw quite an assortment of birds – most of them moped and heavy with the cold. I noticed a single song thrush – I have only seen a few of these birds since I came to France – and two or three marsh tits. These latter were in a rather dirty state, no doubt from contact with smoke-begrimed boughs. They were searching the crevices of a tree trunk for food and were clinging to the bole like nuthatches. In appearance they were greyish in tone, but this may have been due to the dust and dirt.

Later I shot a marsh tit[14] for my collection. The stomach contained a mass of unrecognisable dark, gritty substance, which was probably the remains of small insects – a fair-sized grub was in the midst of this.

Saturday 27 January, Hesdigneul

A fellow named Crossby gave me a 'joy ride' this morning, which was interesting on two accounts – firstly because it was my first view of the front line trenches and Hun-land and secondly because of the charming winter effect of the sunlight on the snow. Bitterly cold on the ground, one expected to find it still colder aloft and yet the reverse was the case for at 3,000 or 4,000 ft the atmosphere was certainly warmer.

The horizon was lost in a pearly grey haze, which faded into a sky of arctic hues – an apple-green light fringing the cold blue of the upper vault. The town and woods were more conspicuous than ever. The former appear strangely drawn together, for height seems to annihilate distance and a wearisome four miles of road looks a stone's throw from above. The poplars threw long blue shadows over the snow and the roads stretched like dark lines across the white sheet.

Although we were above the range of minor detail, there was a sense of desolation about the strip of no-man's land – a blighted zone that had the appearance of being slightly discoloured. Loos of hateful memory[15] was almost directly below us at one time – even from 5,000 ft it looked battered and deserted, while to the south a more symmetrical array of houses showed where Lens lay. Apart from a few bursts of our shrapnel over the German trenches, the zigzagged lines of the opposing defences appeared very quiet and deserted, for the roar of the engine drowned all other sound and the eye failed to detect any other sign of life.

Sunday 28 January, Hesdigneul

Three of us walked in to Bruay to dine at the Sanicklet Restaurant where one can still have a passable repast at the moderate sum of four francs – a pleasant change from the abortive efforts of the soldier cooks who deem it desirable to burn the meat until it becomes a toughened unrecognisable mass of fibres, as indigestible as it is unappetising. A half moon cast a steely light over the snow-covered fields – the air was sharp and invigorating and the frosty soil crisp and firm under foot. No wonder we set out with a light heart and brisk step, for the night was one in a thousand – a night to store away amongst one's ideals.

As we passed a wood on our left, I heard a hubbub of corvine voices – rooks and jackdaws. Surely this is not usual two hours after sunset? Perhaps the bright moonlight had kept the birds awake, but usually they are silent once they have gone to roost. The other night the firing, which is almost always audible from here, became greatly intensified during the small hours and as I lay in bed it shook the house until it reminded me of the effect of boiling water in an overheated cistern. It was good hearing today that this 'strafe' preceded a highly successful raid into the enemy's trenches.

Monday 29 January, Chocques
Before sundown this evening I had a walk round the grounds of the château that is now the HQ of No. 10 Squadron. I noticed a redwing and later a fieldfare, both birds being very weak and tame from the effects of the prolonged frost. Blackbirds, a song thrush and a mistle thrush were also recorded, so that the *Turdidae* were well represented.

In a thin wood of tall, scraggy trees, a flock of stock doves came in to roost and later a couple of wood-pigeons. This spinney was also the home of a kestrel, who flew round and round giving vent to its annoyance at my presence by uttering a *kek-kek-kek* cry which preceded its querulous cachinnation. A party of six or seven magpies were equally upset and chattered loudly. Starlings, blue tits and a few other small birds also came in to roost, while finally a green woodpecker came sweeping in to plaster himself against a tree trunk. Silhouetted against the coppery afterglow, I saw his strange form as he yoicked his way, with great bowing jerks, up the side of the vertical bole.

In this part of Artois the trees are proportionally taller than those of the same species in England; they appear to have had their growth forced by the dampness of the soil in which their roots find nourishment and to be weedy and lank like hot-house plants. In a way this gives the place a foreign aspect, which is by no means displeasing to the eye. These lines of towering poplars are typically French and must look beautiful when their flickering

shadows are cast across the meadowlands on a summer's day.

Their far-away boughs must shelter many orioles, whose mellow notes must mingle with those of the warblers singing amongst the rushes of the roadside dykes or hidden in the silvery foliage of the fat pollard willows that lean across the water. Tree-creepers haunt these trees and the apple orchards that adjoin the old, squat farms. I watched one for some time today, hunting the rough bark of one of these fruit trees and, much to my surprise, his sickle-shaped bill drew out a juicy grub, and this despite many degrees of frost.

Friday 2 February, St-Omer

Yesterday afternoon I returned to this place, where I shall be glad of a few days' rest. Folk are already beginning to talk of this cold spell as being something unusual and quote their aged relatives as not having experienced such a severe frost since the year eighteen hundred and something[16] – the date does not seem to matter much and differs according to the individual. A cirl bunting was moping on the sunny side of a hedge – the first I have seen since I came out.[17] A sparrowhawk flew overhead this evening and a couple of pheasants ventured out of a spinney to search a snow-covered field in the hopes of finding a little food. All the birds are famished and hunger-bold; the mistle thrushes flop lazily about the cottage gardens while the blackbirds, robins and other more familiar species are tamer still.

The rooks are playing havoc with the ricks and like all the other birds are much tamed by weakness. Hoodies seem rather more plentiful. They join the rooks and jackdaws in pilfering the stacks.

Tree sparrows are fairly frequently met with and join their commoner relatives around the farms, where yellowhammers and more particularly chaffinches are also found. Tree sparrows, with their plumage puffed out by the cold, appear to have a little white ruff around the back of their necks, which sometimes gives them quite a strange appearance. A fair sprinkling of white wagtails has been observed in the last week or so and a few song thrushes.

My old friend the gardener at the château has been trapping the blackbirds and thrushes and was enjoying a stew of five or six at midday when I called.

I spent a short time in M. van Kempen's museum[18] and jotted down a few notes.

Sunday 4 February, St-Omer

In the afternoon I was able to take a walk and went out through the pretty village of Longuenesse with its wooded château grounds and high-hedged lanes. A couple of grey wagtails were dabbling in a roadside spring; open water must be hard to find with a daily frost from 12 to 16 degrees. In a spinney that runs along the gravelly edge of the plateau and just where it ended in scattered clumps of birch intermixed with gravelly patches, I flushed a couple of woodcock. They rose from near a rushy spot where a little spring sweated out of a hillside, piling up strata of ice in its efforts to keep flowing. The birds made off with strong rowing flight, the swish of their pinions being clearly audible.

Wood-pigeons were busily feeding on ivy berries and, like the rest of the bird world, their fears seemed numbed by the cold. One, at any rate, sat gazing at me wall-eyed from the dark foliage scarce three yards from me. Later on, these birds settled for the night among the black branches of some fir trees but were disturbed by me and left with a great clatter and whistle of wings. Several marsh tits were seen and their scolding cries heard, while the plaintive note of a tree-creeper sounded very lonely in a deserted part of the wood.

Monday 5 February, St-Omer
I revisited the same spinney this evening, but could make no addition to my yesterday's list. One of the woodcock was near the spring again and would have made an easy mark for a shotgun as he flew away against the white background of snow.

I never recollect a more exquisite evening. A still frosty air hung with a hazy opalescence over the snowy landscape – a landscape so strangely hushed that a child's voice, half a mile away, seemed to jar upon the silence. As the bloodshot sun sank with an effulgence of orange light into the grey mists of the horizon, a full moon climbed into the opposite sky. There, as the warm tints of the afterglow gradually faded from the snow, the cold, steely blue light of the moon gained mastery, and threw harshly outlined shadows across the spotless folds. At first merely a pallid phosphorescent gleam, it later intensified into a harsh brilliance that flooded into the whole country with a wintry light – cruel and unsympathetic in its silvery harshness.

The last two days German aeroplanes have flown over at a great height (17,000 ft it is estimated), their advent being announced by a clanging of church bells in St-Omer. Dazzling white against the profound blue of the sky, they were clearly visible and, with glasses, the black cross and glistening propeller could be easily seen.

Friday 9 February, Filescamp[19]
After a week's rest at St-Omer I have been sent southward to No. 26 Squadron, which shares this aerodrome with two other squadrons (11 and 60). All the way partridges were seen in considerable

numbers along the roadside. Whether they were attracted thither for the purpose of warming themselves on the sunny banks I cannot say, but they were often loath to make way and as a rule merely fluttered a few yards into the fields to let the rattling tenders pass. Rooks must be very destructive in this weather. They literally swarm about the stacks, tearing great holes out of the thatch, while they even attack the sides by fluttering up and snatching at the straw ends with their bills. Hoodies and jackdaws and probably carrion crows form part of this crowd of black thieves.

I had occasion to visit the HQ of the RFC at St-André a few miles out of Hesdin, a huge and imposing château with walled grounds set amongst avenues and belts of tall trees. On one side is a spacious stable yard surrounded by buildings that could hold perhaps a hundred horses. The whole place has fallen into disrepair and there is an atmosphere of decayed prosperity about the place that reminds one of the frowsty palaces that line the Grand Canal of Venice. Magpies were characteristically abundant all the way from St-Omer – perhaps more in evidence than usual, for parties of half a dozen or so were commonly seen. I think I heard a nuthatch this morning.

In reply to my enquiries as to whether any of the pilots in this squadron had ever met birds at considerable elevations, McCudden[20] declared he had seen some once, apparently geese, at 9,000 ft. This was near Abeele.

Tuesday 13 February, Filescamp

This afternoon several of us motored over to the headquarters of the 'Tanks', those weird-looking engines of war that took the world by surprise last summer. I must say the oft-repeated comparison to some prehistoric beast is a very apt one, just as the outline of a huge bird or dragonfly is irresistibly suggested to the mind by certain types of aeroplanes. The blind resistless aspect of the thing as it crawled towards them must have filled the Germans with awesome wonder, and indeed the readiness with which they surrendered to the Tanks is abundant proof of their effect upon the enemy's morale. I had a long talk with an officer who took one of the first lot of Tanks over the line. He said that on one occasion when he was a mile or so ahead of the infantry, the Huns came crowding out of their trenches to gaze at the new and wonderful thing, either at a loss to understand its presence among them or failing to realise that it had a sting. For a time the Tank withheld its fire and then opened up simultaneously with five machine guns! Although tucked away in an out-of-the-world village, their presence in this part of France must be an open secret. Their tracks scar the country like those of a traction engine and at the present moment several are lying derelict and frost-bound in a field within a few yards of the public road.

Two fellows from this squadron (which is equipped with FE2bs) had a wonderful experience about a week ago. An Archie blew the tip of one of the wings off and the observer, Lodge by name, climbed out along the lower plane to balance the machine, which was out of control. By this means they were able to land by 'stalling' the machine at the last moment. Lodge was very modest when describing the incident and gave the pilot credit for making the suggestion in the first place.

Wednesday 14 February, Filescamp
No. 11 Squadron lent me one of their horses (most squadrons have three for their officers to ride) and I had a pleasant jog across the fields and through a big woodland. The ground was too slippery for cantering and even at the moderate speed I took him at, the sturdy little cob managed to fall with me. Besides flocks of greenfinches, yellowhammers and tree sparrows and the usual hosts of the crow tribe (rooks, jackdaws, hoodies, carrion crows and magpies) the open fields contained very little bird life. A few coveys of partridges and some wood-pigeons, which were evidently feeding on cabbage leaves, were noticed, but no larks or pipits etc.

The wood was very quiet – so quiet that the footfall of a frightened hare made a very audible crunching noise as it scuttled through the undergrowth over the frozen snow. The talkative twitter of a large party of long-tailed tits was therefore a positive relief. As is their wont, they drifted with a fretful energy through the upper branches, passing from tree to tree as though they hadn't a day to live. They seemed to be searching, and possibly consuming, the buds of oak and other trees. So far as I could see none of the thirty – there must have been at least that number – had white heads, so I conclude they were all *rosea*.[21]

Thursday 15 February, Filescamp

On revisiting the wood of yesterday, I again encountered a large party of long-tailed tits and, aided by my glasses, I am now sure that none had the white head of the typical northern form. Great and marsh tits were also present in this woodland and quite a lot of chaffinches came in at sundown, but thrushes, blackbirds, wrens and robins were conspicuous by their absence.

A restless sparrowhawk – a small male – kept flying over one corner of the wood and constantly settled on one or other of the scattered pines. His peevish cry – a sort of modified nasal screech – was repeatedly uttered and carried far in the hushed silence of the frosty evening. Now that the frost shows signs of breaking, the crested larks are inclined to turn their call notes into a semblance of a song, while a great tit tried a weak attempt at his vernal see-saw song, but it sounded rather out of place with the snow still lying in the orchard.

Sunday 18 February, Avesnes-le-Comte (No. 12 Squadron)

The thaw has set in with a vengeance and a mild steamy atmosphere has dispersed the last vestige of snow – already forgotten by man and beast. A chaffinch was proclaiming quite boastfully this morning that spring was here, while a yellowhammer was singing with equal confidence from a leafless elm. A crested lark was making the most of a limited but tuneful vocabulary *whegee-e-eo whee-eo whee-e-e-eo* and there seemed to be more than the usual light-hearted buoyancy in his flight as he fluttered round in aimless small circles. Even the rooks' voices seem modified by the mellifluous influence of the soft air and their cawing was evidently full of the memories of homeland rookeries.

Under these conditions it was nice to have a horse under me again. The squelching clatter of the hoofs upon the road beat upon my own thoughts until they harked back to boyhood recollections of

Old Mill

the Thanet Harriers,[22] my first love of hunting. The wide sweeping expanse of arable – but for the long avenues of trees – made a very good setting for these memories and I half-expected to see the green watchful form of old Collard appear over the brow, very patiently casting his hounds on a somewhat stale and apparently cold line. 'Spangle has it – yoick to Spangle – yoiee me little bitches' and away we would go, the pack feathering very prettily over the plough. … The muttering of gun fire and a hurrying Red Cross ambulance are rude reminders of a very different reality. … But Spangle was an uncommonly good bitch and so was that old white-faced Welsh hound that used to be such a marvel on roads. … My thoughts refuse to be diverted from those happy bygone days.

A cirl bunting was singing this morning near the aerodrome. A flock of peewits,[23] twenty or thirty in number, spent the morning on the aerodrome – restless and nervous as migrants will be – they were frequently in the air wheeling and settling again. A party of ducks were also answering the call of spring and passed over flying a steadfast nor'-nor'-easterly course. A great grey-backed shrike was lying dead near the sheds, evidently the victim of a thoughtless officer.

41

Tuesday 20 February, Avesnes-le-Comte

In the fog I heard and indistinctly saw a solitary golden or grey plover (I am not quite sure which) among the lapwings that were feeding on the aerodrome. By the note I am inclined to think it was the latter, but the bird was too shy to allow even a distant view and made away with strong driving wing strokes into the mist. I fancy a great many species must have worked their way southwards during the frost, for there seems to be a distinct increase in bird life since the weather broke. Chaffinches, yellowhammers, sparrows, titmice, crows and crested larks were amongst the birds that 'stuck it out' and were constantly present in large numbers, but skylarks, thrushes and robins seem to have disappeared altogether towards the end of the cold spell, at any rate in the neighbourhood of Filescamp.

Wednesday 21 February, Savy

I rode over to No. 13 Squadron yesterday afternoon, visiting No. 29 and No. 11 at Filescamp on my way. It was a misty ride and I saw little of interest in the way of birds, save a kestrel.

This morning as I lay in my Armstrong hut I heard the pleasant ditty of a hedge sparrow and later saw the dusky songster on some roadside bushes. On the whole this bird is not very abundant just now in north-east France and the few one sees are usually in or about village suburbs. A blackbird was also tuning up his pipes and a robin sang a short refrain, a refrain that lacked the long-drawn pleading and melancholy notes that one hears in the mountain forests of the Alpes Maritimes. This local difference – dialect, as it were, in the voice of birds – is very interesting. An odd chaffinch and a yellowhammer or two must be added to the would-be vocalists, but they won't be in full song for some time.

On the aerodrome a party of twenty or more meadow pipits were noted, busy feeding on the saturated grassland, where an immense flock of rooks and jackdaws were similarly occupied. It is curious how crested larks cling to the roadways and especially to those in the immediate vicinity of villages – they are very fond of keeping round about the huts and sheds of an RFC squadron, no doubt attracted by scraps of food. Several pairs may be seen on most aerodromes, while on a cross-country ride of four or five miles none may be observed. In the mist I heard the unmistakable twanging note of a brambling. Tree sparrows have also been observed.

2.
Abandoned battlefields and Bloody April (25 Feb.–10 Oct. 1917)

IT WAS ON 25 FEBRUARY *that Ingram heard rumours of a German retreat along a section of the Western Front, although at first not even the Allied generals understood what was happening. The enemy's aim was to relinquish a weak portion of the line and to establish another, shorter and stronger: the Hindenburg Line. The retreat was carried out in the utmost secrecy, being masked from the air by smoke screens, and from observers on the ground by diversionary firing: tactics designed to conceal for as long as possible that the trenches were being vacated.*

The ploy was successful, although the British, finding on 17 March that they could advance unopposed over what had so lately been enemy-held territory, were puzzled and suspicious. The scorched earth policy with which the Germans accompanied their withdrawal distressed Ingram: 'anything beautiful or useful', he wrote, had been destroyed.

For the RFC, the following month – 'Bloody April' – was the worst in the entire war. The Corps' sorties in support of the spring offensive resulted in unsustainable losses. 'In roughly twelve days,' wrote Ingram on the 13th, 'there have been over a hundred wrecked machines brought into No. 2 Aircraft Depot. … What a terrible loss of life and capital this represents.' The superior speed and manœuvrability of the enemy's planes were matched by the confidence and daring of the men who flew them, as epitomised by the air ace Manfred von Richthofen.

Despite the high cost of 'Bloody April', the spring offensive had little lasting success, and stalemate on the Western Front was soon re-established. Only the entry of the United States into the war on the sixth of that month provided a glimmer of light.

Sunday 25 February, Savy

The evacuation of a large tract of country by the enemy on the Miraumont Front resulted in a rather strange question being put by Major Powell (OC 13 Squadron). He asked several pilots, as they came in from patrol, whether they had seen anything of the Huns – 'Headquarters VII Corps have rung up to say they have lost the Bosches and ask if we have seen anything of them??!' Later I heard it said that we did not know the enemy had abandoned certain trenches until we noticed that they were shelling their own line – evidently under the impression that we had 'taken over'.

To further show its total disregard for any foolish superstition this squadron, No. 13, has a magpie as a pet and a very friendly chatty fellow he is too. They also had a barn owl taken from a shell-shattered belfry, but preferring freedom this bird abused the liberty that had been given him and made good his escape. I obtained a crested lark for my collection yesterday. It was in heavy moult and had new contour feathers coming on the head, back and breast.

Monday 26 February, Sombrin

I am now with No. 8 Squadron whose huts are prettily placed between two strips of woodland. The morning being warm and sunny the birds were making merry when I woke and a song thrush was in fairly good voice, the first I have heard since St-Omer. Yellowhammers, robins and skylarks were also singing. A brambling's note was heard. Before leaving Savy yesterday afternoon, I had a stroll through the outskirts of the village and down a winding lane between high hedgerows of pollarded beeches. These hedgerows are a picturesque feature of many of the Artois and Picardie villages, as are also the old farmsteads built partly of weathered blocks of chalk. The farmyards are often encompassed by a quadrangle of such buildings and through a broad-spanned arch one sees their high red-tiled roofs all mossy from the drip of the overshadowing poplars.

A marsh tit was chanting in a dialect that struck my ear as somewhat unusual. I wrote it down as *Tshish-se Choo, Tshish-se Choo*

at the time. Tree-creepers, hedge sparrows and commoner species were noted.

Tuesday 27 February, Sombrin

During the course of a short ride I came across two rookeries, one of between thirty and forty nests in a corner of a beech wood near Grand Rullecourt and another of about a dozen nests near Warluzel. I questioned a woodsman about the Rullecourt colony and he said the nests were systematically destroyed every year before the War. He also informed me that there was a larger rookery near Cauroy to the north-west. These are the first rookeries I have come across this year.

A little party of nine woodlarks was a pleasant encounter. Their notes intermingled as they rose from the ground and sounded to me like the fluty tinkling of distant bells – an extravagant simile perhaps, but nevertheless the confused sound was so bell-like in quality and so musical that a better comparison fails me. Greenfinches, linnets, grey partridges (now all in pairs) and the usual common species came under observation.

Yesterday afternoon Tagent,* a young pilot in this squadron, took me up for about half an hour in a BE2d. The visibility was excellent and we obtained a fine bird's eye view of the trenches near Hannescamps beyond the Arras road. Recent shells had punched neat conical craters in the ground, splashing the surrounding grass

46

Woodlarks.

with fresh brown earth. These were the latest pock-marks on the poor disfigured countryside. Troops and transport seemed to be plentiful and the roads were lined with interminable columns of the latter. On No. 59's aerodrome a machine could be seen lying on her back with crumpled wings and a crowd of men standing round – evidently an ill-judged landing that had ended in a 'crash'. Two fellows from this squadron were shot down and killed this morning, Pope and Johnson.[24]

Added 6 April: Tagent was killed towards the end of March.[25]

Wednesday 28 February, Sombrin

A 'beautiful' misty day – any dud weather, even rain, is spoken of eulogistically in the RFC after a spell of flying days, and lowering clouds are always welcomed.

The rooks were busy with sticks today in the Warluzel wood and were evidently patching up their old homes. A largish flock of wood-pigeons pitched among the tallest beeches, but they incontinently fled as soon as they noticed me standing in the ride. A pair of kestrels evidently had an eye on one of the rooks' nests and there was some querulous bickering and aerial manœuvring over the affair.

47

Thursday 1 March, Sombrin

The cirl buntings formed a little party sunning themselves on a thorn-covered bank. They appear to be tolerably plentiful in this part of France and are probably residents, liking the dry chalky soil as do the woodlarks. The song of this bunting is very different to that of the yellowhammer – and this is especially noticeable when both are heard together, as was the case today. It reminds me more of the lesser whitethroat and its notes are shriller in tone than those of its ally, *chi-lil-lil-lil-lil*. The greenish hues of the female serve to distinguish her even at a distance from the female yellowhammer.*

A blue tit was very prettily engaged feeding on the buds of pollarded willows, the supple drooping twigs of which caused the bird to utilise all its acrobatic activities in order to get at the swaying buds. The woodlarks were still in a small flock.

*Added later: The cirl bunting's song reminds me somewhat of the chirruping of a cicada. This species occasionally emits a thin, piercing call-note quite distinct from anything I have heard from a yellowhammer.

Friday 2 March, Sombrin

A sharp snap of frost caused wreaths of mist to hang over the chilled ground during the early hours of the morning, but towards midday the sun lapped this up and finally a blue sky stretched from horizon to horizon. A large mixed flock of rooks and jackdaws evinced their pleasure at the improved conditions by soaring in sweeping circles some few hundred feet above the ground emitting sundry chortling sounds of delight. The *joie-de-vivre* in some was further evidenced by lightning, tumbling dashes towards the ground. Once, so many indulged in this aerial form of playfulness that the loud lapwing-like swish of their wings caused me to turn quickly in my saddle.

Although it was now bright sunlight, a little owl was abroad and with his rounded wings flew ahead of me from tree to tree along the edge of a wood. Fieldfares and a few redwings were on the move – two or three song thrushes were also seen and from the fact that they were together and very shy I presume they were

likewise travellers. Forty or fifty wood-pigeons, a sparrowhawk and two kestrels were among the birds noted. It is somewhat strange that I have detected no crested larks in the immediate vicinity of Sombrin and Warluzel.

Sunday 4 March, Candas

Travelling down a pleasantly wooded valley we passed through Doullens and thence over whale-backed shoulders on to a dry plateau upon which Candas is situated. Crested larks were absent all the way, but I have seen a few today near No. 2 AD Aerodrome.

Hedge sparrows seem to be particularly plentiful round this village and the short cheery song of one – a jumble of pleasant notes – sounded almost in my ear as I lay in my Armstrong hut early this morning. Perhaps their predilection for suburban gardens may be traced to their comparative immunity from cuckoos in such situations – for this parasite would hardly venture into the very heart of a village. A grey wagtail was feeding in a farmyard, looking very sleek and handsome with his canary-coloured waistcoat.

A sparrowhawk surprised me by boldly passing within a few feet of my head. He (for it was a little male) then dashed down the length of a goods train close under the foot-board, when – flick! – over he popped to the other side and then – flick! – back again. This manœuvre failed to yield a chaffinch – of which there were quite a number pecking about the rails, but no doubt he had

Pollarded Willows — Picardie.

practised it successfully on previous occasions.

Bramblings, greenfinches, linnets, and two goldfinches have been noted.

Tuesday 6 March, Candas

Last night snow fell and there was a sharp frost in the early hours, followed by a cold mist. I heard a curlew and saw a party of twenty or thirty peewits. The birds seemed very pinched by the sudden return of wintry conditions and starlings, yellowhammers, sparrows, chaffinches and rooks were pecking tamely about among the rails of the goods station where I also noted crested larks and hedge sparrows.

A marsh tit sang like the Sombrin bird – *sen sen sen* or it may be rendered *sun sun sun.**

*Added later: Today (10.3.17) I heard two singing quite differently from either the Savy or Sombrin birds. They rattled out a series of clear notes in quick succession – the sound of which I will not attempt to translate into black and white.

Thursday 8 March, Candas

Woodlarks are fairly numerous hereabouts and this afternoon a flock of nearly thirty were haunting a stubble near this village. They do not seem to mingle with other birds and a larger flock

of skylarks seemed quite 'on their own' in the same field. The country round here must be well suited to their requirements – chalky slopes with wooded valleys of beech and other trees. Woodlarks seem to like hilly country.

Cirl buntings are fairly common but are considerably outnumbered by yellowhammers. A cutting east wind has brought with it a sprinkling of those 'northerners', redwings and fieldfares. The peewits are still frequenting the uplands near the aerodrome. I have found one or two old nests of song thrush – weather-worn relics of last summer – but the birds themselves are absent. Presumably, therefore, they largely, if not entirely, abandon their breeding quarters during the coldest parts of the year.

Just beyond the station, an old mill stands by the roadside looking delightfully quaint with its fat round body of brick and stone, its wooden (I believe wooden 'tiles' of this description are called shingles), hat-like roof from which depends a sort of pigtail; and its four arms, supporting the tattered remnants of brown sails.

Its owner is no less quaint and is a whimsical, toothless individual much be-powdered with white flour. He informs me with pardonable pride that the mill dates back to 1427 and certainly the interior has every appearance of being *très ancien*, it

having a very charming oak staircase with banisters beautifully polished and toned by the hands of many millers.

The walls of the château where I mess are adorned with trophies of the *chasse* in the form of feet and heads of wild boar. It appears that these animals still exist in the woodland to the north of Candas and a Picard peasant, whom I questioned on the subject, waxed eloquent as to their enormous size. Only the other day one was seen as tall as that – and the good lady held out her hand as high as her waist!

Saturday 10 March, Candas
The weather has turned dull and muggy again and the fieldfares, redwings and peewits seemed to have suddenly taken their departure – at least I have noted none today or yesterday.

Sunday 11 March
Being Sunday, I took an afternoon off and walked back from Hem across the fields to Candas. Near Doullens (where I happened to meet a friend with whom I lunched) there passed along the road

an almost endless stream of troops and their listless appearance evidenced a long and muddy march.

In the river valley, a heron flew over, ponderously beating the air with arched and rounded wings, and out of a reedy backwater surrounded by pollarded willows there rose two mallard who made off with a forced and hurried flight.

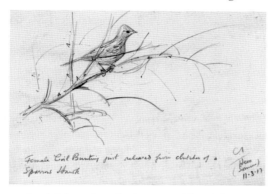

Female Cirl Bunting just released from clutches of a Sparrow Hawk

A cirl bunting had a providential escape today. Just beyond Hem I noticed a sparrowhawk skimming through the lines of tall poplars and I noticed that it was carrying something in its feet. I was amused to see two carrion crows attack the marauder with such vigour that it was forced into the bottom of a hedge. The two crows and a magpie thereupon settled above it, evidently waiting to renew the attack at the first opportunity. The hawk remained in hiding until I approached within fifteen or twenty feet of it when it fluttered noisily out of the brambles. What with the crows and myself, the hawk had had no time to commence its meal – in fact its prey was still alive and unhurt. The poor cirl bunting was too bewildered to realise at first it was still alive and only flew away when I tried to catch it. Cirl buntings are quite common in this neighbourhood – I noticed quite a lot today.

The sparrowhawk disappeared into a small copse and this had the effect of scaring out quite a number of small birds, including song thrushes. A song thrush was singing well from one of the wooded slopes overlooking the broad marshy valley of the River Authie.

An emphatic staccato *check* – then a pause – *check, check*, drew my attention to the upper branches of a tall black poplar where my eyes fell upon the busy form of a greater spotted woodpecker, loping his way upwards. Just then a spatter of rain came down and, after driving away two inoffensive greenfinches, he rested on the topmost twig to shuffle the drops off his pied wings and to preen his plumage.

Flocks of linnets and skylarks were in the open fields and enormous numbers of rooks. An assembly of twenty-eight magpies was noted, also a fair number of starlings round Candas, some of which seemed to be taking an interest in the condition of the church steeple.

A mellow evening of pink and primrose light brought forth praise from unseen blackbirds, while the jarring song of greenfinches was also heard as I entered the village.

Monday 12 March, Candas
Captain Dunn – one of the crack test pilots – took me up for a short flight in a BE2e this morning. It was a drab day and the landscape was a study in grey and sepia, showing no sign of awakening spring.

Tuesday 13 March
A party of meadow pipits alighted on the aerodrome. Just before

seven I heard a barn owl screeching in Candas: by the changing direction of the sound I imagine the bird was beating about on noiseless wings.

Wednesday 14 March
The audacity of the Candas sparrowhawks is remarkable. This morning a fine female dashed between our huts, topped an adobe wall and settled in a pear tree that was growing in a tiny kitchen garden surrounded by houses. Here she remained for some minutes, sitting bolt upright on a bough and in such a way that her plumage melted very completely into the similar browns of the rough bark. She seemed so well at ease that I think she must have been quite accustomed to making forays upon the town-haunting *Passeres* whose association with mankind had doubtless blunted their alertness by giving them a feeling of security.

Thursday 15 March
On my way home from the aerodrome I turned aside and passed through the corner of Longuevillette Wood. In some straggling poplars a flock of fieldfares were resting head to wind – probably

tired from a long stage on their homeward journey.

Some twenty-five magpies and upwards of thirty carrion crows had collected in two separate parties to roost in some big timber on the outskirts of the woodland. Such an aggregation of carrion crows must be unusual. Although the evening was closing in, their outline etched against the sky, and more particularly their harsh cries, left no doubt as to their identity and I feel confident there were no rooks among them.

A large number of wood-pigeons had also assembled for the night in the same corner of the wood and these clattered out of the trees and made away, showing me their full crops and outstretched necks as they swished over my head. Jays, a green woodpecker, and a few great and marsh tits were the only other occupants of the wood I encountered.

Saturday 17 March

Went to Amiens and visited the Natural History Museum to see the specimen of great auk.[26] This example is in excellent preservation – 'much better than the Abbeville specimen', as the concierge informed me.

Five or six hoodies were seen near Amiens – there have been none near Candas lately.

Sunday 18 March, Candas.

My Sunday afternoon walk has yielded little of ornithological interest beyond an observation of a pair of venturesome long-tailed tits busily engaged on constructing a nest. The site selected was among the drooping branches of a spruce about twenty feet from the ground. This tree was one of a small clump planted by the side of a deserted woodman's cottage and these were the only evergreens within sight.

The last few days, song thrushes have made themselves heard and have evidently returned to their summer quarters. One was singing very lustily in the woodlands this afternoon and his voice gave life to the otherwise silent valley, which was still destitute of foliage and filled with a damp blue haze.

The rooks have diminished somewhat, having withdrawn more

Craä

Brambling.

to the neighbourhood of their rookeries,* but a goodly number of carrion crows remain and these were scattered in pairs over the plateaux. One sat on a telegraph post and croaked for some time. I noticed that he always raised the forepart of his body before croaking, the sound being emitted with a bowing movement.

Yellowhammers are exceedingly common in this district and dozens roost in the tangled hedgerows. Tree sparrows, greenfinches and linnets were noted, but chaffinches predominate – they are even commoner than the house sparrows.

Skylarks were showering music over the fields and especially when the sun broke through the patches of fleecy clouds. Blackbirds, robins, hedge sparrows, a sparrowhawk, kestrel, green woodpecker, magpies, white wagtail, wrens, marsh, great and blue tits were also noticed as well as two bramblings which settled, as is their wont, near the top of a tall tree in the middle of the wood. Their twanging note attracted my attention.[27]

*Added later: There is one near Occoches and another at Gézaincourt.

Monday 19 March, Candas

The last two nights – dark and showery – I have heard the cry of migrant curlews passing over this village between 9 and 10 p.m. By the sound I should judge that they were passing in a more or less north-easterly direction. Two peewits flew over this morning and these were also heading towards the north-east.

Thursday 22 March, Candas

There have been intermittent flurries of snow all day. These swooped upon us as great blue–black clouds rolling up out of a sunny sky, and all of a sudden they would obliterate the landscape with a murky driving swish of snowflakes. Between whiles the sun shone crisply over a bright and charmingly coloured scene – a harmony in browns and blue – outlined with dazzling white the contours of the round-bellied clouds that raced across the forget-me-not sky. An exquisite translucent blue filled the distant valleys and masked the cloud shadows as they moved across the rolling downs, while in the clean atmosphere, the details of the brown and purple woodlands stood out with marvellous distinctness.

Overtaken by a snow shower, I willingly accepted the shelter of a Frenchman's cart on my way home. It happened that the fellow was a sportsman and the conversation soon turned upon birds. He informed me that a few red-legged partridge (an odd covey or two) existed between Outrebois and Le Meillard where the soil was *bief* (clay? gravelly?) – ordinary grey partridges had greatly increased since the commencement of the war. Stone curlew[28] were seen occasionally – he *thought* they nested near Villers-Bocage and felt sure they did on the chalky ground near Corbie. There was a big rookery in the Occoches wood.

Saturday 24 March, Candas

My eyes were gladdened this morning by the sight of the first summer migrant in the shape of a wheatear – a dapper male, with a clear, blue–grey mantle.

In the small garden at the back of the château, which forms the HQ of the RFC in Candas, a pair of magpies roost every night in some shrubs. They appear to take not the least notice of the orderlies that are constantly plying to and fro along the path, a few feet below them. Their last year's nest forms a great dark 'blob' near the summit of a tall Lombardy poplar standing near by.

This afternoon a pilot from No. 32 Squadron landed a captured German machine at No. 2 AD. He had shot it down somewhere near Péronne, having wounded the pilot – Prince Frederick Carl of Prussia – in the leg.[29] It appears that the Prince made a very plucky attempt to escape and despite his injury started to run for his own lines but was brought down this time, mortally wounded in the back, by an Australian. The fuselage of his Albatross Scout was bright apple green and on each side was painted the hideous emblem of his regiment – the Death's Head Hussars – i.e. a large skull and cross-bones on a black background.

Sunday 25 March, Candas
For my Sunday afternoon walk I turned to the Longuevillette

woodland in the vague hope of chancing upon a wild boar. If disappointed in this respect, I was lucky enough to obtain a fairly good view of a roe-deer – the animal being wholly unaware of my presence although I approached to within forty paces – no sooner did it catch sight of me, than it sped away, with a loud rustling of dead leaves, panic-stricken into the deeper thicket.

Tuesday 27 March, Candas

I returned this morning after an intensely interesting visit to the newly gained ground in the vicinity of Péronne. After dining with Bruce, General Perkins and Pleydell-Nott at Amiens on Monday evening, I went on with them to Cappy where I spent the night in one of the dug-outs that formed the HQ of the III Corps HA.

On Tuesday morning, Bruce had to visit the COs of several battalions as well as the proposed site of the new HQ in Stable Wood (Bias Wood on French maps). It was during the course of this excursion that I first came into actual contact with the horrors of this War – the uncared for dead, lying upon fields, mutilated and disfigured beyond recognition by many months of shell fire. The year-old rat-eaten corpses, the shrivelled dismembered limbs, still booted or clothed, the half-bare skulls – these are not subjects to dwell upon – but they tell their tale of heroism – for surely only heroes or madmen would have attempted to cross that open stretch of pitted ground between those ugly barriers of barbed wire.

A red turban or a printed page in Arabic scattered here and there among the usual debris of the battlefield – shells, hand grenades, rusted rifles and all kinds of trenching tools – proved that the attacking troops, at this point, were French 'Colonials'. Close to a shallow dip that had once been a lane, and where the attackers had very obviously suffered heavy casualties, I came across a shattered bugle – it did not leave much to the imagination to realise that a last rallying bugle-call, sounded above the intolerable din of the battle, had been suddenly cut short and that the bugler now lay among the blue-grey rags or under a loose scraping of soil.

Today the desolation was complete. Beyond the countless shell holes (nearly all of which were filled with pools of slimy green

Yellow hammer

C1
25.3.17
Candas

The trunk of an oak   Longuevillette wood

Candas
25/3/17

water) there once stood the village of Barleux but today it was only a silent heap of bricks and beams, so inextricably mixed with broken crockery and furniture that the whole place looked more like a dust tip than a ruined village.

It is a commonplace platitude to say that modern warfare is devoid of romance. Romance indeed? It seems to me that war is merely legitimisation of murder and (in the case of the enemy at any rate) the sanctioning of all the more brutal instincts of mankind. Is it not murder to place a clock fuse in the Bapaume

Beyond Peronne   23/9/17

town hall so that unsuspecting occupants may be blown up a week later – or a carefully hidden bomb under a plank of the Péronne footbridge to annihilate the first man that crossed? Dozens of such hellish death-traps have been recorded and yet their devisers have no doubt gone away with a perfectly free conscience – nay so topsy-turvy has the world become that I dare say they have carried with them a sense of extreme satisfaction of a good day's work done. For brutal and carefully planned vandalism nothing could have been more thorough than the work of the retreating Hun, and there was abundant proof that he retired at his leisure.

The unshelled houses had evidently been systematically ransacked and then burnt or blown up, while all the bridges had been demolished and the road junctions destroyed by huge yawning craters. But to me the most galling evidence of wanton devastation was the fact that, without exception, the trunks of all the fruit trees had been cut through at their base. The beautiful poplars and elms that formed the roadside avenues had suffered in a like manner, only in their case, a deep wedge-shaped impression had been carefully cut on the inner side of the trunk so that the trees might fall with the first gale, one by one inwards across the roadway. Even the rose bushes in the châteaux' gardens had been ruthlessly hacked to pieces. In short anything that was either

Cappy.

beautiful or useful had been brutally manhandled.

The Péronne museum, like its fellow buildings, was a mere ruin and of its contents only the books remained. These were strewn in heaps across the floor or loosely littered across the shelves – old, uncared-for tomes, inviting the first-comer to help himself. If the empty bottles were any indication, the German troops must have consumed vast quantities of liquor. They were scattered in all directions or heaped outside the officers' dug-outs. In most cases these more or less elaborate dug-outs had been burnt or rendered useless.

In peace time, the gently undulating country between the chalk quarries of Cappy and Péronne is largely devoted to the cultivation of sugar beet. This is evidenced by the shattered remains of huge refineries at Flaucourt and Herbecourt – their distorted machinery and riddled vats being ocular proof of the violence of the bombardment to which the whole country had been subjected. But of all the erstwhile villages visited by us, Biaches was the most complete ruin – it and its long contested wood had been literally wiped off the face of the earth – so much so that had my attention not been drawn to the place I could never have noticed that a village had ever stood on the site. The wood was like a Dantesque nightmare or the fantastic drawings of a petrified forest, for only the torn trunks of the larger trees remained.

And now let us turn to pleasanter topics. Near Cappy itself, I saw numbers of rooks together with jackdaws and carrion crows,

Blackbird 1.4.17

and later a fair sprinkling of hoodies. Tree sparrows seemed quite at home in the chalk quarries and no doubt breed in the crevices of the cliffs when the time comes. Three corn buntings, a few crested larks and many skylarks were also noticed, likewise starlings, common sparrows, chaffinches, magpies, yellowhammers and a white wagtail.

The neighbourhood of the trenches was too destitute of vegetation to be very 'birdy', but I saw a few crows and a kestrel or two, and some skylarks were singing overhead.

Further back where the ground was covered with un-gleaned corn crops or withered grass, grey partridges were common enough, as were the more ordinary species. A fine great grey-backed shrike, when disturbed by the passing car, perched upon one of the abandoned German field-telegraph posts.

The marshy valley of the Somme looked very pretty today, with its yellow reed beds, pollarded willows, tall poplars and wide expanse of water reflecting the blue of the sky. An open sheet of water opposite the site of Biaches was thickly spotted with wildfowl – the majority of these appeared to be coots but there were quite a lot of tufted ducks as well, their broad white flanks being very conspicuous. On the whole coots seem very abundant in this district. A few moorhens and a couple of wild duck must be added to my list, as well as a mistle thrush and linnets. I thought I saw two corn buntings east of Amiens, but we whizzed by in the car at too great a rate to be sure.

Wednesday 4 April, Candas
After a snowy night – for winter still seems with us, so backward

is the season – a strong south-easterly wind swept the sky bare of clouds.

Saturday 7 April, Candas

The last day or two, I have seen a few white wagtails about, but as the icy hand of winter still refuses to relax its grip, summer migrants are naturally shy about putting in an appearance. For some time now I have had my ears attuned for the ding-dong song of the chiffchaff, whose pleasant voice rings up the curtain of springtime – but in vain.

Rooks, always precocious in their matrimonial affairs, are undaunted by the chilly north-easters, that is to say, if one can judge by the posturing attitudes of the males who may now be seen strutting in close attendance of their spouses – often in single pairs like the carrion crow and not the great black flocks of a few weeks ago. There is a rookery at Autheux.

Yesterday I explored the outskirts of Candas and found a one-storied cottage with a small, hedged garden in which there was an old man pottering over some bee-hives. These formed the subject of several questions on my part. The old fellow, a bent, blue-eyed Picard peasant, proved to be one of nature's gentlemen and answered all my impertinent questions with grave politeness and ended by courteously inviting me into his cottage. Here I found his aged spouse – if anything, more bent and wrinkled than he – seated huddled close up against the fireplace.

The front door opened directly into the dwelling room which

A Picard Peasant.

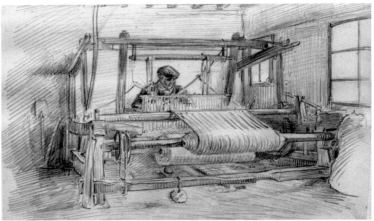

was in every way typical of this part of France – a bricked floor, a few chairs and, in one corner a large *armoire* supporting a row of ornamental plates, comprised its principal features. Through the doorway I saw their wooden bedstead and the inevitable big-beamed loom – for all the poorer folk in Candas make sack cloth. This is very apparent on walking up a street, for on such occasions, through the open windows, one constantly hears the busy click-

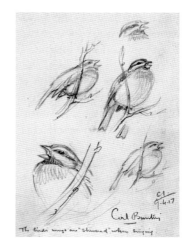

clack of the flying shuttle.

This evening, when I returned with my sketchbook, I received the hearty welcome of an old friend and was hailed as 'Kamerad', and patted on the back with almost embarrassing fervour.

The tide of war has twice swept past their cottage and yet their peaceful peasant life has remained undisturbed. Exempt in 1870 and now, of course, far too old, Dumetz must have stood and watched the armies of three nations march, day after day, through the muddy streets of his little old-world village, usually so sleepy and silent.

Sunday 8 April, Candas

Easter Sunday – the first real spring day we have had – warm and sunny.

Curiously enough, only last night I remarked that I had neither seen nor heard a chiffchaff. Today one was threading its way through the leafless boughs drifting northwards – moving ever northwards towards the land of its birth. Occasionally the bird made a halting attempt to sing, but the voice was weak and broken and on the whole it seemed too busily engaged in searching for food to be vocal.[30]

A single migrant meadow pipit was noted, also kestrels soaring in the warm sunshine and some wood-pigeons. One of the latter came zooming (to use the Flying Corps slang term) out of a sloping wood and clapped its wings loudly over its back as, with curved flight, it crossed the valley.

In a passionless fashion, a cirl bunting reeled out its monotonous song from an apple tree in the middle of Autheux. I have noticed that this bunting is more often encountered in the village gardens and circumjacent hedgerows than its congener, the yellowhammer. The cirl bunting's song lacks vivacity and seems to be uttered as a tedious duty rather than an expression of joy.

Last night, at 11.30 p.m., when quite dark, I heard a hedge sparrow break out into song close to my Armstrong hut. After a brief outpouring of song, it subsided again into silence.* Tonight at 10.45 p.m. a flock of curlews passed over, flying fairly high judging by the sound of their oft-repeated cries. It was raining slightly at the time.

*Added later, 15 April: I have heard the hedge sparrow singing at night – 10.30 p.m.

Thursday 12 April, Candas

Winter again! The last two nights snow has fallen and this morning I woke to a dazzling world of white. Despite these discouraging conditions, a song thrush challenged the morning with a full-throated song – which, however, remained unanswered. (Song thrushes seem to be few and far between.)

Nor has the cold weather damped the fervour of the chaffinches and great tits – both these birds being ardent vocalists notwithstanding the snow-laden branches. The birds appear to be the only part of nature that is adhering to the calendar for there are no other signs of springtide – the fields are bare and the woods as stark and comfortless as in mid-January.

Friday 13 April, Candas

Had a flight in an FE2d this morning. The pilot (Wood) 'lost his prop' and landed in a ploughed field.

Since the first of this month – in roughly twelve days – there have been over a hundred wrecked machines brought into No. 2

Roadside Pear-tree.

Aircraft Depot – 28 in one day! What a terrible loss of life and capital this represents. And to this formidable total must be added the machines brought into No. 1 AD and those shot down beyond our lines.[31]

Saturday 14 April, Candas
The first swallow! What a welcome sight it was to see the steely glint of sunlight upon its back as it sped with sharply pointed wings across a field that, only 48 hours ago, was a white sheet of snow! Indeed the snow was still lying in some old bomb-craters on the aerodrome.

A flying officer of No. 57 Squadron – Lieutenant E. Pope – informed me that about ten days or a fortnight ago he saw a single sandpiper (species?) over Arras at 12,000 ft. The bird was travelling in a more or less easterly direction.

A party of about a dozen meadow pipits were seen this morning.

Sunday 15 April, Candas
A steady downpour of rain lasted all day. This must have interfered with the passage of spring migrants, for during a short evening walk I saw quite a number of newcomers. Possibly the most

interesting of these was a handsome male pied wagtail[32] with a pure black head. There were two females with him – but these may have been *M. alba*.[33]

In the same corner of the aerodrome there were also seven yellow-breasted field wagtails[34] – six handsome males and a female. Three of these were typical *flava* with dark grey heads shading into deep slate round the eyes – a distinct streak of white being noticeable above and behind the eye. The bright canary yellow of the underparts faded into whitish near the chin and round the forward fringe of the dark hood. The other two males did not appear to have the white spot-like streak above the eye.

I wonder if *lugubris*[35] is as rare in the north-east of France as some writers would have us believe? Or is this supposition due to the dearth of reliable observers?

Of three wheatears noted, two were females. Since 24 March I have seen none: probably the bulk of males have passed unchecked by meteorological conditions in the interim and the females will now predominate.

A sparrowhawk dashed under an archway heading out of a farmyard, across the road and thence over a cottage roof in the village of Autheux. This habit of boldly visiting villages seems to be prevalent with sparrowhawks of this district.

Monday 16 April
A single swallow was circling around the Candas church steeple this morning and I heard and saw several field wagtails (species?) and meadow pipits on the move at intervals during the day. The coldness and lateness of the season is truly remarkable – the naked boughs and verdureless fields show no promise of awakening life.

Again, for the third time, I have heard the hedge sparrow 'talking in its sleep' as it were.

Captain Bransby Williams took me for a short spin this morning in a Sopwith – a most exhilarating flight. As is his wont, he 'stunted' most of the time. A vertical dive, with the air shrieking through the wires, is certainly a novel experience.*

*Added later: Bransby Williams – perhaps the finest pilot in the Flying Corps – was reported missing about the second week of May. There is very little hope of his being alive, as a machine – apparently a Spad – was seen to crash to the ground with broken wings on the day he disappeared. His extraordinary pluck, good nature and bonhomie made Williams one of the most popular fellows in any squadron.[36]

Wednesday 18 April, Vert Galant

Yesterday morning I came over here and am now attached to No. 56 Squadron. A steady downpour of rain enabled me to spend the afternoon in Amiens where I had some shopping to do.

I heard several corn buntings singing a few kilometres north of the city – they seem to prefer the country surrounding the town, since I saw a fair number on the east side when returning to Cappy on 28 March whereas I have noticed none near Candas.

Jackdaws were wheeling about the towering spire of the cathedral and I thought I heard a black redstart singing among the

Black Redstart.

71

sculptured masonry. The spluttering song of one of these birds was repeated several times from the farm roof when I woke this morning – later in the day I saw the vocalist and also a rival – both males in immature dress.*

There is, I understand, a rookery at Villers-Bocage.

Added later, 20 April: These two fought battle royals both this evening and yesterday.

Friday 20 April, Vert Galant

Crested larks are not uncommon on the aerodrome. I forgot to record that, in March, I saw one of these birds perched on a small post which appears to be a somewhat unusual habit with this ground-loving species.*

Starlings are fairly numerous, as they were also at Candas. There seem to be no signs of their commencing to nest.**

Tonight I thought I heard a little owl: this species seems to be more numerous in Flanders – i.e. Cassel, Abeele (and also St-Omer) – than further south.

Added later: Often seen perching on some gorse bushes near St-Omer.

***Added later, 22 April*: Today I saw a starling trailing a piece of straw from his bill.

Monday 23 April, Vert Galant

During the course of an evening walk, I came across five fieldfares which flew chattering out of a wooded dingle. The cutting north wind and the stark trees supplied the suitable wintry surroundings, but otherwise it would have appeared strange to have met these birds so late in the spring, while the swallows were glancing back and forth in the sheltered hollows – for today I saw at least six of these summer migrants.

A shepherd boy told me his brother had robbed a magpie's nest on Sunday last containing eggs already partly incubated – but a subsequent colloquy revealed a certain laxity as to the details of the information he was only too eager to impart.

Tuesday 24 April, Vert Galant

By the side of the road leading eastwards across the open country

shepherd boy   Vert Galant.

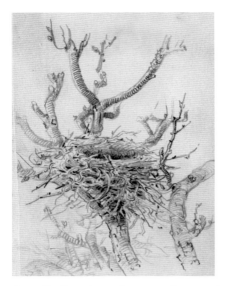

from Le Rosel stand two ancient apple trees – alone in their gnarled and venerable old age and fully exposed to the four winds of the heaven. Of all conspicuous places, for a pair of carrion crows to build their bulky nest these leafless trees would be hard to beat. And yet, as I passed, a black form slipped away to advertise the fact that the obtrusively conspicuous nest was tenanted. I had no difficulty in clambering up the 18 feet to reach the five eggs – two of which I took and subsequently found to be 'frosted'. The nest was largely composed of coarse straw-coloured roots with which were intermixed some large twigs. The lining was made of fine roots, dried grass and a feather or two, a little moss and a fair quantity of hare's fur. Hares are plentiful hereabouts and the scrapping of the 'Jacks' during the last month or so has made this material easy to obtain. Carrion crows at this season indulge in a curious nasal sound – a sort of bleating *caw*, more like the cry of a young red deer than anything else I can think of.

A female chaffinch was busily engaged in constructing a nest supported only by a few twigs sprouting from the bare trunk of an elm, about 30 feet from the ground. Swallows were noticeably more numerous today, the weather being vastly improved.

Saturday 28 April, Candas

Back again in Candas. This afternoon a south wind swept away the clouds and the sun shone with spring warmth. All nature seemed to respond to this belated change and the buds on the trees seemed visibly swollen before nightfall.

A cuckoo calling in the poplars gave the lie to the wintry aspect of the leafless hedgerows, while swallows have now probably reached their normal numbers, and glance up and down the village streets, and in and out of the open barn doors uttering their pleasant twittering song, as they inspect their last year's nests. The summer sounding *jerr* of the greenfinch comes from the tree-tops: blackbirds pipe and robins, yellowhammers, cirl buntings and linnets join the chorus. At Autheux a song thrush claimed one's ear, his clear-toned melody echoing from afar above all the other bird noises. Thrushes are thinly distributed and if there are one or two pairs in each parish that is about all. A cuckoo was heard yesterday by several members of No. 70 Squadron. I heard a willow warbler singing today.

The rookery at Autheux is an important one and occupies a broad strip of the sloping wood. There must be at least 400 nests since a rough count totalled 396. In one tree alone there were seventeen nests. The majority appeared to be built in the tallest

beech trees whose branchless boles would defy the ordinary bird-nester. By the aid of climbing irons however the villagers take toll of their numbers and destroy as many nests as they can. To judge by the uncouth cries the most precocious nestlings were still callow and this assumption was borne out by an old woodman who said they were still too small to take for eating purposes. The cawing crowd wheeled overhead, the whole colony infected by the nervousness of the nearest birds. After a while some flopped clumsily down on to twigs far too small for their weight when I could see that many had their throats distended with food.

A male common redstart is an addition to my list. A yellow wagtail (race?) flew over calling. These birds have been noticed thus on several occasions and presumably migrate at fairly low elevations and travel by day.

Tuesday 1 May, Estrées-en-Chaussée

I came here yesterday to do work with 34 Squadron, passing through Amiens and the war-struck zone area on the way. The latter was as deserted as the Sahara and, in parts, as bereft of vegetation. On the outskirts of this desolate area I saw a long-winged grey harrier flapping over in leisurely fashion, but otherwise bird-life was singularly scarce. This seems to indicate that man and his cultivation are to a certain extent essential for the maintenance of the typical avifauna of this region. Swallows were the only exception and appeared to be quite as plentiful as elsewhere among the ruined houses. Magpies, too, were to be seen here and there, and a few house sparrows still lingered among the piles of bricks.

A nightingale was heard singing in some wooded château grounds at Misery. House martins were observed for the first time. Some field wagtails[37] were also seen, presumably on passage. This morning a solitary swift flew past in a more or less northerly direction. By some flooded meadows near Le Roisel two common sandpipers were feeding, also a mistle thrush. A few rooks were noticed near this village but there are none around Estrées-en-Chaussée.

Friday 4 May, Le Roisel

I am spending a short time with Bruce,[38] whose HQ are a little beyond the wrecked village of Le Roisel. On my way here I passed a closely populated rookery in a small copse in the midst of the undulating plain – this is seemingly the only colony hereabouts.

After lunch, General Perkins took me with him when visiting some of the forward batteries near the village of Sousson. Although there was no activity as far as these guns were concerned, we were witness to an exciting incident during the course of the afternoon. The sunny sky of a sudden became dotted with puffs of smoke and the hot air filled with throbbing, rending bursts of sound. These 'Archies' (Anti-aircraft guns) directed our eyes to some aeroplanes. As two of them sailed into the field of my binoculars their peculiar shape, and especially the rounded form of the tail plane, proclaimed their enemy origin. One turned eastward, but the malignant intention of the other was soon apparent. With nose down and engine full out, this machine dived towards one of our observation balloons.[39] The occupant of the nearer balloon, taking no risks, sprang into space and was soon seen drifting to the ground beneath the white expanse of his parachute. But to us on the ground, the Hun's real objective was only too apparent. Why didn't the other fellow jump? Would he be too late? But just as a fresh salvo of 'Archies' began to burst about the attacking Hun, the balloonist leaped from his basket and none too soon – for a moment later the hurried *poop-poop-poop* of the German's machine gun fell upon our ears. For once our 'Archies' seem to have found the range and as the hawk-like aeroplane circled gracefully round its huge defenceless prey, spitting destruction, burst after burst seemed within an ace of bringing it crashing to the ground. And then – a sudden flare and the great fabric melted with yellow flames – and was no more. Its fateful mission accomplished, the aeroplane headed eastwards and was soon lost to sight.

In a wood where the enemy had felled all the trees, leaving nothing but the scrubby undergrowth, I found two magpies' nests respectively within four and seven feet of the ground and in ordinary thornless bushes. Nightingales, two or three, willow warblers, many, hedge sparrows and two jays were also noted.

Some goldfinches were feeding on the seeds of a pine tree – the hot sunshine causing the cones to open with a crack and so release the coveted seed.

Greenfinches, linnets, wood-pigeons and a few carrion crows likewise came under observation. Tree sparrows are building in the chinks of a chalk quarry here – also a white wagtail, whitethroats, whinchats, starlings and many grey partridge must be included in my list for today.

Saturday 5 May, Le Roisel
This morning I rode over the rolling down-like country that stretches from here to Péronne – seven or eight miles of uncultivated chalk land bearing, in its present grassy state, a strong resemblance to Salisbury Plain. Camps, horse-lines, ammunition dumps and all the other paraphernalia of war were obtrusively visible on all sides, while the nearer slopes of the Somme were all

disfigured with whitened trenches and shell-holes.

Skylarks rejoiced in these open lands but otherwise, save for a few corn buntings and numerous couples of grey partridges, bird-life was not plentiful on these grassy fields. Nearer the villages or wherever there were trees or scraps of hedgerows, yellowhammers, chaffinches and sparrows were noticed and, of course, magpies and a few carrion crows.

Having arrived at Péronne I put up my horse in an empty stable, gave him the feed I had carried with me, and walked to the river-bank in search of aquatic species. The croaking song of a great reed warbler and the soothing cackle of moorhens from a large reed-bed below the citadel walls was a promising start, which however was not maintained. The shattered orchards, battered gardens of a favoured *faubourg* held a certain number of the commoner warblers – blackcaps, whitethroats and garden warblers, but on the whole this attractive-looking district yielded comparatively poor results.

Hedge sparrows, yellowhammers, blackbirds and mistle thrushes were all there – indeed, I found a nest of the latter species in a rather unusual position, i.e. on the beam of a broken-down *baraque* scarcely four feet from the ground. This nest contained eggs a few days incubated. The poor sitting bird was evidently suffering from the oppressive heat since her bill was agape and she

sat panting in the fierce sunlight.

The broad span of the Somme opposite Péronne was liberally dotted with coots just as it was about five weeks ago, but the tufted duck had now all gone. I saw two common sandpipers feeding on the floating patches of weeds.

Sunday 6 May, Estrées-en-Chaussée

One of the pilots of this squadron, No. 34 – O.B. Wills[40] by name – tells me he has fairly frequently met with birds when flying and mentions having seen waders (species?) and peewits (March) at heights between 4,000 and 5,000 ft, swallows (swifts?), 3,000 ft, ducks (winter) about 4,000 ft, heron (one – autumn) about 3,000 ft – redwings (or fieldfare) (March) about 3,500 ft.[41]

Monday 7 May

The river Omignon just below Monchy-Lagache runs through a swampy wood of willows and poplars. Where the ground slopes upwards to the south, oak and beech replace these riverine species. No wonder such a mixed woodland proved a happy hunting ground for the ornithologist. A cold east wind more than tempered the bright sunshine in the early morning and this was no doubt responsible for silencing a number of birds that would otherwise have been vocal. A few nightingales babbled in the sheltered thickets where the wood anemone and Solomon's seal ran riot – a robin sang fitfully and a cuckoo called in the distance.

As the morning wore on, the wind subsided and the concert of loud voices swelled proportionately. The most interesting performance was a blackcap. This individual possessed a peculiar genius for mimicking other species – in its way this bird was almost as skilled in this respect as *Hippolais*[42] and to the listener nothing was lost by the fact that it lacked much of the latter's blatancy. This blackcap seemed to be 'trying over' the songs of its various imitants – as though attempting to recall its more favourite snatches of song. I recognised the robin's piercing note, which was repeated frequently; also the blackbird's alarm rattle and the starling's 'twang', while the willow warbler's simple little refrain was beautifully imitated. The nightingale's rich voice and the song thrush's melody also contributed to the repertoire. When later the blackcap became more ardent, its louder song more nearly approached that of its own species – a typical outpouring of pleasant warbled notes.

In the fork of an ivy-clad oak, a kestrel was nesting. I tried to reach it by means of a borrowed rope but failed in my attempts to throw it over the lowermost branch. These efforts were strongly resented by the little falcons who fluttered round on quickly beating, depressed wings, screeching invective pretty well all the time.

Close by, two firecrests were busily feeding, uttering the thin shrew-like call notes of their genus and one every now and again broke into a sizzling song. It struck me that these firecrests had a cleaner-cut outline than the goldcrest – looked less portly and more warbler-like – and a shade larger. The song too was distinguishable, although not strikingly distinctive.

The *check-check* of a greater spotted woodpecker drew my attention to a spreading sycamore. His scarlet under-tail coverts were very conspicuous – indeed he was an altogether noticeable bird with the sun shining on his parti-coloured dress, vividly patched with red. A turtle dove settled close to me and started bowing to his mate, crooning throatily the while.

Near the village of Estrées I was shown two crested larks' nests. It is really remarkable how this species always seems to keep as close as possible to populous roadways and the outskirts of towns and villages. Both these nests were in fallow fields, sunk under the lee of a clod of bare earth and were placed in spots where they were in daily danger of being tramped on by passing troops. The nest itself was a slight affair – a few wisps of dried bents lining the rather deep hollow. The clutch consisted of four in both cases and incubation was only just commenced. I was also shown a skylark's, a linnet's and a chaffinch's nest – the last in a strikingly conspicuous place, i.e. on the dead branches of a small pear tree that had been felled by the retreating Huns and lay close by the side of a pathway.

En route for Péronne and thence to Nurlu, I caught fleeting glimpses of the marshy Somme with its great reed-beds and sallow-grown islets. I noted a party of waders that were probably reeves, a common sandpiper or two, a stone curlew (flying down the valley in a northerly direction), a wild duck and another duck (with longish neck and much white on its wings) that I was not able to identify. Great reed warblers were noisily plentiful – I saw also common reed warblers, white wagtail, coots and moorhens and would unquestionably have noted many more species had I the chance of exploring these attractive localities. A wood-pigeon was sitting on a very exposed nest on a branch of one of the still leafless elms that lined the highway between Péronne and Nurlu.

Tuesday 8 May, Nurlu
A partially cleared wood fills a hollow just below this aerodrome. Among the tins and wire and dug-outs that mark the recent

German occupation, bird-life is extraordinarily plentiful. I watched a cuckoo for some time to see if it opened its bill when calling. If it did so at all it is very slightly on the first syllable. During the performance the head is very slightly ducked and the lower throat inflated – the wings are drooped and almost meet under the raised tail.

Wednesday 9 May, Nurlu
This evening I revisited the wood I explored last night and was rewarded by seeing many interesting species including a greater spotted woodpecker, golden oriole and fieldfare. Above the chorus of nightingales and warblers I was more than a little surprised to hear the *chuk-chuk-chuk* of a fieldfare. There was, however, no mistaking the sound and, indeed, I clearly heard and saw the bird on three occasions.

The grasshopper warblers were reeling away in the sultry evening air. I watched one rise on to a spray of tangled honeysuckle, open what appeared to be its black-lined gape and emit a monstrous ticking sound for some time. Does this black lining indicate an affinity to the fantail warblers? The 'tongue spots' in the young of both genera are somewhat alike.

Wood-pigeons were again indulging in their special flight. Rising with a series of exaggerated wing beats, causing the pinions to meet over their back with an audible clapping sound, they then float with a graceful curve downwards on slightly depressed wings. The whole performance conveys the impression of enjoyment – as though it were an expression of happy emotion. Turtle doves will also take somewhat similar joy flights.

Two rival nightingales were having a vocal battle and singing with loud defiance and throbbing insults at one another. Beautiful as the full rich notes were to my ears, it was patent that they were really expressing bitter anger between themselves, as was evidenced by the up-raised russet tails and puffed-out dorsal plumage. Later indeed they actually came into conflict, with shrill small notes, the more masterful bird driving the other away.

This afternoon Ellis took me up for a short flight in a BE2e.

Thursday 10 May, Nurlu
Rising at 5.30 a.m. just as the sun capped a low bank of haze, I set forth through the dew-spangled grass to some flooded fields I had noticed yesterday from the aeroplane. These proved to be much further than I had thought, and must have been over 3½ miles from our camp. To my surprise I again encountered fieldfares[43] – two being seen and heard in some tall poplars near the canal bank. These birds sat and preened themselves in the morning sun until driven away by a bullying magpie, so were evidently in no hurry to reach their northern fells.

A slope embracing a re-entrant, containing a small winding stream and its bordering meadows, was beautifully wooded, the finest timber being beech, larch and oak. In places shell-fire had combed through the wood, and many of the trees drooped shattered limbs among the budding green, while others had been killed outright and their splintered trunks lay crashed upon the ground. Golden orioles were piping in the upper greenery and these birds have no doubt arrived in their full numbers. A chiffchaff or two were singing. Although thinly scattered in the larger woodlands, it would appear that this warbler is a fairly common summer visitor to this part of France, its numbers being equalled and possibly slightly exceeded by the willow warbler. A spotted flycatcher was noted but this bird has evidently not settled for the summer.* The soil hereabouts seemed to be a stiffish clay on chalk: a few pairs of partridges were seen but they do not appear to be nearly so abundant as in some parts.

A single female wheatear was flitting along the parapet of a disused trench: she was evidently a belated bird of passage.

Added later, 11 May: Saw several in Gurlu Wood – no doubt nests fairly commonly in the district.

Saturday 12 May, Longavesnes

Yesterday afternoon I came over here to No. 52 Squadron and before dinner had a stroll in Gurlu Wood. Entering this from the Templeux end, I found two hobbies perched in tall oak trees. One uttered a *peep-peep-peep* cry, distinctly reminiscent of a wryneck's call – the other made a weak querulous noise and bobbed its head nervously up and down after the manner of falcons. Shortly after, they both rose into the hot afternoon air and soared in small circles over the wood at a great height. Their wings struck me as not only being longer than the average falcon, but proportionately longer. I should imagine the lifting surface is greater in proportion to the birds' weight than in any of its European allies.

Corn buntings are remarkably plentiful round here – this is somewhat surprising since at Nurlu, only about a couple of miles away, I saw none. The soil is certainly lighter round Longavesnes and this probably accounts for their presence in large numbers. A cirl bunting was heard singing near Templeux-la-Fosse.

One or two *Hippolais* were seen in the wood – the first of the year. They were shy and mostly kept to the upper branches so I could not identify the species. Not being in full song their voice was no guide.

Tree-creepers, many orioles, a marsh tit, a greater spotted

woodpecker and a fair number of song thrushes were noted as well as all the common species. As I went to bed I heard a stone curlew wailing on the open lands behind the aerodrome. A lesser whitethroat was seen and identified today – the first of the year.

Sunday 13 May, Longavesnes
The stone curlews were calling again today. In a small spinney near the aerodrome I found a song thrush's nest containing two eggs:* this bird was actually nesting *on* the ground among some stubbed growth.

Found a kestrel's nest in the fork of a beech tree: the first branching of the larger boughs seems to be a favourite site of this bird's nest.

*Added later, 14 May: A third egg was in the nest this morning.

Wednesday 16 May, St-Omer
Yesterday morning Captain Probyn flew me here in a BE2e. We expected to return again in the afternoon in an RE8, but the weather changed suddenly and we have been obliged to remain.

Hearing that Lieutenant Colonel Drury – an army chaplain – was anxious to meet me, I called on him and found him to be an honest and fairly keen ornithologist. He gave me several interesting pieces of information. He said the only rookery he had seen in the neighbourhood was one at Dunkirk where the birds were practically building in the town itself:* last year he had found a colony of little bitterns nesting near Clairmarais and two heronries in the forest of that name.

After lunch Drury arranged to motor me out to Clairmarais. After passing through a quaint Dutch-like district for three miles (in one place a canal separated the houses from the road and this waterway was consequently spanned by an immense number of bridges and carried a flotilla of picturesque boats) we pulled up opposite an old convent. Here we embarked, and the boat was half punted and half paddled along an intricate system of canals and dykes to a mere that was not more than a couple of hundred yards from our starting point.

Being exceptionally clear of reeds or rank growth of any kind,

I hardly expected to find the little bitterns, but in some willows that surrounded a wildfowler's hide one sprang into life and sailed away over the water with strong buoyant flight.[44] A moment later this bird was attacked by another male, and the two disappeared among some distant willow trees. With their light creamy shoulder patches and dark backs these birds were strangely conspicuous – their flight too struck me as being remarkably agile for a member of this family, especially when they were chasing each other in and out of the branches. Although we later came across two or three more specimens, there was no sign of their having commenced to breed. Drury says they place their nests among the branches of willows where they can be easily robbed. It seems probable, therefore, that they are nearly always disturbed, as people are constantly working in the surrounding fields which are highly cultivated.

There were only two herons' nests in the portion of the forest behind Clairmarais church, but at least a dozen birds were reposing in the surrounding oaks when we appeared upon the scene. Considering the small size of the trees it is surprising these had not been *dénichant* by some enterprising youth: it was only later when I was warned that the birds would peck my eyes out if I attempted to climb the trees that I understood their immunity.

The unmusical cry of the oriole, which the bird sometimes mingles with his mellow flutings, might well be likened to the mewing caterwauling of a cat. Spotted flycatchers are fairly plentiful in this forest. This bird cannot be described as a songster but occasionally he makes a feeble effort, which consists of three or four shrill chirping notes with but little variation.[45]

Added later: This statement has been stoutly denied by Commander Chambers RNAS – he says that there are hardly any trees in Dunkirk and certainly not a rookery.[46]

Thursday 17 May, Longavesnes
Drove back from St-Omer – probably about 90 miles – the greater part of the way in rain and, from Albert, in a heavy downpour all the way. No rooks were seen during the earlier part of this journey and afterwards the weather conditions precluded observations.

Friday 18 May

Before dinner I visited Tincourt Wood but an overcast sky and rough wind seemed to dispirit the birds and kept most of them silent. In this wood chiffchaffs were quite as common as willow warblers if not actually more numerous. In one corner I heard a note that I am almost positive was uttered by a scops owl:[47] when I made further attempt to locate the bird it immediately lapsed into silence. A tremendous hubbub drew my attention to a concourse of magpies – twelve or more – and upon approaching I found the cause of all the commotion was a dead jay! A few wrens and robins were included among the usual woodland species.

Saturday 19 May, Villers-Bretonneux

On my way here I passed through Tincourt and in the wooded grounds of the château I saw and heard an assembly of rooks, so presume there is a rookery there.

One of the crested lark's nests at Estrées (see 7 May) now contained young. These are fairly heavily protected by very pale straw-coloured down. This down differs from that of the common skylark by being of a rather finer texture: in the latter bird the nestling down is not only comparatively coarse, but has a 'pepper and salt' appearance and seems to form a very dense covering. In the crested lark the colour is quite uniform, a pale creamy or yellowish buff. The tongue-spots of the bill are conspicuous in this lark.

Saw a grey shrike near here – whether a greater or lesser I would

not like to say as the car whisked by before I could get a decent view of it.*

Added later: Saw this bird again: I think there is no doubt it is a lesser grey shrike.[48]

Sunday 20 May, Villers-Bretonneux

This afternoon together in company with four fellows from 35 Squadron, I visited the marshy valley of the Somme below Corbie. Overshadowed by tall poplars, the reedy lagoons and lush meadows looked like being very attractive to swamp-loving birds. One inland sheet of water with no communication with the canal or river (and therefore normally inaccessible by boat) was teeming with common and greater reed warblers, the latter being especially noisy. By carrying our boat over a narrow strip of land, we were able to invade their domain and this resulted in the discovery of three nests of the greater reed warbler,[49] containing respectively, two, two and one eggs freshly laid. The nests were in the reeds and typical in every respect from what I could learn. Although I searched pretty carefully I neither saw nor heard any signs of marsh or icterine warblers. As a matter of fact there did not seem to be any very suitable spinney for the former, but the shrubby railway embankments and tree-lined dykes ought to have held some icterines.

In the well-tended garden of M. Boullet – a rich banker naturalist whom I called upon – I heard a cirl bunting singing: there is no doubt that this bunting is much more of a suburban bird than the yellowhammer, but is not so strictly confined to outskirts of human habitation as the crested lark. This latter encroached right upon Amiens, where I have seen it in one of the boulevards surrounded by houses. On my way back between Corbie and Villers-Bretonneux I heard several quails calling in the vetch fields.

Tuesday 22 May, Boulogne

On my way down here I had to report at Hesdin. In the château garden I heard an icterine warbler singing. Before dawn I took the tram up to the high bluff half way to Wimereux. I saw five or six field wagtails, all of which were unmistakable *raii*.[50] Meadow pipits were abundant and I was shown a nest containing four young, about as many days old. A few crested larks claimed the sky. Starlings as plentiful as in England.

In late May, Ingram returned to England on leave.

Wednesday 30 May, Westgate-on-Sea
Found a yellow wagtail's nest in a clover field containing five much-incubated eggs. The nest was sunk into the ground almost flush with the surface.

Wednesday 6 June, Stoke Golding
Examined a young starling about seven days old. Apart from the pale greyish down still adhering to the tips of the ordinary feathers, in parts there was a fairly profuse secondary growth of down in the interspaces between the feathers and the feather tracts. This down (also pale, smoky grey) was sprinkled over the 'bare' spaces on the sides of the body but was thick, one might almost say copiously distributed, on the upper surface of the wing between the tertiaries.

Friday 8 June, Stoke Golding
Tree pipits are abundant here. Last night there was a heavy

thunder shower which perhaps brought down some caterpillars from the oak trees or may be they were dropping out of their own accord. Be this as it may, birds were finding no difficulty in gathering beakfuls from the roadway this afternoon and a tree pipit was plying to and fro at regular intervals between its nest in a clover field and the shadows of an oak that stretched across the Daddington Road.

Yesterday I found a baby plover in a meadow. The old male peewit, although he was punctiliously performing his duties as sentinel some hundred yards away, did not rise soon enough to give the warning note – or perhaps I was too old a hand to have my attention diverted by his cries and demonstrations. Anyhow I spotted the fluffy youngster before he had time to sink into a tuft of grass, when the cryptic effect of his black and brown back caused him to become immediately lost to sight among the surrounding lumps of semi-dried dung.

Standing up, the young plover instantly became a conspicuous object. It is difficult to understand the use of this, so called, warning colouration – the white under-surface and more especially the very noticeable white patch at the back of the head. Is it really a 'warning' mark? To me it is much more probable that it is nature's device for enabling the young birds to keep together. This suggestion is supported by the fact that species marked thus are generally silent (cf. ringed and Kentish plover) whereas chicks lacking any conspicuous mark – such a game birds – keep together by means of a cheeping note.

Willow Warbler

Found a nest of willow warbler containing young about four days old. Down apparently on capital and humeral tracts only.

Saturday 9 June, Streatley-on-Thames

There are several kingfishers about here and they come and fish in the little lake behind the house. As they dart, with headlong flight, down the backwaters or between and under the willows, they often rush into what might be a hidden danger – they come upon a human being before they know where they are and brush by one's cap with startling suddenness. While dashing about with hurried, direct flight in this manner, they utter a shrill call-note which is sometimes disyllabic *cheee-ze cheee.*

It is remarkable how all haunters of running water possess a high-pitched voice as witness the dipper, grey wagtail and common sandpiper. Moorhens, as they swim, have a habit of jerking their tails and thus display the white feathers. They have a very pleasant rippling cry.

A lesser whitethroat has a nest in the garden – in a privet some three feet from the ground. The parents are much concerned about their young and became very excited when I attempted to sketch them. The alarm note is an oft-repeated *tchak* – not unlike that of a garden warbler. This is reiterated at quicker intervals as one nears the nest, until it changes to an agonised little squawk as the poor birds become frenzied with anxiety and resort to demonstrative, noisy flutterings in the undergrowth – the usual avine ruse. *Three* birds took part, but whether they were all actively interested in the same nest I cannot say. Green caterpillars were being given to the young.

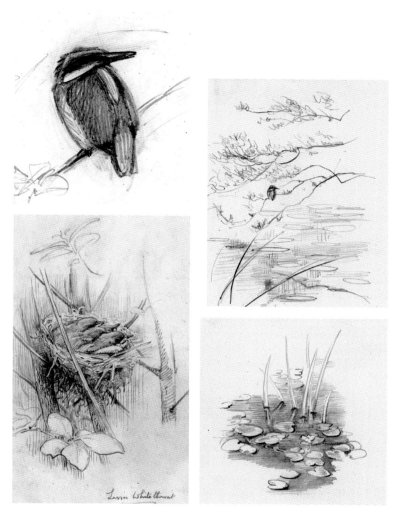

Lesser White Throat

A blackcap's song strikes me as being richer and more varied than that of a garden warbler: the notes seem to range to a higher key and the whole effort seems to be more of a finished tune, much as a coaching – or bugle – call leaves an impression of completeness on the ear. The song of a garden warbler on the other hand is more of a rambling warble – a jumble of musical

♀ Chaffinch trying to cover
well-grown fledglings

notes. In quality these notes are rather like those of the blackcap and for this reason the songs of the two birds are rather easily confused by inexperienced naturalists.

Chaffinches are just on the wing or else fully fledged in their nests. The parents feed the youngsters with quite large insects at this stage. In the beak of one I noted a large dragonfly which must have been rather difficult to ram down the purple throat. Green caterpillars form a large portion of their food.

A pair of sedge warblers have built in a low box bush: their nest contains two sterile eggs and two young about a couple of days old. These are quite innocent of nestling down and their naked skin is of a blackish hue, rather shiny and a little creased, especially about the head and back. This pigmented skin is not confined to the young of the sedge warblers but is common to several acrocephaline species and is possibly a generic character.

In a dovecote, not more than a dozen yards from the front door, several jackdaws have clamorous young. A kestrel also visits this dovecote and presumably has a nest there also. A willow warbler has built its nest in a tangle of roses that overspreads the bridge carrying the drive. It is at least seven feet above the roots of the plants and about 4 ft 6in above the level of the bank and bridge.

A family of eight moorhens formed a charming picture in the sunlight as they ran about among the white water lilies, trotting

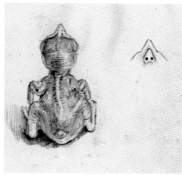

over the wide leaves like miniature jacanas. The mother clucks occasionally and is constantly flicking her tail as she paddles in their midst. Upon a sudden alarm, the little black balls of fluff scatter in all directions.

Wednesday 13 June
At the British Ornithologists' Club[51] meeting, a black-eared wheatear was exhibited. A specimen from the Witherby collection killed in Crete (1.4.06) had been feeding on 'flies, beetles and two large hard seeds'.

Saturday 16 June, Stoke Golding
This morning I was surprised to find a young hawfinch in the garden – it was only barely able to fly and I had little difficulty in catching it in my hands. At this age their massive bills appear to be even more of a disproportionately large size than in the adult and altogether they are very quaint-looking birds.

Generally speaking the plumage is a dull edition of that of the old birds but a very conspicuous feature is the mottled breast and distinctly barred flanks, these markings being of a dusky or smoky brown hue. A broad diagonal bar is formed by the white, or whitish, upper wing-coverts and secondary coverts. During flight these and the white inner webs to certain flight feathers render the owner very conspicuous. Another characteristic of the fledgling is the canary yellow wash round the base of the bill

95

Young Hawfinch.

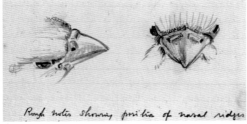

Rough notes showing position of nasal ridges

and lower cheeks. The lores are dusky. Running from the nostrils inwards are two ridge-like bosses. These are very pronounced. So far as I remember these are not present in the adult. Inside of the mouth purplish crimson.

Knowing that the nest must be very near, I searched the orchard and found it near the top of one of the apple trees about twenty feet from the ground. At first I thought it was a last year's nest, for one could see right through it from below. On going up to it with a ladder, however, I found it was quite new and still contained a lot of nestling down from the young birds with which in their early stage they are plentifully supplied. This down was almost pure white. Externally, the nest was composed of coarse black twigs, but the lining (which came away as a distinct layer) was of very much finer material – chiefly straw-coloured rootlets with a few grass bents intermingled.

Thursday 21 June, Candas

Back again in France. Candas looks a very different place from when I saw it last and the leafy lanes overhung with hornbeam give it quite an attractive appearance. By the way, in the winter I mistook these roadside hedges for beech and referred to them as such on several occasions in my last journal. At midday I walked from the aerodrome to the village. As I saw no corn buntings *en route*, my previous supposition that this bird is wanting hereabouts seems to be confirmed, although it is so common near Amiens – it is not a species one can easily overlook.

Hippolais are fairly common in the lanes round the village. There is every reason to believe these to be *icterina*.[52] I tried to obtain a specimen to make sure, but could not obtain a shot among the dense foliage. Of course they are more or less silent now – at any rate in rainy weather as today – so it is extremely difficult to detect them.

Saturday 23 June, Treizennes

Arrived here yesterday morning to visit No. 100 Squadron who are now on the aerodrome formerly occupied by No. 4 Squadron which I visited during the cold spell last winter.

In the open country – among the beet and pea crops – I have noted several blue-headed wagtails and meadow pipits. Crested larks are common and are even more vocal than the skylarks. Icterine – I believe they are icterine warblers – are quite numerous. Each bird seems to have a slightly different song owing to one individual preferring to mimic the notes of certain species, while the next will harp on the notes of another species. Today one of these warblers repeatedly, and very perfectly, reproduced the trilling of a skylark, while its neighbour showed a partiality to the song of a whitethroat and a few piping notes of a blackbird. All, however, possess the characteristic twanging notes which always seems to intimate a close affinity to the acrocephaline warblers.[53] Sparrows' chirps and the swallows' alarm-cry nearly always form part of their repertoire. Tree sparrows are common and are no doubt nesting in the pollarded willows. I forgot to mention that I saw a great grey-backed shrike between Frévent and here.

Aries
25/6/17

Young Whitethroat

Sunday 24 June

Last night I heard quails calling in the tall grass near our huts – they continued until I fell asleep about 11 p.m. (summer time). Being Sunday, I spent a few hours birds-nesting, but with singularly little success. In different places I heard four or five icterine warblers singing, but search as we would (I was with a companion) we failed to discover their nests.

Tuesday 26 June, Aire

Icterine warblers are very plentiful. They seem to prefer the gardens of the low-lying country where the soil is a rich alluvial, and reed-fringed dykes reflect the pollarded willows. In this district they also frequent the cornfields and several times I have seen them fly out and drop down among the growing crops. Today I met with one in an open wheat field at least three hundred yards from the nearest tree or hedgerow. My presence seemed to excite this individual into loud song and it flew here and there pouring out a volume of notes which were continued even on the wing.

When it settled it would sidle up to the tip of the stalk singing all the while after the manner of a reed warbler among the reeds. Its song-flight was intentionally laboured and fluttering and the wings continued to vibrate for a few seconds after alighting, beating an accompaniment to the rich flow of notes – among

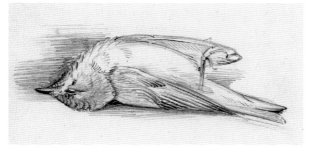

which I frequently recognised the voice of the skylark and the loud alarm of the swallow; but the twanging, violin-like notes characteristic of the species recurred throughout the strain.

A pair of common redstarts was noticed by an avenue of old pollarded willows. These grey-leaved trees lined a narrow lane that led to a pretty, red-roofed farm which was completely overshadowed by tall elms. The male occasionally indulged in its short musical refrain: the alarm cry is a clear liquid – *wheeeetcher* – the first long-drawn syllable is very like the alarm note of a nightingale and can be reproduced by a low-toned whistle.

In an icterine warbler I shot today, I noted several hair-like feathers projecting from the hinder portion of the head. Similar appendages have been observed in other species including, I believe, the blackbird.

Wednesday 27 June, Lealvillers

After reporting to HQ at Hesdin I came on here last night. It was an entrancing day, sparkling sunlight, a soft summer breeze and a marvellously clear atmosphere. For miles we sped over great rolling plains that stretched away in blue-shadowed folds to far horizons where they met a fairyland of clouds.

Dropping down into the valley of the Authie we followed the course of this river for a considerable distance. At one point I was tempted to stop the car and explore a very attractive looking marshy woodland. The luxuriance of the vegetation was something to remember and with its towering poplars, tangled undergrowth and trailing creepers – for there was a riot of wild hops – its resemblance to a tropical forest was more than a suggestion.

The play of sunlight in the foliage of a poplar that is being gently moved by a light breeze is always a thing of great beauty, and this effect was to be seen at its best among the huge trees that spread their branches over the acres of alder scrub. The whole scene seemed punctuated with little dots of light and shade – of light green and dark green, yellow green and blue green and whenever the breeze stirred among the upper branches these dots danced and scintillated like the sparkle of rippling water.

With the watery dykes, rank undergrowth and shady trees I had great hopes of meeting the marsh warbler in this swampy wood. I heard the few opening bars of a song that may have been uttered by this bird, but could not swear to it – had it been earlier in the season of course it would have been an easy matter to have named the bird population, but now the great majority are silent and in the dense thickets it is impossible to distinguish them.

Thursday 28 June, Lealvillers

One of the officers here said he had seen a large grey bird (which, by his description must have been a Montagu's harrier) frequenting one of the valleys near here. In the hopes of meeting with it, we sallied forth this afternoon but after wandering over the open fields for some time we were obliged to return disappointed. The butterflies, and especially the wild flowers, more than repaid us for our trouble. Marbled whites were flitting about in all directions among the blues, meadow browns and tortoiseshells. There were quite a number of flowers altogether new to me, and one or two of very striking appearance. A plant bearing a spike of lemon-yellow flowers centred with mauve hairy stamens struck me as being especially handsome,* as also a more lowly plant with a bright purple inflorescence.

Although crested larks** appear to be absent, skylarks are common enough.

A pilot named Turner informed me he had seen two swallows at 2,500 ft last summer (July) near Arras.

*Added later: Black mullein.

**Added later, 29 June: Crested larks are only absent in the open country. By the sides of the roads leading out of Harponville I saw several couples today.

Friday 29 June, Lealvillers

I took a stroll before dinner through Harponville and into the large wood that covers the chalky hillside a mile beyond. On the outskirts of the village I came across two fledgling wheatears and an adult male – the former were, I think, too young to be migrants so presumably the species nests in the district.

The loud twanging notes of an icterine announced the presence of this warbler in a village orchard. There can be no doubt that this species prefers such places – shady gardens and orchards – to the wilder localities. For instance I heard none in the big wood, which by the way seemed to be the home of innumerable garden warblers, many of whom were warbling softly to themselves or tending to the wants of fully fledged youngsters. Possibly these warblers were attracted by the wild strawberries and cherries. I noticed them feeding greedily on the latter.

Sunday 1 July, St-Omer

In a heavy cold rainstorm, which was borne on a strong north wind, I motored here yesterday. Although the rain has ceased, it is still so wet and cold and threatening that the birds are, for the most part, sulking in the undergrowth.

Swallows and martins of course are always *en évidence*. The former are no doubt hard put to it to supply the wants of their newly fledged youngsters. They may be seen skimming very low over the grass, occasionally checking their flight to snatch a fly from some flower-head. A man mowing a hay-field is a great attraction on such occasions and he is sure to be closely attended by a cloud of grateful swallows, which will be greedily attacking the insects that are forced into the air by his operations. Song thrushes were singing this morning despite the depressing weather. Stonechats and meadow pipits were noted on the aerodrome.

I looked up Drury last night. He told me he had seen grey wagtails while fishing at intervals throughout the summer and was sure they were nesting. He had also noted a grey-plumaged harrier in the marshes – either a hen harrier or a marsh harrier. Near the aerodrome, a short while ago, he observed a great grey-backed shrike being mobbed by small birds. I noted a red-backed shrike on my way up to the aerodrome this morning.

Monday 2 July, St-Omer

After tea I borrowed Drury's bicycle and made my way out to Clairmarais to visit the lagoons where we had seen the little bitterns in May. Although I had no time to make a thorough search of these lagoons – now vastly changed by a growth of reeds, sedges and other water plants – I beat about their former haunts without any kind of success. A couple of grey herons were flapping and croaking in the heavens, a few common reed warblers darted out of the reeds in front of me and a cuckoo flickered into a grey willow – otherwise these lagoons seemed very deserted.

In another place I saw a duck – it appeared to have too plump a figure for a mallard – fly off to a more distant part of the marsh. Greenfinches were love-making and evidently contemplating their late second brood: among the trees, too, blackbirds, chaffinches and other small birds were noted including, I think, a tree sparrow.[54] A field wagtail of sorts[55] was calling in a cabbage patch on the fringe of marsh, but I could not spot him.

There was a sand martin on the aerodrome this morning. In St-Omer itself I was surprised to hear a blackbird singing in the very middle of the town where there seemed to be no gardens of

Old Windmill
St Omer.
3·7·17

any description. On looking up, I found his black head and yellow bill projecting over the edge of a chimney-pot where he had taken his stand to carol in the westering sun.

House martins are common in St-Omer and today half a dozen or more were settling on the ground among the cobbles of the Grande Place. So far as I could make out they were gathering the dry chaff-like remains of desiccated horse dung that had lodged in the crevices between the sets – presumably for the purpose of constructing their nests although these should have been built and finished months ago and, moreover, one usually sees these birds gathering *mud*, not a dry crumbling substance. Probably house sparrows had driven these birds from their rightful homes. Swifts were very conspicuous at nightfall round the cathedral and etc.

Wednesday 4 July, St-Omer
Stonechats and meadow pipits are very abundant among the gorse bushes that surround the grassy plateau that forms the aerodrome. These birds seem to be chiefly confined to this gravelly district – a light soil on which the crested lark also thrives. Linnets, whitethroats and yellowhammers are likewise fond of the district and are common there. Partridges, corn buntings and skylarks seen.

Young Stonechats

Thursday 5 July, St-Omer

In the marshes near Arques, meadow pipits and blue-headed wagtails are quite common and I found a nest of the latter containing young about five days old. The distribution of the field wagtails[56] in north-east France is a very interesting subject. Near Boulogne all the birds I saw, and they were quite numerous on the arable east of the town, were undoubtedly *raii*, whereas round Aire and again in this neighbourhood typical *flava* occurs. As we are such a short distance from Boulogne – about thirty miles – this must be very near the meeting point of the two races.

The nest was tucked away in a tuft of rank grass, a semblance of a 'run' leading up to it. The slight hollow that contained it was lined with fine grass-roots and bents and this was followed with a warm, inner lining of wool and hair (both cow's and horse-hair). It struck me as curious that the nest had not been destroyed by the many beasts that were grazing in this field. By some guiding instinct the birds had selected a patch of grass that was evidently distasteful to the animals and this had now grown up, with many others, into a dark island or tuft in a sea of short-cropped turf. For

some reason, probably a collection of cow droppings – the herbage at this point was darker and ranker than the surrounding meadow and unpalatable to the animals.* In the distribution and colour of the nestling down the young appear to be indistinguishable from *raii* – the down being of the same pale creamy-buff hue, the colour of a lightly cooked biscuit.

Field wagtails are noticeable birds and generally claim attention by their far-reaching note. With modifications this may be used either as a call-note on the wing or as a sort of song uttered from the top of a meadow plant. In the latter case, the bird sits on some prominent spray – as likely as not swaying to and fro in the breeze – and repeatedly delivers this monotonous strain – a rather plaintive, rasping note. Sometimes it is more distinctly disyllabic and when it has this flourish in the middle, it is a pleasant sound and falls upon the ear with a cheerful ring – *choo-we* – *cho-eee* and then perhaps *choo-we* again.

A number of sand martins had mixed with their commoner brethren and were hawking for insects in the marshes. Their note is a little, rough, self-satisfied purr.

*Added later: Two days later I was chagrined to find the nest crushed by what appears to have been the hoof of some passing beast. Although the bird's 'guiding instinct' could ensure that their special patch of grass would not be eaten away, it could not

safeguard them from the roaming footsteps of an irresponsible heifer.

Saturday 7 July, St-Omer

Last night was one in a thousand – a full moon riding in a mellow summer sky and not a breath of wind to stir the soft scented air. As I was walking back from St-Omer – where I had dined – the silence of the night was broken by occasional bursts of melody from that inimitable songster the icterine warbler. Bird song always sounds more beautiful – more soul-stirring – at night when the notes fall upon an undisturbed ear and when they need not be disentangled from the thousand and one that always fill the daylight hours. Certainly my icterine was in happy vein last night for he united the charm of many species – and especially those of the whitethroat and skylark – into a charming rhapsody. But the most interesting point of this observation was that the sound came from the midst of a field of oats, a fact which rather corroborates my experiences at Aire (see 26 June). Colonel Drury has also remarked that this bird will, on occasion, frequent the cereal crops.

Much of a nightingale's fame rests upon its nocturnal habits. Poets would not wax so eloquent if it was purely a day singer as is the thrush whose music would be thought every bit as fine if it competed at night.

'The nightingale, if she should sing by day
When every goose is cackling, would be thought
No better a musician than the wren'.[57]

The little owl appears to inhabit the trees of the ramparts of St-Omer. After nightfall a chittering or chattering sound is heard and I attribute it to this species, although I am by no means sure.

Sunday 8 July, St-Omer

Drury and I were invited over to Rollencourt to the HQ of the war correspondents. There I met Beach Thomas, Robinson, Gibbs and others – men whose writings are daily read by millions of people.[58] Their château is superbly situated in well-timbered grounds, through which runs the river and a crystal clear tributary that comes gushing out of a wooded hillside.

In the spring the place must have been ringing with bird-song for even now there were many species to be heard: chiffchaffs, garden and icterine warblers, blackcaps, song thrushes,* chaffinches, robins, golden orioles, yellowhammers, wrens, goldfinches and blackbirds, and all these were in very fair song and especially towards the evening. The goldfinches were haunting a flower-spangled meadow, attracted thither by the purple knapweed, upon the seeds of which they were feeding.

Beach Thomas showed me an old reed warbler's nest in the reeds. This was fairly shallow and composed entirely of fine grassy material and contained no moss or wool – in short it was not the deep elongated structure one is accustomed to meet with in such a situation, but reminded one rather of the alder-built nests I found in the Riviera.

Flattened against the mottled bark of an ash tree we found one of the oak beauty moths[59] harmonising very perfectly with its surroundings. The brown, jagged markings on its wings run transversely in relation to the insect's body and therefore, in order that these may assimilate the vertical grooves of the bark,

the moth has to take up a position with its head and tail lying almost horizontally and this it appears to do invariably. Similarly nightjars will always be concealed among longitudinal twigs etc. whenever possible.

By carefully studying the accompanying sketch (which is as truthful a representation as I could make in the time at my disposal) it will be observed that the moth's lower wing has been drawn in slightly towards its side. Is this purely adventitious or has the insect subconsciously done so in order to bring its markings more into line with the grooves of the bark? The point is an interesting one.

Several of the war correspondents had attempted to amass a collection of eggs, but this had not got further than a few of the commoner species. The most interesting clutch was that of a carrion crow: one was a large, double-yolked egg, with very few surface markings to cover the blue shell, two were more or less normal and the third remarkably small, spherical in form, and of an almost uniform dark greenish-brown colour. One might almost assume that the pigmentation of these eggs was equal in each case and that the colouring matter had been condensed in the small one and thinly scattered over the very much larger surface of the 'double' egg. I was able to identify among the others the icterine warbler, hedge sparrow, cirl and yellow bunting, jay and magpie.

Added later: Beach Thomas told me a few days ago he had found two song thrushes' nests with fresh eggs – evidently a second brood.

Tuesday 10 July, St-Omer

This afternoon I had tea with Captain Whaley, the officer in charge of the Carrier Pigeon Service[60] out here. I asked him many questions and extracted the following general information.

Pigeon fanciers in Europe always prefer to train their birds to fly more or less towards the north as all the big races are in this direction. The explanation is that the birds will not willingly fly into the sun. When lost, therefore, pigeons nearly always make their way north.

The average height at which they fly is 140 ft, but on clear days they will rise higher and on misty ones very much lower – sometimes quite close to the ground. On being released they usually circle three times to attain their height before making off. Whaley was of the opinion, with which I agree, that pigeons are guided by a combination of the senses of orientation and sight – the former leading them to within sight of familiar landmarks. Out here the horse-drawn lofts are all of very similar appearance. After being moved the birds take about ten days to learn their new surroundings. The young birds are first used when about ten weeks old.

Another officer imparted the surprising information that the authorities were now training sea lions with a view to using them to detect approaching submarines! He made this statement in all seriousness and assured us that the experiment was being carried out on Lake Bala in Wales. It appears that a sea lion has an extraordinarily acute sense of hearing and it seems that these animals are being taught to associate their meals with the sound made by a submarine. In anticipation of food the excited aspect of the animal will announce the approach of enemy craft.[61]

Wednesday 11 July, St-Omer
This evening at sundown I again heard an icterine singing from the middle of the oat field behind my billet. The bird probably roosts there every night. The jackdaws quit the cathedral at nightfall in a huge flock and noisily retire at night in the trees of the ramparts.

Before dinner I spent a short while in the marshes near Clairmarais hunting for the little bitterns. Several peasants know the birds well and declared that they had seen them quite recently in the lagoon I was searching and said that they usually nested there among the willow bushes.

Reed warblers seemed to be amazingly numerous in certain reedy corners: I also saw a few sedge warblers and some great reed warblers. The latter were producing what was to me an unfamiliar squawking note, which probably emanated from young birds being fed by their parents. They were unusually loath to take wing, and despite stones thrown at them from close quarters they remained

skulking in the reeds until finally I drove one into a corner and had almost caught it in my hands when it flew away quite strongly. At first I thought that this bird must have been unable to fly well through being in heavy moult, but this was evidently not the case.

Other species worthy of note are: moorhen, grey-headed and white wagtails, herons, reed bunting and tree sparrows.

Thursday 12 July, St-Omer

Yesterday, taking the short cut up to the aerodrome which leads through wooded grounds, I caught a glimpse of a hawfinch – it was only a momentary view, but just enough to be sure of the bird's identity. A bullfinch was also piping in the birch trees so I was able to add two species to my list of probable summer residents.

Today, walking down to the river below Wizernes I saw a grey wagtail. Starlings are much reduced in numbers: I saw a few today, but comparatively speaking they are very scarce. Very few mistle thrushes have been seen lately and no cuckoos. Have the latter gone or are they only hiding away?

Went in an RE8 (Henley was the pilot) this afternoon for about half an hour.

Crested Lark perched on tip of some bush.

This morning I saw a crested lark perch on a spray of gorse where he remained some time singing very pleasantly. I think this must be a fairly unusual occurrence. In the winter I saw one of these larks settle on a stake near Amiens, but otherwise I have not seen them at rest anywhere but on the ground.*

*Added later, 22 July: Since writing the above I have noticed other crested larks in a similar position on many occasions, so conclude that it is not, after all, an exceptional habit. They are able to perch thus in a strong wind.

Friday 13 July, St-Omer

Drury and I visited the forest of Clairmarais this afternoon and were rewarded by a good view of two large birds of prey which I took to be honey buzzards. They were both dark brown, but I based my identification on their outline more than anything else – they appeared more peaky about the head than common buzzards, and generally speaking did not have such a rounded contour. The wings did not seem quite so blunt; the tail appeared proportionally a little longer and the head did not give one the impression of being either so rounded or close to the shoulder as in a common buzzard.[62]

Otherwise the afternoon was not very productive. I heard the half-hearted fluting of a golden oriole, a feeble warbling on the part of one or two small birds, but apart from these the hot, stuffy afternoon was practically songless.

Drury tells me nightjars are common on the heathy ground near Wisques.

Sunday 15 July, St-Omer

Today I met Lieutenant F.C. Brown-Douglas, a pilot who was formerly in 29 Squadron. He told me he had seen some 'black and white birds' (which he thought might have been peewits) flying over Arras in a westerly direction at a height of 7,500 ft. This was in the early spring or late winter of last year.

After dinner I had a walk with Drury through the cornfields. It was a delicious evening, still and cloudless and sounds carried far. On a slope leading down to a hollow, several landrails[63] were uttering their reeling croak – a rough, unmusical sound – and in the distance we heard a quail's *whit-wit-wit*.

I have come to the conclusion the icterines leave their gardens and hedgerows to a great extent at this time of year to frequent the growing crops. This evening in a field of tall broad beans, we heard at least three singing a long way from any trees. For some time Drury and I listened to their wonderful imitations with great delight – as Drury said, it was as good as a star turn at a music hall, only much better. At times the imitation was so quaintly realistic that we were forced to laugh outright. It is so incongruous to hear a nightingale's song coupled with a partridge's creaking note; or a skylark's soaring song with the angry churr of a whitethroat or the fussy chatterings of a sparrow! The chaffinch figured prominently, for not only were their liquid spring call and pink-pink notes parodied but also its full song, which was rattled out to perfection. A blue tit was also imitated as well as the song thrush, starling and whitethroat (song), but the most original and unusual were the partridge call and the chaffinch's song.

Drury says he has often heard house martins 'bubbling' away in their nests long after dark – I suppose this is what Gilbert White quaintly describes as their 'twitter in a pretty inward soft manner in their nests'.

The other night I met Commander Chambers at dinner. He

was by way of being quite keen on ornithology, but admitted that his enthusiasm surpassed his knowledge. Among a few eggs in his possession were two that were possibly marsh warblers', although the site of the nest – among the reeds on a river bank – makes it more probable that they were lightly marked specimens of reed warblers'.[64] They were taken on 8 June near Hesdin. Chambers told me that Dunkerque was a very good place for waders and says he and a friend identified the lesser ringed plover as breeding there.[65] He had shot dusky redshank and black-tailed godwit there.

Ingram spent part of 17 July sketching in the van Kempen Museum. He returned there several times over the next few weeks.

Sunday 22 July, St-Omer

Before dinner I had a walk with Drury in the marshes to the north of this town. At this time of year one cannot expect to see much, and it is only by sitting still for some time that the birds of late summer show themselves at all. A whinchat was an addition to my Audomarois (St-Omer) birds, as also was a common redstart – an individual in very worn and bedraggled garb. The black redstart breeds in the very heart of St-Omer, frequenting the chimneys and house-tops where his dusky dress admirably matches his sooty surroundings.

Studies of a nestling Meadow Pipit
17.7.17

Today I found a meadow pipit's nest containing four young about eight days old, and a few days ago I found another with fledglings about the same age. Icterine warblers are still frequenting the crops; fields of heavy-scented broad beans apparently being the greatest attraction to them. This habit, of disappearing into the standing crops after the breeding season, seems to be a fixed one in this species and is probably shared (but to a lesser extent) by some of the other warblers. Whitethroats at any rate are fond of visiting the open fields at this time of year and later on, when partridge shooting commences, many of them may be discovered skulking in the turnip and wurzel crops, together with thrushes, pipits and other birds.

Commander Chambers gave me a chiffchaff he had shot with his catapult. The breast of this little warbler is really streaked with lemon yellow and not tinged with this hue, as is vulgarly supposed. This streaking effect is due to the outer edges of the feathers only being yellow, the remainder being greyish or white as the case may be.

Monday 23 July, St-Omer

Tonight was what the meteorologists would call anti-cyclonic – fine, still and starry. At 11.30, as I was going to bed, above the distant rumble of the gunfire I heard the clear call-notes of passing curlew, their voices sounding far away in the spangled vault of indigo. So the autumn movement has already commenced.

Friday 27 July, St-Omer

Yesterday I found a spotted flycatcher's nest in a niche of an old gnarled lime tree near the aerodrome. It contained young about eight days old. On returning a couple of hours later I was disgusted to find that some malignant man, bird or beast had torn the whole structure out and the heart-rending cries of the distressed parents were painful hearing.

Tonight I visited the Clairmarais marshes to show a chaplain named Sheldon[66] the haunt of the little bitterns. In our mission we were entirely successful, and saw at least three of these interesting birds. They flew with the same silent direct flight and passed fairly

114

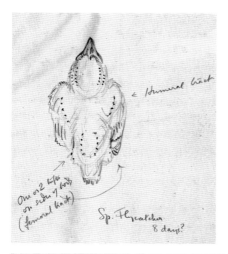

low over the cultivated marsh-fields to a distant willow. They are very characteristic birds and cannot very well be confused with any other species.

Being in a lucky vein, we found a nest of blue-headed wagtails containing a young cuckoo – a very late date for such a discovery. The bird – well advanced and probably about 17 days old – squatted in its adopted home with a ludicrous, statuesque glare, its bill tilted upward and its throat feathers puffed out like a hooting owl. The flanges of the gape – small and unobtrusive – were nevertheless of a vivid reddish-orange colour.

The 'parents' – possibly three birds were attending to its voracious appetite – were bringing beakfuls of very large insects. I think this is always noticeable when a young cuckoo has to be catered for. The nostrils of this parasite are rather conspicuous at this age – they are encircled with a distinct raised ridge. The nightjar has, if I recollect rightly, a somewhat similar arrangement.

Reed buntings, reed warblers, greenfinches, herons – they came in at a fair height from the south – a solitary peewit travelling north, and a moorhen were among those observed.

During the last fortnight I have twice been up in aeroplanes – once to test the new 517 compass with a fellow named Buckridge (in an RE8) and again in a Maurice Farman with a Belgian aviator.

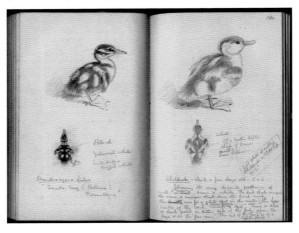

Sunday 29 July was spent in the van Kempen Museum studying and sketching.

Monday 30 July, St-Omer
Today I visited Dunkerque and, having an hour or two to spare, I walked out after lunch to a salting and some sandy country beyond, where Commander Chambers RNAS told me I would find the lesser ringed plover. According to him these birds nested last summer among the dunes. Today they were on the flats, where

dunlin, curlew sandpiper, stints, Kentish and common ringed plover were also feeding. At first I was not quite happy about my identification of the species, for they mixed with their cousins and refused to allow a very close scrutiny. However, later on, I found some apart and their distinctive call-note finally dispelled my doubts. This cry is clearer and pitched in a higher key than the plaintive call of the ordinary ringed plover, with which sound it cannot be confused.

There were a few curlew sandpipers on the naze; although these would rise with the other waders when a panic set them on the wing, they otherwise showed an inclination to feed apart. Two of these were still in their rusty breeding plumage. Compared with the rather quaint short-necked, high shouldered aspect of the dunlin these are shapely, well-proportioned birds. As they rise they utter an alarm call of several notes. Dunlins have a rather rasping note which they utter occasionally while feeding, but when they rise they do so with a chorus of twitterings.

The stints were possibly *minuta*,[67] but I could not pretend to identify the species. Common ringed plovers were the most abundant and among their numbers were several youngsters looking like overgrown Kentish, but very squat and stuffy about the tail. Despite their juvenile appearance they were surprisingly strong on the wing. About 50 per cent of the dunlin had black breasts – they are probably now moulting into winter dress.

The little black-legged Kentish plover claimed attention chiefly by their characteristic call. I suppose I must have seen about six or eight of them. There were several common sandpipers about and I think I saw and heard a green sandpiper in the distance – a clear piping cry. Whimbrel and curlew flew over. A party of common and black-headed gulls were sitting about all the time. The former were all (green-legged) adults, as were the majority of the latter. The black-headed gulls were changing into white livery, but one or two were still hooded.

I found a linnet's nest on the open sandy country, placed in a low herbaceous yellow-flowered plant. It contained five much incubated eggs. Meadow pipits were abundant. I had the idea that I saw a tawny pipit, but on second thoughts I think this doubtful.

The country lying between St-Omer and Dunkerque has a very Dutch appearance with its broad waterways and low red-roofed cottages grouped about their banks. The slow-moving, square-ended barges, the busy windmills, and above all, the rounded heads of the innumerable willows that dot the landscape – all go to make a picture that one is bound to associate with Holland. Why, the very Flemish names have a Dutch flavour about them!

And into this quiet unobtrusive country, what a strange conglomeration of men this war has brought. Today I passed British troops and blue-coated *poilus*,[68] Belgian gunners and German prisoners, Chinese from the northern provinces and the more dusky-skinned Tonkinese employed by the French. And within a few miles I could have seen the Jap-like Portuguese and a few representatives of the American army and all manner of men from our far away colonies!

At 10.30 p.m. I heard a redshank flying southward through the darkness – a confused babble of notes.

Friday 3 August, St-André[69]

For two days it has poured with rain, a continuous driving deluge obliterating the landscape with a veil of water.

Today I motored here (eight kilometres from Hesdin) and saw but little by the wayside. Swallows were resting on the roadway in some numbers, evidently finding it more restful to settle on the hard surface in the wind and rain, than on the trees and telegraph wires. I have noticed this habit before. When on the wing this species seems to show a very marked preference for luzerne fields – evidently this yielded the best supply of insects under these trying conditions.

In the shady depths of Hesdin Forest, a good many carrion crows were to be seen. This habit distinguishes them from the rooks who never settle on the ground beneath a thick canopy of leaf and branches.

Monday 6 August, St-André

In the midst of my work, of a sudden a familiar cry fell upon my ears – a cry that recalled the wilds of Connemara, the treeless coast of Uist, or the wide sands of East Anglia. It came from a lone curlew – a forlorn, solitary individual winging its way towards the Somme estuary.

Wednesday 8 August, St-Omer

The last day or two there have been quite a number of goldfinches about – attracted thither, no doubt, by the seeding thistles.

Chambers sent me a whitethroat he had killed with his catapult. The bird has almost completed its moult, but there were a few sprouting feathers on the breast and flanks. This whitethroat appeared to be a large bird, possibly owing to its new growth of feathers. The wing measures 75 mm.

Saturday 11 August, St-Omer

This afternoon I bicycled with Drury to Clairmarais forest. We saw a large hawk, which was probably a honey buzzard, but I was not able to identify it properly. Where are all the passerines? It is extraordinary how they manage to hide themselves now they are moulting – presumably they retire to the fields for there were practically none in the forest itself – a few robins, jays, a marsh tit or two and several blackbirds were all that were present save wood-pigeons, which seemed fairly abundant. These birds were crooning pleasantly and I saw one indulge in the 'switchback' love-flight for over a mile, in which distance he performed at least ten successful 'loops'.

Drury had heard a song that he could not identify and asked me to go to the place this evening, when I found it to be a goldfinch. Certainly the song was a little unusual but it contained the customary tinkling notes. There were quite a lot of these birds about – young and old – evidently attracted by the thistles now in full seed. I noticed one settle on a sugar-beet leaf and commence to peck at it.

The goldfinches were flitting restlessly about the tops of some tall elms. On three or four occasions I noticed a leaf floating down through the still air to the ground. I imagine these must have been ripped off by the goldfinches since there is no other explanation for why they should fall.

Thursday 16 August, St-Omer

After a spell of comparative silence (blackbirds have been singing for some time past, often using the chimney pots of St-Omer from whence to deliver their melody), there has been a slight recommencement of bird song. After a heavy downpour of rain I heard wrens, hedge sparrows and thrushes and of course skylarks, yellowhammers and cirl buntings who have never ceased to be vocal. Chiffchaffs sang well into last month as did also chaffinches.

Lately a green woodpecker has been yaffling hereabouts. I think this proves that they wander afield at this time of year, since none were about Longuenesse a short while back.

Monday 20 August, Izel-lez-Hameau

At a moment's notice I had to pack up and hie me hence, calling at Albert and Toutencourt (3 Brigade and 13 Wing) on the way. At Albert I heard a willow warbler making a weak attempt to be vocal and also a few notes from a blackcap, while this morning a chaffinch was making ludicrous and almost unrecognisable attempts to repeat its vernal song. Toutencourt is in rook-land. I saw a lot of these birds today, the vast majority being undoubted adults and I am not sure that the few individuals seen with feathered faces were not carrion crows.[70] Where do the birds of the year go? – presumably they migrate southwards. This detail in the life history of the rook requires thrashing out.

Near here I saw quite a little flock of crested lark – they scattered in front of my car. These six or eight birds had possibly been attracted to one spot by some favourite food, for they are usually non-gregarious – linnets, yellowhammers, cirl buntings, swallow, sparrow, martins, kestrels and partridges all forced themselves upon my notice. Swifts have not all gone (18.8.17), but are much reduced in numbers. Wood-pigeons were seen on several occasions. Flocks of starlings noted on one or two occasions. I noticed quite a lot of these birds round Hameau.

Two or three days ago I was taken up in a captured German two seater (an 'Ago'). About the 18th I found a yellowhammer's nest containing young three or four days old. This was in an old dog-rose, just outside St-Omer.

Fledgelings of :—

Blk. Redstart   Com. Redstart   Bluethroat.

Broad-billed Sandpiper

Avocet. (newly hatched)

Monday 3 September, St-Omer

A chiffchaff was attempting its song yesterday morning. This species has been more persistently vocal than almost any other and its little tune was heard on and off into late July, when all other bird voices were hushed save those of the yellow and cirl buntings. I have not seen a swift for days past, but this evening one was flying round the deserted tower of St Bertin in the slanting rays of the setting sun. I should have thought the rain storms and high winds would have swept these southerners completely from the sky.

Monday 10 September, St-Omer

When with No. 100 Squadron (now stationed on an aerodrome close under Clairmarais Forest), I saw one or two lots of peewits. Yellow wagtails – presumably *flava* – were observed on several occasions, flying as is their wont in a rather aimless way, hither and thither, and constantly uttering their call note as if searching for lost companions. Herons, wood-pigeons and starlings are among the birds seen.

Friday 14 September, Treizennes

A number of white wagtails were feeding on a newly ploughed field, and blue-headed wagtails are still about in some numbers, behaving in a manner described on 10 September. This afternoon I rode out to the wood I visited in the winter and found it a very attractive spot. Wrens, great tits, robins, jays, magpies and carrion crows were among its tenants, and on a heathy bit of country adjoining I saw many linnets and yellowhammers, and a few stonechats and whitethroats. This bit of waste-land was looking very beautiful with its masses of sheep's bit scabious and St John's wort. On the lilac flowers of the former, large numbers of tortoiseshells and a few red admirals were feeding and spreading their gaudy wings to the sunlight, thereby adding bright patches to the already gay surroundings. Meadow pipits and grey partridge were seen. The other day chiffchaffs and willow wrens were heard singing.

Wednesday 19 September, Chocques
On several occasions during the last two days that I have been here, I have seen a grey wagtail flitting somewhat dubiously about the moat that surrounds this château.

Sunday 23 September, St-Omer
Two officers of No. 55 Squadron – Lieutenant B. J. Silly[74] (pilot) and 2nd Lieutenant A.D. Taylor (observer) – told me that, on 22 August last, they saw three small birds when over Béthune at a height of 10,000 ft. They said that these birds had a dipping flight and were about the size of linnets. It appears that they both observed them and that they did so independently. They are quite positive as to the above facts. The hour was about 10 a.m. and the birds were travelling in a more or less southerly direction. When I was at Bruay two days ago, I noted several meadow pipits and field wagtails.

Tuesday 25 September, St-Omer
While working at the Van Kempen Museum today, I heard a black redstart singing from a house-top: this is the first I have seen or heard of this bird for a long time. The last week or two starlings have been on the increase.

The last four Sundays I have had to report at GHQ at Hesdin. Between here and that town I have seen no rooks, but just beyond, near St-André, where the château is, there are often some about. Chiffchaffs are still singing vicariously. Peewits have come into the marshes in some numbers. Wood-pigeons were numerous in Hesdin Forest: I had heard marsh tits and jays there, also a phylloscopine warbler.

Wednesday 3 October, Izel-lez-Hameau
An Irish pilot in this squadron (No. 102) – 2nd Lieutenant W.H. Pierce – tells me he has frequently seen geese when flying over Salonika at about 8,000 ft. It would seem from his statements that these birds were passing between their feeding and resting grounds since he said they used to be observed pretty regularly in the mornings and evenings.

Pierce also informs me that he has seen eagles at about 6,000 ft. He also referred to the French aviator's notorious feat of killing two eagles in the air with a shot-gun. This was Louis Noël![75] (Pierce's statements were not wholly convincing as he seemed a little vague as to detail.)

Having got hold of a gun, I had a short walk round when everything was quiet – for it would not do to be caught by the military authorities! There were not many partridges about and I only had a couple of shots, one of which I bagged.

On Sunday last near St-Pol I saw a buzzard – it seemed rather greyish in tone but I thought it was undoubtedly a *buteo*[76] and not a honey buzzard. On the whole I have noticed very few big raptors since I have been out.

Friday 5 October, Treizennes
During an early morning ride I saw a big flock of tree sparrows, a few white wagtails, greenfinches, crested and common larks and one or two lots of starlings. A fair number of meadow pipits are still about – also a few house martins.

On 9 October Ingram returned to England on leave.

Wednesday 10 October, Stoke Golding
Crossed yesterday afternoon, in a driving rainstorm. All this morning a cold north-westerly wind had been blowing – so strongly that the morning's sailing had to be cancelled.

Some twenty or thirty common terns had sought shelter in Boulogne harbour. Most of these could be seen fishing at the tail of the rip below the sluice gates separating the inner basin from the main harbour – the remainder sat in mopey attitudes upon a beam, evidently most discomforted by the biting wind. These terns all had the white forehead of immature dress. A few black-headed gulls were also frequenting the harbour. A flock of starlings passed fairly high, travelling in an easterly direction at about 4 p.m.

While on leave he sketched all his children (clockwise from top left): Ivor,
Mervyn, Alastair and Certhia.

3.

Night bombing and boar-hunting
(24 Oct. 1917–24 Mar. 1918)

DURING THE SECOND HALF *of 1917 the RFC gradually recovered from the trauma of 'Bloody April'. As British planes improved, so did the pilots' chances of survival; for the extreme bellicosity of their Commander, Hugh Trenchard, which had earlier contributed to the carnage, came into its own with the new aircraft. In October the RFC was enlarged by a Wing dedicated to long-range bombers, which, often flying by night and beyond the enemy's front line, brought within range not only strategic targets but also the civilian population.*

The new bombers meant more compasses to service, and when Ingram returned from leave at the end of October he was immediately sent south-east to Toul. Admiring the beauty of the Avre Valley in flood, his words remind us of the torrential summer rains that had condemned so many soldiers to live and die in Flanders mud.

By the autumn both sides were tiring of the war. Mutinies in the French army were weakening Allied capability. In Russia, bread riots had led first to civilian turmoil and then to revolution. In November Lenin, carried forward on fierce anti-war sentiment, seized control, and in December Russia withdrew from the war. With the eastern front virtually shut down, Germany could now focus on the west.

At Toul it had not taken Ingram long to make the acquaintance of the local boar-hunters.

Wednesday 24 October, Treizennes
I returned to France three days ago to find a great change in the landscape, the woods having taken on the brown and gold hues of autumn. Drury tells me hoodies arrived last week and are now here in considerable numbers. Rooks have also appeared and there

are large flocks of starlings about. House martins have not all left and a dozen or more were hawking over the sheltered moats of the St-Omer ramparts. Wagtails (white) are to be encountered here and there, meadow pipits and crested larks in their usual numbers, and wood-pigeons – a few seen.

Saturday 27 October, Compiègne

At about eleven yesterday morning I received an urgent message instructing me to proceed forthwith to Toul – where, I understand, there are now several night-flying squadrons. Owing to the trend of the trenches, it was necessary for us to describe a rather more angular route than would have been the case in peace time; consequently we had to travel southwards as far as Compiègne.

The flooded valley of the Avre between Amiens and Montdidier looked very picturesque in the many colours of autumn. The great brown-tinted reed beds were deep in water, while the poplars and alders, many being still full-leaved, ranged through a variety of tones from green to golden–yellow, while to the west a lurid sunset added to this varied palette.

Sunday 28 October, Toul

Astir betimes, we took the road in a cold white fog at 8 a.m. heading for Reims. It was plain sailing for the first twenty or thirty miles, but between Braine and Fismes we fell in with endless convoys of French troops that obliged us to proceed at a walking pace.

These blue-clad troops formed an interesting contrast to our everlasting khaki, but their transport impressed me as being decidedly inferior to our own and especially in regard to the speed at which they travelled. Beyond Fismes there was less congestion and we were able to make good mileage until we came to the almost deserted streets of the city itself. A very few civil pedestrians, their footsteps echoing down the vacant highway, only enhanced the impression of emptiness.

The western portion of the town was little damaged, but in the Hun's unpardonable and deliberate bombardment of the cathedral, the circumjacent buildings had suffered considerably. If to me, a foreigner whose former knowledge of the cathedral was that of a curious tourist, the sight of its ruined splendour engendered feelings of bitter indignation, what must be the sentiments of the Reimsois. I was informed by one – a Commandant of the 16 Chasseurs – that Joffre had pledged his word of honour not to use the towers as observation posts, so that the Germans can claim no military motive for their vandalism.

The direct road to Châlons being under fire from the German guns, we were obliged to make a detour via Epernay, where I lunched. Thence onwards through Châlons, Vitry-le-François and St-Dizier our way led across open plains, for the most part low swelling hills, rising in gentle cultivated folds. In summer this is the country of the little bustard, stone curlew and tawny pipit. Between Epernay and Châlons I saw vast flocks of rooks, as also a little west of Reims (where there used to be a rookery). In the afternoon, a cold rain began to fall and, before we reached Toul, this turned to a mushy snow.

Tuesday 30 October, Ochey
I arrived here yesterday morning after reporting to 41 Wing HQ[77] at Bainville en route. The journey from Toul was very exhilarating and the view of the deep wooded valley of the Moselle near Villey-le-Sec was one to remember.

A sprinkling of snow lay upon the ground and heightened the

Hooge (Pilot

MacRagan

marvellous tints of the almost endless woods – mile upon mile of the most brilliant gold, orange and brown, with here and there a dark patch of pines. The country hereabouts is very wild and hilly and the steep-sided valleys hold most of the scattered inhabitants.

The southern slopes are sometimes cultivated with vines, but the 'fruits of the earth' must be wrung with difficulty from the thin stony soils. I saw a great grey-backed shrike near Villey and, in the valley of the Moselle, a largish flock of goldfinches among the vines.

In the evening we accepted the invitation of some French officers to attend a military concert in the neighbouring village of Allain. This was held in a large barn which we found to be packed with *poilus* of the 16th Chasseurs. A few civilians, including several girls, were also present – and these latter had every opportunity of being shocked, for most of the songs were distinctly broad, to say the least of it. Afterwards we English officers split up into small parties and dined at different messes – personally I was entertained by the very hospitable Commandant.

Wednesday 31 October
This morning I motored into Toul. The Moselle had rid itself

C. Knabbe

Cd. 1917

Chambers (N.3. Pilot)

of much water, for yesterday, when we passed along the same road, the river was greatly swollen and had flooded its bordering meadows until the trees stood several feet deep in turgid water.

Thursday 1 November, Ochey

Having with some difficulty borrowed an old pin-fire gun, this morning I joined a party of boar-hunters who were shooting in a neighbouring wood. A start was made at 7.45 a.m., at which hour a frosty mist hugged the ground, but when the sun strengthened this dispersed and left a bright sparkling atmosphere.

The pack consisted of ten – a heterogeneous assembly of various breeds and half-breeds, ranging in size from a diminutive dachshund to a grizzly griffon. The old *piqueur*, save that he wore a trumpet wound round his shoulders, looked more like a disreputable tramp than a huntsman, but nevertheless he possessed a good hound voice and sounded a true note on his horn, and both rang very pleasantly through the forest glades.

The eight guns were posted in rides and surrounded a large section of the forest, much as pheasant shooters would a smaller woodland beat at home. The hounds were then thrown in and hunted in the ordinary way. While drawing they were cheered with

Werk. (Pilot)

Hibbard
Camp Commandant (St André)

a *hoo-la hoo-la* or a loud grunt sounding like *how! how!* or sometimes a brief flourish on the deep-toned horn. The cries recalled to my mind a deer-hunt in the 'high woods' of Trinidad and I think it probable that the methods practised there have been handed down from the early French colonists.

The hounds were a riotous noisy lot, but by and by they opened out in earnest and it was obvious that something was afoot. A distant report echoed through the trees – had a boar been killed? It transpired subsequently that one – of course an 'enormous' one – had been missed and the tow-rowing of the mixed pack advertised its passage through the forest. A little later two of the dogs came back with tusk wounds in their buttocks.

Several foxes were seen and fired at, but the bag was nil when we knocked off for *déjeuner.* I now had the opportunity for 'weighing up' my hosts. The 'master' was a kind-faced elderly man in corduroys and brass buttons, these latter being of the usual type, ornamented with boars' heads, pheasants etc, so dearly beloved by French sportsmen: there were three *militaires*, a farmer and his son, a cheery, plump-faced old fellow and the master's grandson. During *déjeuner* a collection of one franc each was made for the benefit of the *piqueur.*

Unluckily I had to leave after lunch so cannot say if they bagged anything in the afternoon, but they were all sanguine of doing so.

Wild boars have become very plentiful in this region and last year 96 were killed by this coterie of sportsmen.

Tuesday 6 November, Ochey

I again joined the boar-hunters for a few hours, but unfortunately left them before a kill was effected in the afternoon. We were working a more remote part of the forest – the high ridge above the Moselle – and there was abundant evidence that our quarry was there in plenty. Every ride was marked with their footprints and on all sides the ground showed traces where they had been rootling among the dead leaves and this was especially the case under some of the larger beech trees where they had been attracted by the mast. On one occasion we heard a troop quite close to us – loud, angry snufflings and the drag of their feet among the leaves – but the undergrowth was too dense for us to get a shot in. Walking home we had to traverse about six miles of forest, which gave me a good idea of its vast proportions. The timber was mostly oak, beech and hornbeam.

I saw several hawfinches, bullfinches, greater spotted

Waiting for wild boar.

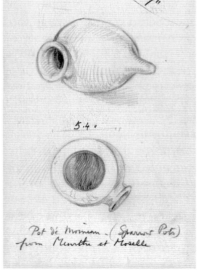

Pot de Morinam. (Sparrow Pots) from Meurthe et Moselle

E. T. Carpenter (Pilot)

woodpeckers, green woodpeckers, and nuthatches were again seen and heard in some numbers. A few migrating song thrushes flew over – also rooks and skylarks. A party of long-tailed tits were also noted. Saw a grey wagtail at Ochey.

The following are the measurements of a sparrow pot[78] taken from the side of a house at Toul. Back: greatest diameter 5.4 inches; diameter of opening at back: 3.2 inches; length from back to tip of projection 7 inches; internal diameter of spout 1.9 inches; length of spout 1 inch.

Sunday 11 November, Ochey
There was another meet of the local wild boar 'hunt' this morning – on the right bank of the Moselle where it rolls its oily waters between butting woodlands by the village of Pierre.

The *chasseurs* gave us a cordial welcome – a fellow named Carpenter was with me – and we were soon posted in a dripping ride in the Forest of Chaudeney. The day passed very pleasantly although we saw no boar, but both Carpenter and I had a shot at a roe buck.

Bullfinches were fairly numerous – also the birds mentioned before. In addition I saw several tree-creepers. In the damp portions of the valley robins, hedge sparrows (heard) and meadow pipit were noted. Rooks passed high overhead, evidently on passage. A woodcock crossed a ride at dusk.

We had a seven or eight kilometre walk home and it was past six when we fetched up at the little *estaminet* belonging to Mme Leloup. Here we decided to dine and invited one of the *chasseurs* – M. Henry Cesar – to be our guest. After a very excellent little meal

we repaired to his house in the village and chatted over a cup of coffee and a glass of wine, Mme Cesar and their daughter taking part in the conversation.

Wednesday 14 November, Ochey
A pilot in this Squadron (No. 100) – Parnell by name – says he saw plovers on two occasions at 4,000 ft in February last over Auchel. I saw a black redstart near the hangars this morning; it was a male.

Sunday 18 November, Ochey
I have had a very interesting day with the boar-hunters. The meet was at Bicqueley and we worked the woodlands on either side of the Toul road. A party of five boars were early set on foot, the hounds opening out with a heartening crash of music. This herd finally broke through a wide gap in the line of gunners and escaped without a shot being fired.

The rest of the morning was blank. We had an early lunch seated round a small wooden fire which we kindled at the junction of two

large rides. Most of the Frenchmen seem to carry their victuals in a spacious pocket let into the back of their coats – this appears to be quite a sensible arrangement, since it allows free movement of the arms and does not interfere with the shouldering of the gun. Considering each sportsman carries a quart bottle of wine and a very liberal supply of food, a receptacle of large dimensions is certainly needed.

We had not been posted long after lunch before M. Rousseau's excited 'Souyez! Souyez!' set us all on the alert. In a few moments his cries had gathered the pack, which immediately broke into an angry, clamorous baying. The loudness and tone of the outcry left us in no doubt as to the presence of our quarry and when the sounds came nearer and nearer the excitement was intense. Clutching our guns in eager anticipation, we heard the oncoming throng crashing towards us through the undergrowth. The next moment a huge boar burst into view – a great, shaggy-maned monster that it seemed impossible to miss. And I don't believe I *did* miss him, for although the ride was narrow and he was soon across I am sure I had him well covered when my finger pressed the trigger. But surely it's expecting a lot of an old 16 bore to hope that it will stop a beast of that size at 25 yards? But hope springs eternal and in a twinkling I had dived after his retreating figure, fully expecting to find his dead body lying among the undergrowth. With the rank porcine smell in my nostrils, I forged through the thicket, a French officer (who had also fired) close at my elbow.

Alas! The receding cries of the hounds told us that our hopes were vain. Several distant shots followed and then all was silence. The exchange of our various experiences caused much animated conversation when we re-united. The old *piqueur* was particularly vociferous – and especially when the *patron* seemed inclined to blame him for our failure.

The next beat yielded a fox – a large-sized animal with a much greyer and more dusky pelt than our British fox. I was rather amused when the *piqueur* came up and asked for the carcass to eat! Presently a distant *hallali* came to our ears and upon going to the sound we found that our friend the bearded *poilu* – a curious-looking man with bland eyes and a pale, Syrian-like beard – had shot a large female boar weighing probably about 160 lb or 180 lb. It transpired that he had posted himself in a remote valley and while the hounds and we were harassing the old male boar, a party of eleven tried to escape in his direction and he had shot this one at point blank range – a few paces only from the muzzle of his gun and it had fallen dead in its tracks *comme un lièvre*.

The old *piqueur* unslung his horn and sounded the *morte* or *hallali* – a mournful call that echoed through the misty woodlands to the accompaniment of the angry snarling of the hounds as they savaged the grinning carcase. With ropes tied to its feet and jaw, four of us hauled the grizzled body to the nearest road – about a kilometre distant. Long before we reached our destination we fully appreciated the great weight of the ponderous body. The tiny eyes, high withers and long and heavy black coat were the most striking features of the beast.

The huntsman plucked a big handful of the long bristles that formed the mane.[79] It appears that these are used by cobblers, in lieu of needles. The thread is presumably attached to the frayed extremity. Thanks to the pliability of the hair, the thread may then be drawn through the most awkwardly situated awl holes – holes that would be practically inaccessible for a rigid unyielding needle.

A four-mile tramp in the dark brought us to a little roadside *estaminet* where we regaled ourselves with long draughts of cool beer – a very light and harmless beverage in these times. After supper I bade farewell to my three companions and trudged the last mile home by myself.

It appears that the owner of the hounds – M. Munier – holds the title of Lieutenant de Louveterie (literally 'wolf-hunt'), presumably conferred on him by the communal authorities or some other local body. This gives him the right to hunt non-game animals – such as foxes, boars etc. – out of season in any part of the forest.

M. Henry Cesar

Monday 19 November, Ochey

I dined tonight with the Cesar family and partook of the *sanglier*.[80] Properly cooked and served with a delicious sauce, it proved a most delectable dish – a tender close-grained viand equal to the best venison, if not better.

We fed in the kitchen where these homely folk set before me a simple but excellent repast. We commenced with a slice of home-cured bacon and a steaming dish of greens. Then came the *pièce* *de résistance* – the *sanglier* – after which we had a beautiful blanched salad,* an apple sweet and a well-browned pastry tart. A local wine was followed by a bottle of old crusted burgundy. A cup of tea and a home-made liqueur called Mar concluded the dinner.

Added later: They told me that they gather the lettuces with a ball of earth attached to the roots, and place them in the cellar. After a time they become etiolated. They can be kept for many weeks in this manner.

Friday 23 November, Tantonville[81]

I came here two days ago and am now with 55 Squadron. The French interpreter here is the Marquis de Bonardi du Ménil – a keen sportsman whose country seat is the Château of Plancy in the Department of Aube. So far as I know the rookery in this park is the most southerly in eastern France and is very extensive. According to Bonardi, before the war the nests could be numbered by thousands, but, the government having requisitioned much of the large timber, the colony has probably diminished. There is also a heronry at Plancy, consisting of sixty nests. Bonardi also told me of two other large rookeries – one which he thought was even more populous than the Plancy rookery – on the estate of the Marquis d'Aligre about 30 kilometres from Chartres and the second at Orgères (Eure-et-Loire).

Sunday 25 November, Tantonville

After a wet, cold morning the north wind drove the grey pall of cloud to the southward in one long sharply defined line that stretched from horizon to horizon. This gradual unfolding of the blue sky was like the rolling up of a huge grey carpet or the slow withdrawal of a lid from a vast limitless box.

Starting from the aerodrome I crossed a bleak wind-swept plain, seeing but very little life on my way – a few skylarks and a couple of magpies being the only birds that I encountered. Quite unexpectedly I came upon a steep declivity, an abrupt slope, that fell away to a broad grassy valley down which a flooded stream* raced in winding curves. The striking feature of the landscape that stretched below me was the remarkably vivid colouring of the naked trees. The willows that lined the river bank and grouped themselves at the foot of the slope formed patches of the richest orange-yellow and apricot-red; while in the thickets the low dogwood scrub glowed a dark brownish purple, and the white-trunked birches still held a few golden leaves to contrast with the sombre green of the spruces.

There are an enormous number of mice in this country: the fields are riddled with their holes and the wood seems infested with them.

Added later: This was the River Madon.

Saturday 1 December, Hesdin

Awakened at 4.30 a.m., I drove through a cold grey dawn to Nancy, where I caught the Paris train. In the 'piping times of peace' an ordinary omnibus train could have shown this one a clean pair of heels and it was nearly 4 o'clock when I left the Gare de l'Est in a taxi and made my way in perilous darts – for the Parisian traffic is as reckless and undisciplined as of yore – to the Gare du Nord.

In the flooded valley of the Marne, hoodies were in abundance. At one spot I noticed a jackdaw wading up to its belly in water; ever and anon it plunged its entire head below the surface, evidently gathering something from the submerged grass.

One of my travelling companions was a French interpreter on the French Headquarters Staff. He was an Alsatian by birth and had recently returned from England where he had been interviewing German prisoners with an idea of finding compatriots desirous of joining the French forces. He told me that no less than 18,000 had expressed sympathy with the Allied cause and were now enrolled in the armies of their former country.

I dined quietly at a Duval restaurant near the Place de l'Opéra. An old French woman, garbed in the weirdest and shabbiest of costumes, came in and sat down at my table. Only a person of nobility or notoriety could have afforded to be so wholly indifferent to public opinion – for her eccentric dress and still more eccentric manners were causing people to stare and titter on all sides. Presently she addressed me in excellent English and did not take long to prove by a versatile conversation that she was a travelled and gifted woman. My surmise as to her birth was not wrong. Presently it transpired that she was a marquise and had formerly lived in Picardie. I asked in what part. 'Near Hesdin,' she said. 'The château is at a place called St-André – it now belongs to my nephew.' My destination – the present HQ of the RFC!

Sunday 9 December, Treizennes

Two cold, frosty days have restricted the birds' feeding grounds to narrow limits. Where the overflow of the Treizennes sugar refinery has flooded the corner of a field this soft muddy margin offers great attraction, and quite a number of species had congregated there: white wagtail – there may have been pied amongst them, at a distance I would not like to swear to them in their winter dress, meadow pipits – again I would not like to swear that one with an aberrant call-note was not a rock pipit[82] or some other species, peewits, rooks, starlings, grey[83] and carrion crows, tree sparrow and last, but not least in interest, three snipe.

Monday 10 December, Treizennes

Today I had occasion to visit 101 Squadron at Clairmarais. The vast multitudes of rooks and jackdaws – especially the former – that converge on this forest as twilight comes on is a really remarkable sight. It is of course impossible to hazard a guess as to their numbers, but there cannot be less than hundreds of thousands. Black flocks crowd in from all sites – probably the rook population from twenty to twenty-five miles around nightly wing their way to roost in the depth of the extensive forest.

At St-Omer the other day I saw grey wagtails and kingfishers frequenting the small stream that flows below the ramparts. Grey-coated water shrews were also busily feeding along its banks.

An article in a recent number of *Country Life* describes the spring notes of a little owl as an excited chattering. This conveys an idea of the sound I heard last May in this neighbourhood.

Sunday 16 December, Ste-Marie-Cappel

The last few days I have been with 57 Squadron on 45's old aerodrome. The place awakens sad memories, for how many of the old crowd are still alive? Lubbock, Bransby Williams, Truscott, Griffiths and a dozen others have been killed since then – in fact, I should say that not more than four or five are still alive. And what good fellows they were too!

On Sunday I reported as usual to GHQ near Hesdin. A flock of a dozen or more black-headed gulls were tacking inland against an icy wind as we breasted the hill near St-André. 'That means bad weather,' said my platitudinous friend, and he was not mistaken. That night the wind freshened to half a gale and a sprinkling of snow fell on the frost-bound ground.

Wednesday 26 December, St-Omer

Christmas Day I spent in company with Drury. Taking a few sandwiches with us we set out to explore the Clairmarais Marshes, our objective being a wide stretch of water marked on the map as Canarderie – an alluring name suggestive in this winter weather of many varied species of duck. A bitterly cold wind blustered across the level marshland, bringing with it flurries of sleety snow out of the north. A storm of this description drove us into an *estaminet* for shelter and here we ate our lunch before embarking on our venture.

The small, two-prowed marsh-boat that we hired was equipped with the most primitive of oars – short, shapeless things devoid of balance and very clumsy to handle. What with the wind and this unhandy means of propulsion we made little progress and in the end we had to abandon our quest. In this decision we were guided by a wildfowler who informed us that the Canarderie and Romelaere (another large mere) were still frost-bound. This fellow had killed five wild duck and a coot on a small sheet of water, the corner of which he had freed of ice. He had made a very elaborate *hutte* and had six decoy birds tethered a short distance out from the bank.

Sunday 30 December, Hesdin

The last few days I have been at No. 2 ASD near Candas. A

heavy fall of snow accompanied by an intense frost made the living conditions somewhat trying – especially in my case as I was sleeping in a stoveless Armstrong, by no means weather tight.

Before retiring on Thursday I went for a brisk walk. It was a heavenly night and the woods were a fairyland of beauty. A moon of unsurpassable brilliance flooded the silent landscape with a cruel glare of greenish light, which traced sharp inky shadows of the trees on the rounded white folds. The snow crystals caught and reflected the moonlight upon a myriad facets until I appeared to be walking in a world of sparkling diamonds – never have I seen this effect so exquisitely produced. The frightful stillness of the woodland at midnight was almost startling – everything seemed to be frost-bound and nerveless – even the icy air seemed frozen into immobility. The crisp crunch of my footfall appeared to my fancy to be an unpardonable intrusion, while the scars they made upon the smooth field of scintillating white seemed a positive sacrilege.

The next night it came on to blow, and the snow crystals were swept along with a little twinkling rustle until they filled the hollows and road cuttings with great impassable drifts. On Saturday, therefore, it was impossible to reach Abbeville by the direct route and in order to get there we had to make a long detour to Auxi.

Having an hour to kill at Étaples between two trains, I walked down to the tidal river to see if there were any interesting birds along its banks. Skylarks were coming and going in large flocks – evidently they were finding food of sorts on the sands and muddy banks in lieu of their normal diet, deprived them by the hard weather. Chaffinches, starlings, hoodies and two pied wagtails were also gleaning the same harvest. Black-headed and common gulls were also working the river, but I saw no waders. A dabchick was diving close to the further bank. A fair number of meadow pipits were also about and, of course, sparrows.

Sunday 6 January 1918, Marquise.
The countryside is under a shroud of snow and the air possesses a frosty piquancy with a bitter winter bite. The birds are again

hard put to it for a living and their hunger begets an unwonted familiarity.

The crested larks and chaffinches are especially fearless and come up to the very doors of the huts. The little top-knot of the former gives it a quaint, perky appearance and enables it to express its emotions – either of fear or contentment, according to whether the crest is lowered or raised. One or two bramblings have been about and black-headed gulls have frequently passed, beating inland from the coast, which is but three of four miles distant. Rooks are crowding about the ricks, making serious inroads upon the precious stores of grain. Round one particular stack, which they have partly demolished, they swarmed like bees about a honey pot – the conical top was one seething mass of black objects.

On the snow I saw marks that puzzled me considerably at first – quadruple dots, widely spaced and leading down a long furrow. In the end I came to the conclusion that these must have been the footprints of a weasel, formed as it progressed with a quick looping gait. The inturned tracks of a swaggering rook were nearby.

Robins frequent the hedgerows near our camp.

Friday 18 January, Ste-Marie-Cappel
After a stormy spell of snowy weather, the temperature has risen

until the air caresses the cheek with a soft, silky touch of a spring morning. This sudden change has filled the birds with hopes of better days, and at dawn this morning I heard the loud carolling of a mistle thrush from the high poplars that surround the grassy enclosure – a heartening sound after so many months of avian silence.

Rooks and jackdaws are very plentiful hereabouts – indeed these birds are extraordinarily abundant in this part of France, while starlings are also more plentiful than they are further west. I noted a hawfinch near Cappel yesterday.

2nd Lieutenant J.S. Rissen of this squadron says he saw 'two large birds' at 15,000 ft between Boisdinghem and the coast about mid-August. He says he is certain of the height.

Tuesday 22 January, Bailleul
Heard and saw some meadow pipits today and yesterday – in fact these birds appear to be fairly common around Bailleul just now. The mild spring-like weather that has prevailed the last few days may have accounted for a local movement and their presence may only be a temporary one.

A song thrush has been singing a full-throated melody from a distant orchard the last two mornings – a rare and precious sound in this part of the world. Rooks and starlings are very plentiful – the latter whistle freely from the chimney pots. Great tits, crested and skylarks, yellowhammers, hoodies, blackbirds and sparrows are birds that I have noted round the immediate outskirts of the town.

To the above, add blue tit and chaffinch.

Saturday 26 January, Droglandt
A still air and a strong sun gave the day an unwonted warmth. Birds were few in number or neighbouring woodland would have been filled with melody. As it was, a blue tit rose to the topmost twig of an oak and repeated over and over again its trilling song which is not a very frequent sound even in summer. The CO of No. 32 Squadron, Major Russell, tells me that he once met swallow-like birds at 10,000 ft.

Tuesday 29 January, Poperinge

The last two nights I have watched the starlings come in to roost at Couthove Château – a truly wonderful sight. In no part of the world have I seen a denser aggregation of birds – they might be numbered by hundreds of thousands, possibly millions and as they swirled and circled overhead they literally darkened the twilight sky. They flew round in an uncertain manner for nearly twenty minutes. They wheeled in wide flocks, towering upwards in a black spiral; then they would spread their ranks in broad sweeping phalanxes, alternately closing and opening, circling and towering. Of a sudden, a hundred or so would drop precipitately upon a tree, crowding close upon the branches.

Later, when the majority had settled, they swarmed so thickly upon the boughs that, in silhouette, they blackened the branches of one or two oaks as though these trees were in full midsummer foliage – but most of them selected the spruce trees where they were partly concealed by the leaves.

Just as the starlings were settling down for the night, a peregrine appeared upon the scene, gliding easily between the tree-tops. What a commotion he caused! The black throng wheeled up again with a roaring rush of wings – countless thousands of them and they recommenced their manoeuvring overhead, herded by the falcon who seemed to play about them with devilish enjoyment. Presently, without much apparent effort, he clutched one in mid-air and disappeared. Whether this tiercel ate his prey I know not, but at any rate before many moments he, or a counterpart, reappeared and the panic-stricken hordes again took to the air.

Settled for the night, the twittering, whistling and chirping of a million voices blended into one continuous roar, which sounded to my ears like the backwash of waves sucking downwards over a pebbly beach, or the even clamour of a waterfall. I understand that this sound is maintained all through the night. Starlings have roosted in these château grounds for a number of years, so their presence is in no way due to the War. An orderly who had been quartered at the château since August says that they put in an appearance about three or four weeks ago.*

*Added later: The next night, I noted a sparrowhawk cruising

round and I have no doubt that he found a ready meal.

Added 31.1.18: I passed Couthove at 11 p.m. Although it was pitch dark (being a misty night) the birds were keeping up a continuous din of chirping notes.

Wednesday 30 January, Poperinge
Yesterday (29.1.18) I motored out to Bergues to see if I could trace the two great auks' eggs[84] that were once in M. Stanilas de Meesemaerker's collection. I heard that he had left all his natural history specimens to the town. I therefore made enquiries at the *mairie*, whence I was escorted across the square to a large room containing the collection. During the bombardment of this town about three years ago the collection suffered considerably, and it was now in a sorry state of disorder – the hundreds of stuffed specimens being heaped together behind the shattered panes of the cabinets.

For some time I searched in vain for the great auks' eggs – hunting diligently among the dusty debris. I then opened a case and found two impressions in a compartment among the guillemots' eggs that, from their shape and size, left no doubt that they once held the two rarities. The natural assumption was that they had been stolen during the excitement of the bombardment. I therefore hastened back to interview the Mayor himself. That individual was able to set my fears at rest. It seems that M. Meesemaerker left these eggs to his daughter and that they are now in the possession of his grandson, M.S. de Praneuf of 40 Rue Carnot, Bergues.

Yesterday this squadron had a record day – every pilot had a scrap and three German machines were shot down in flames and five others driven down, apparently out of control. Unfortunately my room-mate – a cheerful Scot named Rodgers – failed to return and as he was last seen with a Hun 'sitting on his tail', it is feared that he has been killed. The matter-of-course attitude of the rest of the squadron struck me as somewhat remarkable and his absence from dinner in no way interfered with the riotous bonhomie that prevailed during the meal, for it chanced to be guest night, and a very cheery one at that.

Friday 1 February, Poperinge

A fellow named Gordon – a New Zealand pilot in 70 Squadron – has given me some interesting photos of the Australasian gannet (*Sula seriator*). The most remarkable fact displayed by these photos is the symmetrical distribution of the nests. A careful scrutiny of the pictures shows that these are not only very nearly equidistant from one another, but that they are arranged in rows running both diagonally and at right angles, like a carefully planted orchard. Of course these positions are not mathematically exact, but this disposition is sufficiently pronounced to be detected at a glance.

It would seem that this is in no wise due to the stratified formation of the ground for Gordon says that 'the rock is very smooth except at the highest parts of the saddle, where there are small ridges'. The nesting season lasts from 'late September or early October to the end of February'. Apparently a second brood is reared in a large percentage of nests.

The colony is situated on Cape Kidnapper, which is the most easterly point of Hawkes Bay, North Island, New Zealand. The photos were taken by M.S. Gordon, Tadworthy, Northam, Devon.

Sunday 3 February, Poperinge

2nd Lieutenant W.E. Wood of 70 Squadron says that he saw three herons about mid-January at a height of between 5,000 ft and 6,000 ft. They were flying in a north-easterly direction. He dived at them and they manœuvred out of his way. Lieutenant M.S. Gordon also saw these herons.

Tuesday 5 February, Hesdin

The weather has turned so mild that this evening the frogs were uttering their musical bell-like call in the pond of the old courtyard at St-André. A stroll round the well-timbered grounds and through the mossy orchards showed me several birds of interest – tree-creepers, a greater spotted woodpecker moving restlessly about among the higher branches and shrieking a loud *check, check* at intervals – and several little owls. In the late afternoon one of these uttered a soft mewing call from the orchard, while another in the wood answered with a rather more usual, but much harsher, note.

Sunday 10 February, La Gorgue

Four pilots in No. 43 Squadron inform me that they have seen birds at considerable heights. Major Miles last autumn noted plovers (lapwings) over Lens at 8,000 ft. Captain Balfour met birds 'flying in formation' between 8,000 ft and 9,000 ft. He was uncertain as to their identity. 2nd Lieutenant King saw some small birds at 9,500 ft on 18 December, flying in a southerly direction. Lieutenant W. Carson observed fifteen green plovers on 1 February 1918. They were flying roughly in a south-westerly direction – the wind was westerly. These plovers did not seem to mind the anti-aircraft fire which was being directed at him at the time.

Considering the number of fellows I have questioned, I should very roughly estimate that birds are not seen over 3,000 ft more than about once in 2,000 hours of flying. Although the average man might be accused of being unobservant, the pilot is usually alert and on the look-out for enemy machines, so that he would stand a very good chance of seeing any birds that passed reasonably close to him.

I was at Treizennes (near Aire) two days ago. Meadow pipits were still about, so it would seem that these birds are resident in the neighbourhood. One or two wagtails (?white) were noted in the distance. Jackdaws and rooks are very abundant. At one time I was inclined to believe that the latter 'paid' for their winter board by the number of insects that they consumed during the summer months, but these last two winters have changed my opinion. Their ravages on the crops must be immense. Stacks are demolished and the newly sown fields robbed of most of their grain – and this at a time when grain is of vital importance to the future of the Allied nations.

Saturday 16 February, Camblain l'Abbé

Major C.F. Portal (OC of this Squadron, No. 16) happens to be the author of two interesting communications that appeared in *The Field* about a year and 18 months ago, describing birds migrating at considerable heights. I subjected him to a rather severe cross-examination, as he is one of the few pilots I have met who possesses more than a layman's knowledge of ornithology.[85]

Portal appears to have encountered birds at over 5,000 ft on at least five occasions during the 800 hours he has flown. Once he met geese (or ducks) at about 9,000 ft and four times he has observed lapwings at over 5,000 ft. On 26 February last year he encountered a flock of these birds at 6,000 ft near Candas, flying at an air speed of about 50 mph. As they were heading more or less north, from which direction a very strong wind was blowing, their progress was almost negligible. At lower elevations the wind was more favourable, and had they chosen to fly close to the ground it would have been very nearly behind them. Why did they choose such an unfavourable current?

This pilot once saw very large numbers of wood-pigeons at 1,500 ft. They were circling round and evidently not migratory. Portal believes that the majority of the flying men here have, at one time or another, seen birds at considerable heights, but taking little interest in ornithology they make no mental note of the fact. On his questioning two other fellows who had done long hours in the air, they both declared that they had seen birds, but their observations were too vague to be worth chronicling. One had seen geese at a considerable height. Geese (or ducks), peewits (and ?golden plover) and wood-pigeons (1,500 ft only) are the only species Portal was sure of. He believes it would be a common thing to meet birds at 1,000 ft to 2,000 ft during the migrating season 'if one went out to look for them'.

A large flock of linnets remained on the upper branches of a tall ash for some time, their breasts turned towards the westering sun. They maintained a happy twittering chorus all the while – a loud clamour for an assembly of such small birds.

Sunday 17 February, Hesdigneul
Heard a meadow pipit flying over today. Last night we motored out to see a large twin-engined German machine that had been brought down by gunfire. A Portuguese as well as an English guard were mounted over it. Between the two, I fancy the souvenir-hunters will be successful in satisfying their extraordinary passion for collecting absolutely useless objects. Already two of the 'Iron' crosses had been cut out of the fuselage and several sparking plugs

Old chalk-built windmill
Boisdinghem

had been stolen from the engine.

When an English officer appeared to be taking more than an ordinary interest in a part of the machine, the Portuguese sentries would expostulate, saying 'Camarade – no bon – allez', of which no notice would be taken. Similarly it was difficult for our men to interfere with the Portuguese officers.

When at Savy a few days ago, I heard one or two hedge sparrows singing very sweetly. This seems to be a favourite district with the species.

Wednesday 20 February, Boisdinghem
This country west of Omer is a pleasant breezy space with rounded, whale-back hills, open to the skies. There is something rather fascinating about this clean, flinty country that appeals to one all the more after the grime and dirt of Bruay.

This morning a chaffinch sang quite lustily for the first time this year – I have heard faltering, broken attempts before, but not the full song of today. A few skylarks, crested larks and partridges were about all I met on a cross-country walk, save a distant flock of rooks and one or two magpies. Robins (singing), hedge sparrows, blackbirds and house sparrows are to be seen in the hedgerows round the camp.

The hill-tops usually carry a round, fat-bellied windmill capped with a shingle roof. They stretch four thin arms to greet the breezes and on a windy day these turn with a busy air and give a touch of life to the otherwise quiet and sleepy landscape.

In coming from Bruay yesterday, a child ran from behind a van just as we were passing and we unavoidably knocked the poor little youngster down. To see him lying white and bleeding, spread-eagled upon the *pavé* gave one rather a shock, but before we got him to the Casualty Clearing Station he had recovered so far as to cry – which was a pleasant sound when one was fearing the worst.

On 21 February Ingram returned to England on leave.

Friday 22 February, Stoke Golding
At the Visitors' Château near Hesdin (where I stayed the night) the spruce trees were filled with goldcrests yesterday morning – their feeble song being heard at frequent intervals as they busied themselves among the shadowy branches. A wren was also vocal, the soft, spring-like morning causing it to be more than usually boisterous. Long-tailed tits were also in the high trees of the château grounds. At Boulogne, both in the harbour and above, along the river banks, black-headed gulls were numerous.

Today a high wind was blowing almost a gale. Near Hinkley I saw what I took to be a kestrel capture a small bird in mid-air. From a distance, the latter appeared to make no effort to escape. Both pursuer and pursued seemed to be manoeuvring in the wind when suddenly – so it seemed – they drifted together and the hawk clutched its prey without trouble. I shot a jack snipe today at Kirkby. It was in heavy moult, both on the back and breast, but none of the quill feathers were being shed.

Saturday 2 March, Dartmouth

Went up the Dart to Totnes. A typical March day, sunny but with an icy north-east wind that had powdered the distant moorlands with snow. Gulls, curlews, redshank and a number of herons were seen. The latter were statuesquely awaiting the ebb of the tide, and in one ploughed field opposite the heronry I counted seven, six of which were lined up in the sun under the shelter of a hedge-topped bank.

Rooks scavenge Dartmouth harbour like crows, settling on the moored dinghies, buoys etc. Jackdaws do much the same, as of course do the gulls. These latter are of at least three species, black-headed, great black-backed and herring gulls and, I think, common gulls. The first named are acquiring their dark hood, which spreads forward from the posterns and upper margin; the forehead being the last position to become brown. These and the herring gulls are constantly soaring high over the harbour and circumjacent hills.

Tuesday 5 March, Dartmouth

Rode to Prawle Point to find a pack of harriers meeting there. The long stretch of inland lake or lagoon called Slapton Ley was peopled with many waterfowl – hundreds of coots, gulls and flocks of duck – tufted duck and pochard predominating, but a few pairs of mallard were also to be seen. The tufted duck were feeding in the afternoon and they usually remained submerged for about 18 seconds each time they dived. Their cry is a grumbling croak – the pochard also had a harsh cry. Ringed plover were fairly numerous and were running about on the short rabbit-cropped turf and shingle by the roadside.

Heard woodlark singing near Tor Cross and saw a cirl bunting. Jackdaws haunt the rocky bluffs and cliffs. Two guillemots were feeding by the mouth of the Dart. They remained under water about 35 or 40 seconds at each dive – I timed them on four occasions.

Saturday 9 March, Hesdin

After a night disturbed by gunfire – for London was visited by

What is left of Champin March 1918.

enemy aircraft[86] – I returned from my leave yesterday and reached here late in the afternoon in glorious weather, which still continues. Hesdin seems to be a favoured spot with birds. On the mossy trunks of the huge trees that surround St-André Château, tree-creepers are common and in the broken light its little monotonous song comes from an unseen throat. Hedge sparrows and robins were also singing, the refrain of the former having its usual sweetness, but, in one individual at any rate, I fancied a slightly different expression from that of our English birds.

Faillouel

Motored through from Amiens, passing Roye and Noyon *en route*, to visit Bruce whose HQ are now in the shattered village of Faillouel. The Hun seems to have discriminated between some of the towns and villages in this district in what seems to me an inexplicable manner – one will be badly knocked about, the next entirely destroyed and a third almost intact. Noyon, for instance, is very much more fortunate than Roye in this respect and its cathedral – possibly on account of its lack of venerable beauty – is outwardly whole.

About Noyon the country becomes quietly hilly, the tops being generally crowned with woodland. The fields are thickly studded with well-grown apple trees. These must give a singularly beautiful aspect to the landscape when draped in pink blossom for north-west of Noyon they stretch for miles. The ground has lain

fallow for so long that it is now yellow with the dead stalks of the weeds and grasses that have grown up. Just now some endeavour is being made to reclaim this territory and it is being burnt and motor-ploughed by British troops.

Thursday 14 March, Champien

The last three or four days have been amazingly fine, a still sunny atmosphere during the day and a bright frost at night. Everything has been laced with a delicious network of gossamer, intangibly light and nearly invisible until the sun lowers and its rays strike aslant across the spreading web. At such times one sees it glistening in a shimmering path, like moonlight on water and one realises for the first time what an immense quantity of the web must have been floating about unseen.

A number of magpies and a crowd of rooks busily picking on an apparently bare road makes me believe that they were feeding on these little aeronautic spiders, whose web transport had no doubt failed to carry them over the sunken roadway – possibly on account of the still air below the embankment.

Captain Taylor[87] of this squadron shot the pilot of a two-seater the other day. As the observer had apparently exhausted his ammunition and was seen to be stretching over to the forward cockpit in a harmless endeavour to reach the controls, Taylor did not fire upon him, but flew close up and pointed in a westerly direction indicating that he was to steer to our side of the lines. Unluckily for the Hun, an SE5, not realising what was happening, dived down and put a burst into him and Taylor saw the machine crash.*

Added later: Taylor has since been killed.

Friday 15 March, Cachy

Some corn buntings were sitting on some telegraph wires near Roye – the first I have seen out here this year. Evidently the district lying east of Amiens is favourable to this species, for they are common also near Villers-Bretonneux, Péronne and other villages (see last year's notes).

An odd meadow pipit or two has been seen flying over 'cheeping' in a more or less north-easterly direction. Song thrushes were singing beautifully in a wood across the aerodrome. Linnets, robins, wrens, carrion crows and immense flocks of rooks (with a sprinkling of jackdaws) are among the birds worth recording. The latter are still at their depredations and blacken the surface of newly sown fields. Magpies very plentiful. Later, greenfinches and mistle thrushes also seen

Heard from J.H. Gurney.[88] He says that Belon describes the nesting of spoonbills on the Loire. Belon's work was published in about the middle of the sixteenth century, if my memory does not fail me.

Sunday 17 March, Villers-Bretonneux

Monsieur J. Delacour has an exceptionally fine collection of living birds at his château – many of the species being unknown to me.[89]

The collection is especially rich in toucans, but many families are represented, from ostriches to tiny sunbirds. A male of the former honoured me with a very remarkable display this afternoon. This bird appeared to be angry at my presence and made several vicious rushes at the high fence that separated us. All of a sudden it dropped down into a sitting posture facing me, with its weight (as is usual in many ratite birds) resting on the leathery heel pads.

Spreading its wings it thereupon commenced to rock violently from side to side, which alternately raised and lowered the white wing feathers. The neck, with throat laterally inflated, was curled backwards and with each swaying movement the bird struck its head on the hinder side of its body producing thereby a hollow knocking sound, the resonance being no doubt due to the inflated throat. Above is a very rough and inaccurate note of the general effect – for one thing the head is not properly represented as striking the femoral region and is not sufficiently in perspective.

A male Mikado pheasant is just now in perfect feather and its blue-glossed black plumage has hardly a feather awry.

The note of the rhea is a remarkable sound – a soft, throaty, far-away boom, dying away with a sort of faint flourish – the whole sound suggests a distant fog-horn and is no doubt ventriloquistic in character. The keeper informs me that the ostrich frequently display in the way described above. It is no doubt attributable to sexual excitement and is apparently chiefly done for the delectation of his spouse.

In *The Field* (22.9.17) Lieutenant W.N.T. Rooper records a plover (peewit?) at 6,000 ft flying north. Wind at that height 25 mph south. Captain B. Young in the same number describes the rose-coloured pastor as singing with 'wings a-quiver and crest erect gave forth his best efforts in startling (misprint for starling?) song!'

Thursday 21 March, Fienvillers (No. 2 ASD)
This afternoon I walked across the fields to Autheux, a charmingly

Mikado Pheasant.

162

situated old village hidden among trees and surrounded by old orchards. Each of these orchards is fenced about by those quaint hornbeam hedges so characteristic of this part of Picardie. Its lanes tunnel their way under the branches that spread from the crowns of these ancient pollarded hornbeams and are as deeply sunk as any Devonshire byway. The moss-covered apple trees are scattered over the moist pastures, which are just now studded with the white stars of wood anemones. It is small wonder that this shady, tall-timbered village should be an alluring spot for birds!

This sunny afternoon I was amply rewarded for my two-mile trudge and in quite a short space of time saw about thirty species. A big flock of redwings puzzled me for a while, for they uttered a chorus of notes from the tree-tops that sounded new to me. At one time I felt almost certain I heard one sing, but subsequently I had doubts that it might not be a blackbird, dwelling somewhat persistently on an unfamiliar note.

I visited the large rookery (described last year) and in one tree alone counted 22 nests.

Saturday 23 March, Fienvillers
There are quite a number of little owls haunting the wooded valley running northward from the edge of the plateau which forms the aerodrome. At night, their muffled bell-like hoot may be heard at frequent intervals and today one commenced calling as early as 3.30 p.m. (4.30 summer time) in the full glare of the sun. I went down to have a look at him and found him perched among the upper boughs of a stark ash tree. He did not seem in the least shy and, after glancing at me with half-closed eyes, soon re-commenced his musical cry, which he uttered with head thrust forward and throat inflated. At night these birds are very persistent and will call thus for hours on end, the monotonous note being repeated, with occasional breaks, at intervals of from six to ten seconds and often less. I heard one utter its chattering note, but at this season they are generally answering one another with the bell-like calls.

Tonight the soft air and bright moon tempted me out for an after dinner stroll in the woodlands. Considering the hour (10 p.m.) the birds were very wakeful and I heard crows cawing, magpies chattering and a yellowhammer's *cheep* while, of course, the owls' cries punctuated the shadowy woods, the notes ringing out at more or less regular intervals. An answering bird, a quarter of a mile or so down the valley, possessed a note of an altogether higher key. This individual suddenly changed this call into a screech, which is also a familiar sound at the present season. Are these differences sexual?

Sunday 24 March, Fienvillers
I heard today a chiffchaff calling from some tall trees on the outskirts of Hesdin – the first summer migrant I have seen or heard this year. Someone writing over the initials L.J. in *The Field* for 27 October 1917 describes magpies in the war stricken area that formed the Somme battlefields: 'They erected their great domed structures on any part or stump that gave sufficient purchase. Now the magpie in the nesting season is not gregarious, but the force of circumstances so cramped their instinct that in many localities, where one solitary tree or bush had survived the blasting effects of high explosives, three or even four pairs of magpies had each constructed a nest.'

4.

A gnawing sadness
(27 Mar.–30 Aug. 1918)

THE ARRIVAL OF DRIER WEATHER *in spring offered Germany her first opportunity to profit from Russia's withdrawal from the war. Troops from the east were moved to the west, and on 21 March she had launched a massive new offensive. This was designed to separate the British and Commonwealth armies from their French allies and to drive them back to the coast, and to do so before the Americans could arrive in strength.*

The enemy onslaught was initially successful, and within four days she had driven a wedge deep into British positions. So critical was the situation that at Doullens on 26 March the Allies had agreed to a single command: Maréchal Foch was to be Supreme Commander, with Field Marshal Haig under him. Ingram, forced to contemplate the possibility of defeat, felt 'a gnawing sadness' weighing on his heart; and on 11 April, Haig delivered his famous 'backs to the wall' speech: each one of us, he said, 'must fight on to the end'.

Then hope dawned. The British line held; Allied convoys were frustrating the blockade; and American troops, fresh if untried, were pouring into Europe at the rate of 300,000 a month. The tide was turning. One consequence of the German advance, albeit a comparatively trivial one, was the complete destruction of Jean Delacour's bird collection, visited and sketched by Ingram just a few days earlier on 17 March.

Wednesday 27 March, Hesdin

The vaguest of rumours are passing from lip to lip. One will tell you that the Hun is almost knocking at the door, while the next will cheerfully inform you that Ostende is in our hands and that the Americans are landing there in countless numbers! But the fact remains that 2 ASD are moving westward as fast as they can pack up and get away, and the roads are congested with our troops moving in the wrong direction – in short, the outlook is far from cheery and a gnawing sadness weighs heavily upon one's heart, for the enemy's guns are hourly more audible. Yesterday evening I left Fienvillers in charge of two lorries bound for Hesdin, whence 'Issues' of 2 ASD have migrated.

The moon sailed across a cloudless vault of purplish blue and the distant sparkle of 'Archie' bursts showed that the Huns were busy with their night-flying machines. I heard this morning that they actually dropped several bombs on the wireless section of 2 ASD – where I had been working a few hours previously – killing three and wounding 13 others. Of the latter, Lewis (my late room-mate) was one and I hear he is rather seriously injured.[90]

Against the indigo background the distant Archie, dotting the darkness with a progressive series of minute flashes, reminded me irresistibly of the pulsating light of fire-flies hovering on some tropical savannah.

Thursday 28 March, Hesdin
Chiffchaffs were singing in the château grounds and a nuthatch was noisy as he explored the sappy branches of the lime avenue. Nuthatches do not figure prominently in my journal and they appear to be fairly scarce in north-east France. Greenfinches, barn owls and starlings are all to be met with here – also a pair of white wagtails who cling faithfully to the vicinity of the pond in the courtyard. Cirl buntings are likewise denizens of these attractive grounds.

Friday 29 March, Berck-sur-Mer
Meadow pipits seen.

Tuesday 2 April, St-André
Spring is in the air and the greening landscape is flooded with warm sunshine. No wonder the birds are full of joyous melody – the blatant voice of the chaffinch, the see-saw of the great tit, the boisterous outpourings of the wren – all these are constant sounds today.

And this morning from the budding branches of a plum tree I

heard the voice of a newcomer – the pleasant, rambling warble of a blackcap. I heard this early from my bed, but I was not satisfied until I saw the owner, sitting with half-raised crest on a sunny bough.

On the other side of the old chalk wall a redwing was feeding in the orchard, so here we had, side by side, a winter and a summer migrant. Yesterday I saw a flock of these northerners in company with about half a dozen fieldfares, but the latter had all gone today.

Wednesday 3 April, St-André

Today I made a tour of the country south of here, visiting the mayors of certain communes upon which aerodromes are situated. The social standing of these men varied from landed proprietors living in sumptuous châteaux to small peasant farmers. Although I sought favours, they all received me with uniform courtesy and we parted the best of friends, my requests in all cases being conceded without demur.

At Buigny, near Abbeville, the spluttering song of a black

A Picardy lane.   ca. 5/4/18   Pied Wagtail   St André 9.4.18

redstart drew my attention to a cottage roof, upon the coping of which sat a male of the species in immature dress. There is a rookery near Yvrench (south of Auxi), another near Fontaine-l'Étalon (north of Auxi) and a third, west of Campagne.

Friday 5 April, Hesdin
Motoring through the forest of Hesdin today, on my way to St-Omer, I saw a very handsome variety of carrion crow. The bird, when feeding in the roadway, appeared to be quite normal, but as he rose he exposed wings and tail and it seemed that these were symmetrically marked with white. The white appeared to be confined to the inner webs of the remiges and rectrices, so that when the wings were folded and the tail closed, none was visible, and when at rest there was nothing unusual about the bird.

Tuesday 9 April, St-André
Twice today I have seen a handsome male pied wagtail in company

169

with a white wagtail. He seemed quite at home and at his ease, so possibly he has been about for a day or two. He did not seem to have the restless manner usual with birds of passage.[91]

Chiffchaffs, judging by their song, are more numerous in the woodland, while blackcaps are also singing in the garden shrubberies. Two song thrushes, responding to the warm spring-like weather, were busily exploring an ivy-clad tree trunk for a nesting site,* while a pair of mistle thrushes were actually filling an angle between two boughs with moss, which the female (?) was gathering with much tugging and straining from an adjoining branch.

A tree-creeper was also building, carrying little bits of material to an ivy-covered bole. Little owls, yaffles, marsh, great and blue tits, and goldfinches are worth recording – also starlings, barn

170

and (?) tawny owls – the latter two species being heard of nights.

Added later: Song thrushes hereabouts seem very unobtrusive birds and one does not often hear their lusty song, boldly thrown forth from a tree top as in England upon the still evening air. Blackbirds seem to take their place in this respect.

Wednesday 10 April, St-André

Today a swallow flew over, twittering joyously in the bright sunlight as he glanced across the turquoise sky. The first swallow always imparts a thrill of pleasure and is a red-letter day for all lovers of birds. Chiffchaffs are still plentiful.

Friday 12 April

Another swallow passed over, disappearing in a northerly direction. Saw two or three meadow pipits and heard a willow warbler singing – the first and only one I have heard this year. Five or six starlings were whistling and chattering in the tree-tops in thorough appreciation of the finest day of the year. Skylarks are common enough in the open country, but I have seen no crested larks in the immediate neighbourhood. Partridges are all in pairs now, the two birds in close attendance on one another.

Near Reclinghem I saw a stonechat on a dry chalky hillside and a little further on, in a clover field, a couple of meadow pipits.

Saturday 13 April, St-André

Although today and yesterday I have been closely quartering the country north of Hesdin – Anvin to Fauquembergues – in search of suitable ground for aerodromes, I have seen no sign of rooks – only the gruff-voiced crows which are all too plentiful. This afternoon a cold northerly wind was blowing and I felt sorry for the poor crows sitting on their nests in the bare branches of the bleak roadside trees. In quite a short space of time I counted four birds, all sitting, like weather vanes, head to wind.* Two of these nests, which my chauffeur clambered up to, contained three eggs each, but clutches freshly laid.

Both days, English and French cavalry have been streaming along the roads, evidently travelling north to try to stem the

A Belgian refugee

German advance. All the villages and towns are choked with troops. Among these are intermingled refugees from the invaded territory – usually these latter travel dolefully along the highways – family parties with their worldly belongings piled high upon some cart or hand trolley.

As we were passing over the level crossing by Hesdin station a sparrowhawk whisked over our heads, slipping between the traffic, and was gone in a second over the top of a garden hedge. This sudden audacity on the part of such a shy species was really surprising.

*Added later: If the wind is light, carrion crows do not necessarily incubate head to wind as I discovered today (17.4.18). Seen from below, the tail projects fairly conspicuously beyond the edge of the nest. Crows seem to like exposed sites. Near here a large isolated beech tree grows upon the edge of an open expanse of country and this contains a nest fully exposed to the four winds of the heavens, although a quarter of a mile away there is a snug wood in a valley.

Sunday 14 April, St-André
The cold breezes of yesterday have freshened into a searching

172

north-easterly gale. This afternoon I explored the wide marshy valley of the Canche below Maresquel. The keen wind roared in the up-stretched branches of the lank poplars and rasped the young spring foliage with unseasonable violence. It was hardly surprising therefore to find that no birds were showing, and beyond a wind-tossed grey wagtail (he must have found his tail uncomfortably long in the strong wind), a couple of wild duck and a few crows and magpies, I saw practically nothing. Two French *chasseurs* however had secured a teal and a moorhen. In the wood below the château, a mistle thrush's nest with eggs had been torn out by some mischievous individual.

Tuesday 16 April, St-André
Yesterday I motored to Desvres, the weather being damp and raw. About five miles north of Montreuil on the Boulogne Road a party of twenty or thirty rooks were robbing a newly sown field, so I conclude the rookery was not far distant. East of this road (I have now traversed almost every lane and road to the front line trenches) I believe no rooks exist during the summer months. The distribution of this species in north-east France presents a pretty problem. Swallows have increased in numbers, also willow warblers and blackcaps.

Wednesday 17 April
Near Fruges I saw a solitary curlew feeding on a pasture.

Friday 19 April, St-André
The weather remains harsh and cold and intermittent showers of snow have fallen all day, with only an occasional break of sunshine. Both today and yesterday, a handsome male ring ouzel has been haunting the orchards, feasting on the purple berries that cluster on the clumps of ivy that overtop the coping of the old fern-covered wall. The clear black of its body plumage leaves no doubt that its parentage is of the typical race. Compared with the blackbirds that were also feeding on these ivy berries this bird looked noticeably larger, while its secondaries had a faded, light appearance that was very noticeable and of course its whole crescentic pectoral band

was strikingly conspicuous. On the slightest alarm, it uttered a chuckling note, cocking its tail between drooped wings in the characteristic manner of the ouzels.

I climbed up to the tree-creeper's nest located on 9 April and found that it contained five (?) eggs, handsomely marked, as are most examples of the short-clawed race of tree-creepers. It was built between the intertwined stems of an old ivy plant surrounding the trunk of an elm, and was about twelve feet from the ground. Later I discovered another tree-creeper's nest. This was also about twelve feet high up, but placed in the hollow of an apple tree. The bird had access to this through a small aperture, but lower down there was another much larger hole through which I could see the bulky foundation of the nest. This was composed of a mixture of sticks, moss and a few silky cocoons. The sticks were amazingly large for so small a bird to use. One I drew out at random measured about six inches.

Saturday 20 April, St-André

My work took me to Guines, Calais, and thence home via Boulogne. On my way out, I located the rookery on the Montreuil–Boulogne road. It was in the Bois de Longvilliers and appeared to be a very populous one. Later in the day I came across more rooks, near Wacquinghen, and found the trees of the château near the village crowded with nests. I believe this to be the most north-easterly colony in France and, indeed, I was surprised to find rooks at all in this district during the breeding season. An interesting fact is revealed by these isolated colonies – viz. that the birds seldom, if ever, wander more than a mile or two from their nests at this time of year.

About six kilometres south of Samer I saw a handsome male yellow wagtail (*Motacilla raii*) by the roadside. Tree pipits were also seen near this spot. Corn buntings seen near Campagne-les-Hesdin (the first I have seen hereabouts) and also in the Calais district.

When I left this morning at about ten, the high ground beyond the Canche was white with snow. This was dissipated by the sun soon afterwards, but the air retained a wintry bite that refreshed one like a tonic.

A third tree-creeper's nest is in an old decayed stump. The foundation, like those of the others, contained some disproportionately large sticks and twigs. Saw a pheasant near Marquise.

Sunday 21 April, St-André

This afternoon I walked across the skylark-haunted uplands to the marshy valley of the Canche. Here, above a sheltered pool, a number of swallows were hawking and in their midst were a few purring sand martins. The common house martin appears not to have arrived yet.

White wagtails, kestrels, greenfinches and (I think) tree sparrows are worth mentioning. A sandpiper of sorts was flushed by a peasant before I got within recognisable distance – it was probably a common sandpiper.

Wednesday 24 April, St-André

On several occasions I have observed a male sparrowhawk, making for the wood beyond the orchard where it presumably has a mate engaged upon domestic duties. This afternoon it again flew over from a westerly direction, heavily laden with what appeared to be a small mole. I followed its line of flight as speedily as I could, but failed to locate its nest at first. Ultimately, held in the branches of a towering forest tree – a tall, straight-trunked beech – I espied a nest that might well be that of the sparrowhawk. At any rate, as I was resting nearby some time later, one of these little hawks came gliding through the forest and silently pitched on a bough immediately above my head. Unaware of my presence, he sat there alternately preening himself and scratching his head, until a tell-tale movement on my part interrupted his toilet.

A song thrush was singing in the far end of the wood. I believe this to be one of the only pairs within a radius of a mile or two. There is a blackbird's nest with four eggs in a box bush in the garden. A greenfinch was building this afternoon.

Friday 26 April, St-André

A cuckoo was loudly proclaiming its arrival this morning. The soft

Beech
25·4·18

steamy weather made all the birds happy and the château grounds were filled with their many voices – greenfinches from the tree-tops, blackcaps, willow warblers, hedge sparrows, chaffinches, starlings, and half a dozen more were contributing to the avian concert. Last night I dined at Paris Plage by the tidal river at Étaples. I saw a few gulls – one adult and four or five immature great black-backed and an odd black-headed or two.

Saturday 27 April, St-André
A warm caressing breeze crept over the rounded shoulder of the hills but was hardly felt in the broad valley of the Canche. The lank poplars standing in the wet marshland are still bereft of foliage, but they dangle little red catkins from their upper branches and these give the trees an aspect of life and a certain warmth to the landscape. At their feet and especially round the frog-haunted pools, the meadow lands are already ablaze with king-cups and lady's smocks.

Fieldfare.

27.4.18

Just as all these signs of summer were slowly sinking into my senses, to the accompaniment of a faint booming of insects and pleasant twitterings of swallows, a harsh chattering cry brought me back with a jerk. Overhead, scattered through the branches of two tall poplars, were a score or so of fieldfares – birds inseparably associated with wintry memories or the high birch-covered fjelds of the north. I heard a pheasant crowing in one of the marshy spinneys.

I flushed two green-necked mallards, who no doubt had mated, brooding somewhere in the reed beds or among the alders that formed a wooded island.

The blackcap that has taken up its quarters in the shrubbery near my hut is getting into better voice each day and is constantly adding new notes to its rambling song. These are palpably borrowed from his neighbours, and today I heard a very plausible

imitation of the fluting song of a blackbird.

Sunday 28 April, St-André

Went to 2 ASD, which is now near Berck-sur-Mer. On the lowlands between the coast and the rising uplands – small dyked and hedged pastures for the most part – bird life is plentiful: goldfinches, hedge sparrows, tree pipits, willow wrens, cuckoos, black redstarts and green woodpeckers being among those noted. A sparrowhawk flew over at midday, dangling an object from its claws.

On my way home I went by 2 ASD and thence via the valley of the Authie. I saw a fine female harrier quartering the corn lands above Nempont-St-Firmin – most likely a Montagu's. Her wide wing span and leisurely manner of flight were very characteristic of the genus. This slow flapping flight with frequent intervals of glide is a very graceful performance.

From Campagne-les-Hesdin westward, corn bunting became tolerably frequent – east of this point they do not appear to occur over a large tract of country. There is a largish rookery near Maintenay. The one at Brunehautpre contains about 165 nests.

A peasant, speaking of a green woodpecker to a companion, referred to it as *Bec-an-bo* (evidently patois meaning beak-in-wood).

Monday 29 April

At Guines a ringed plover settled in the quarry of one of the cement works. It uttered a note unfamiliar to me – no doubt a migration call. Crested larks are common at Guines.

Tuesday 30 April, St-André

Yesterday morning a nightingale tarried for a few hours in the garden shrubbery and beguiled us with its rich music during its short sojourn – but by the afternoon it had passed on. A male pied wagtail was feeding on a newly turned plough. I am becoming convinced that this species is far less rare in this part of France than is generally supposed.

In *The Field* (16.3.18) Mr Woodruff Peacock writes on the food of the thrushes in winter. Redwings, he aptly remarks, 'suffer sooner because it is more of a ground-feeding and pasture-loving species than the other thrushes.' Song and mistle thrushes, blackbirds, fieldfares, ring ouzels and one black-throated thrush he found to be all feeding on hedge fruits. 'When the migrants arrive the berries of the mountain ash and guelder rose have usually been cleared off by our local thrushes. ... By the middle of January (1917) the blackbirds here were compelled to turn to the buckthorn (Rhamnus) – this is a thing they never do unless forced by hunger.' Ivy berries, he remarks, are not properly ripe until April, so 'it is only when birds are greatly pressed for food that they turn to them'.

The ring ouzel seen here this April, was undoubtedly feeding on ivy berries and, by the purple-stained droppings that had splashed the leaves of this plant, others had been doing likewise.

The same number contains a letter on carrier pigeons. The writer (R.H. Artindale) claims to be a fancier of over fifty years' standing. He mentions the case of an untrained bird returning from Penzance to his home (165 miles). This seems to prove that the homing faculty in some pigeons is so well developed that they can return to their loft without visual training. Mr Artindale says that Frohawk's statement, that pigeons cannot fly over a snow-covered landscape or in a fog, has been disproved by the Admiralty and War Office birds during the present war. 'I have sometimes encountered race pigeons crossing these downs against a strong adverse wind and so close to the ground that in some positions landmarks not half a mile distant could not have been seen.' The first-quoted case of the Penzance bird is quite incompatible with the sight theory, although there are many proofs that migrants and homing pigeons prefer to travel under weather conditions favourable to visibility.

Wednesday 1 May, St-André
In a wood behind the château near the mouth of the Authie, I came across another fair-sized rookery – a rough count made a total of approximately 240 nests. In the same wood I saw two stock doves who made away with their usual driving flight – swift and forceful. No house martins to be seen yet. Heard a lesser whitethroat trilling.

Friday 3 May, St-André
The last two days have been a pleasant change from those that preceded them – warm and summer-like. April has been a cold grey month, which seems to have greatly retarded the vernal progress of nature. All the migrants are backward and have reached their breeding haunts a week or so later than last year. This morning two spotted flycatchers were playing about in the upper branches of the lofty elms and one was making an abortive attempt to sing, which resolved itself into a few squeaky notes. These were oft-repeated and did not differ materially in character from the bird's call note.

Yesterday, being in the neighbourhood of Cassel with a fellow named Godden, we decided to go to the top of Mont des Cats to see what we could of the War. No one said us nay and without hindrance we climbed to the top of this upstanding hill, which overlooks a wide expanse of country including many miles of the line.

Behind us our own batteries were keeping up a heavy fire – great spouts of yellowish-white flame followed by ear-splitting reports and the rushing sound of the projectiles – which could be seen and heard on all sides. For some time we lay on the forward slope of the hill watching the frequent flashes that gushed sporadically from hidden spots in the landscape. Apart from this, the country had a very still and deserted aspect. It stretched away into the bluish haze until it merged with the sky just beyond the vague, familiar outline of Bailleul. The French were occupying this portion of the line and for twenty minutes or so we chatted with a very affable officer in an observation post, who obligingly pointed out all the more noteworthy features of the line.

As we were returning to the car (which we had left under the shelter of a hill), a loud swishing sound told us that the Germans had at last commenced to retaliate, and as we got into the car we saw that they were plopping them unpleasantly near to the road we had to traverse, and especially near Kruystraete where the road forked on the lower shoulder of the hill.

Believing their 'strafe' to be merely chance shooting, we decided to 'carry on' – but we were soon undeceived. Just as we got abreast of the turning, instinct warned me of an oncoming rush and caused me to duck my head. The next instant, not thirty yards away, a great black fountain of dirt shot skyward to the accompaniment of a loud heavy crash and the reeking smell of burnt powder. Evidently it was no time to dawdle, so we bade the driver to press on, but a hundred yards further we were brought to a standstill – a shell had recently burst right in the centre of the highway and a great yawning crater barred our way. I must confess it was not very pleasant having to reverse slowly up this shell-scorched lane and then weave our way round in a narrow gateway in order to face the friendly shelter of the hill. By this time, the air was thick with the smoke and dust of many bursts. During the few minutes we were on the exposed portion of the road, I suppose half a dozen or more shells must have fallen in a very narrow space, and possibly thirty or forty were dropped altogether.

Our curiosity was more than satisfied. I suppose there are not many people left in France foolish enough to travel 60 miles to get under shell-fire. Ultimately we got away by another road, through Godewaersvelde and Steenvoorde and so home, having seen quite enough of the war for one day!

Birds were undisturbed by the shell-fire – neither by our own nor that of the enemy. This of course has been commented on dozens of times before, but two facts made the circumstances worthy of note in this instance. One is that Mont des Cats has only recently been occupied by batteries and the other that many of the birds heard were migrants, such as willow wrens, blackcaps, tree pipits etc., who could have easily travelled further afield to quieter areas. Starlings were very common and were roosting in the monastery roof. Jays and robins were also noted on the wooded hillside.

The warm weather seems to have opened the floodgates of the migrants – swifts, house martins and whitethroats were all seen for the first time this afternoon.

Below are sketches of a wood-pigeon's feather I picked up in the wood here. These are the blue-grey feathers covering the rump and upper tail coverts.

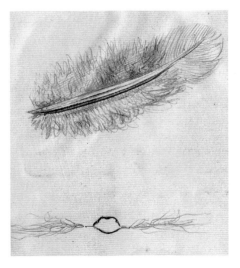

Monday 6 May, St-André

The tree-creeper's eggs in the nest I found on 9 April have hatched at last – unfortunately I did not make a note of when the eggs were laid, but I feel sure the period of incubation must have been unduly prolonged. The nestlings had fairly long and profuse smoky-grey down on the head, but none on the body. Inside the mouth, gamboge yellow: gape inconspicuous.

At 2 p.m., by appointment, I met Sheldon at Clairmarais and we spent the day together looking for birds. The marshes have all been flooded as a precautionary military measure, in case the Hun should press his offensive too strenuously for the Channel ports. The inhabitants declare that this will mean their ruin and certainly their rich market garden, so intensively cultivated, and their meadow crops have all been completely destroyed. The whole district is now one vast sheet of water, from which the trees, cottages and the tips of reeds stand out in wintry desolation.

Naturally bird life has been considerably affected by this change and the reed warblers, reed buntings and little bitterns were nowhere to be found – in their stead we found a solitary shoveller, four or five common sandpipers and a party of twelve greenshanks. The latter rose wildly as we approached and made away with loudish cries, flying with their wings hooked well back and conspicuously displaying their white rumps.

Herons were as common as last year and were again nesting on the western side of the forest. White wagtails, field wagtails (species?), a whinchat (singing), cuckoos, a sedge warbler and moorhens were also encountered during our hour's row through the hidden channels and across fringeless meres.

The underwood of the more open portions of the forest was teeming with whitethroats, all very much on the alert and full of fight for their chosen territories. A *Garde Chasse* showed us a robin's nest in the old monastery wall – it contained two newly hatched young and two eggs just chipping. Willow warblers, judging by their song, outnumbered the chiffchaffs by at least six to one. A wood-pigeon, with its clear colours, plucked insects from the unfolding oak leaves. This bird was evidently a transient. One or two pheasants were heard crowing, followed by the rattling of

Wood Warbler   6 · 5 · 18

their flapped wings.

A corncrake was grating in the monastery meadow and a song thrush was singing in solitary state in the depth of the forest – the only one heard all day. Tree pipits are common through the open glades and are in full song. In an old magpie's nest on the outskirts of the forest, a kestrel was nesting and apparently had young since the female kept flying round with a mouse in her claws uttering a *queck queck queck* of annoyance at our presence. This foolish behaviour betrayed her nest to the ponderous *Garde Chasse* who otherwise would have been too dull-witted and unobservant to have noticed it. I bribed him two francs not to put the threatened charge of shot into the nest on the morrow; this he pocketed with many promises which I have no doubt will be broken at the first opportunity.

185

I heard a golden oriole singing – the first of the year. A tree-creeper had a nest in the crevice of a split bough, about 22 feet from the ground. There was a corn bunting just west of St-André.

Tuesday 7 May, St-André
Two pied wagtails were feeding in the kitchen garden this evening.

Wednesday 8 May St-André
The pied wagtails, or other individuals were seen again today. This morning I spent at the Repair Park 2 ASD (Bahot) and in the afternoon I visited No. 6 Squadron at Le Crotoy. Wishing a small piece of the fabric from Richthofen's machine, I asked the officer in charge of salvage for it. As he gave it to me, he looked over the remaining portions of the fuselage and said 'I am afraid there is no blood left' – apparently the gore-bespattered pieces have been much sought after by the more eager and morbid souvenir-hunters.*

Le Crotoy has always been ornithologically famous, and the greater portion of the Marmottan Collection[92] was derived from the neighbourhood of this village situated on the northern lip of the Somme's mouth. An old bird-stuffer named Yaune was still in residence, but had practically given up his trade on account of his age and ill health. Formerly he apparently prepared vast numbers of sea birds for the *modistes* of Paris – he spoke of 'thousands' in one day. These were mostly terns and were principally caught at night in large-meshed nets stretched across the sandy flats. *Mouettes* (black-headed gulls) and *gaburis* (larger gulls) were also captured, especially the former. Even though he may have exaggerated, it is pretty certain that an immense destruction of these birds used to take place annually[93] – Yaune spoke of one man who brought in 500 at one time and said that they were conveyed to him in 'cart-loads' He said the price varied, but he used to get two or three francs each for the skins.**

The tide was out, exposing an immense expanse of sand. For the most part this appeared to be fairly firm and therefore unattractive to the ouze-loving waders. There may have been better feeding grounds along some of the more distant channels or further up

St andre Hill

the river, but I did not see them and was very disappointed by the results of my walk.

Two old wildfowlers came in while I was standing on the dyke – weather-beaten old fellows, picturesquely garbed in tan-brown blouses, loose blue trousers and slouch boots, and both were armed with prehistoric twelve-bores. They had been shooting over infamously stuffed decoys – curlews and one reeve. Their bag was only five greenshank, birds which seem to be passing just now in tolerable numbers.

Added later: Richthofen was the famous German aviator – the Baron – who is reputed to have destroyed 80 of our machines.

**Added later*: During the period of their migration, common

187

Garden Warbler

and other terns formed a very large proportion of these.

Thursday 9 May
I visited M. le Vicomte Pierre d'Applaincourt at his château (Château de la Triquerie) near Abbeville. He has a fair collection of the species of birds which he considers connected in some way with sport, besides the legitimate game birds – these include gulls, terns, grebes and raptors. During my hurried visit I jotted down a few hasty notes on his specimens – all obtained at the mouth of the Somme. In an aviary he had a fine buzzard, which he took from a nest in Crécy Forest in 1903. Buzzards are seemingly still to be found in this forest and also Goshawks. The *Garde Chasse* always call the latter *faucons.* Quails were heard today.

Friday 10 May
In the marshy woodland just below Auxi-le-Château (Petit Ponchel) I heard a strange sound which I think must have emanated from a water rail. This sound might be described as something between a prolonged throbbing grunt and the lowing of an herbivorous animal. It had amazing and bewildering ventriloquistic properties for I was never certain whether it came from above, in front or behind me – first it was on one side and then on the other.

From the number of chiffchaffs I heard singing, it would seem that these birds prefer marshy woodlands in this part of France to the ordinary forest or wooded haunts of the willow warbler. Generally speaking, the latter considerably outnumbers the chiffchaff, and it is exceptional in my experience to find the latter in preponderance. One might make a similar distinction between the garden warbler and blackcap – in this case the former prefer the humid, marshy woods.

I watched a marsh tit to its nest in an old greater spotted woodpecker's hole. This was in the dead stem of a tall poplar and was at least 65 ft from the ground. It was apparently the male taking food to his mate, for an eager head was protruded to receive the little green caterpillar at the threshold. There was abundant evidence of the presence of the greater-spotted woodpecker, for the dead boughs of almost all of the sickly poplars had been chipped and perforated by their industrious and inquisitive bills. But although this seemed to indicate their plenty, I only once heard the staccato *chek, chek, chek* note. Starlings were making good use of the larger woodpeckers' old homes and they were breeding in the wood in comparatively large numbers.

I watched a grasshopper warbler trilling on a bundle of faggots in a marshy clearing. I believe in my last year's journal I referred to the inside of the mouth as being black. This was most certainly not the case in the present individual, the mouth lining being yellow with only the inner tips of the bill black. The longest trill lasted 42 seconds, but for the most part it broke off after eight or ten seconds. While producing this sound the gape is kept open, the wings quivered and the tail very distinctly vibrated.

At close quarters the young leaves of the poplar have a beautiful glossy reddish appearance, but at a distance these trees appear to be clothed in a delicate tawny yellow or golden green foliage which contrasts noticeably with the fresh green of the surrounding vegetation.

With the drier weather I think food is becoming less abundant for the rooks, and they now seem to forage further afield to satisfy the requirements of the growing family. Carrion crows are very plentiful round Crécy Forest, and yesterday I counted 32 together in one field. Cuckoos were calling in the woods and tree pipits seen near Hesdin.

Sunday 12 May, St-André
Every morning for the last week I have seen a pied wagtail feeding in the garden outside my window and on more than one occasion I have noticed a female with him. This morning they were courting one another, so there seems every likelihood that they are breeding somewhere about the château grounds.

Monday 13 May, St-André
Lieutenant Gordon Sheldon writes to me as follows: 'If you go on the main road from Bergues to Wormhout there is a rookery two kilometres from Bergues and 200 yards on the left of the road. There are about 14 nests but I only saw two pairs of birds. Five hundred yards further on there is another rookery with 21 nests. Here I only saw two birds. They were unmistakably rooks – not crows – and were very shy of my approach. This latter place I examined closely: the trees were oaks and the nests mostly in three or four trees with a few odd ones in other trees.'

Saw the pied wagtail again.

Wednesday 15 May, St-André.
So far I have failed to discover the nest of the pied wagtails and I am beginning to fear that they are a pair of philanderers dawdling on their way to England. Some white wagtails have a well grown family hidden among the polypodium growing in the old pear tree in the middle of the courtyard.

The weather today was deliciously fine and a soft, scented breeze played over the sunny cornfields. Skylarks, of course, were

Young Hedge Sparrow *g. Andrew*
16.5.18

lavish with their music – and there is none so light-hearted and so brim-full of *joie de vivre* as theirs. Found a yellowhammer's nest with four eggs – the lining was composed almost entirely of small rootlets and contained no horsehair etc., as is usual.

A young hedge sparrow was on the wing. The gape of this bird on leaving the nest is tinged with purplish red and is not waxy yellow as in many species. Quails were calling.

The following letter is from Major C.A. Portal (12.5.18).[94]

I have seen a few green plover at heights about 2,000 ft going north-east and one of my pilots (very reliable but no ornithologist) saw about fifty rooks, jackdaws or crows at 6,000 ft over Lens in March. I myself saw about half a dozen birds early in March which I couldn't recognise. They were at 4,000 ft going north-east very fast and looked like small curlews. They were not golden plover but looked exactly like curlews about two thirds full size. Their flight behaviour was between that of a curlew and golden plover. I have since seen several from the ground and still don't know what they are.

One day, 21 April to be exact, my observer and I saw a most enormous bird at 8,000 ft flying north over Lens. We were at 6,500 ft and there was a thin layer of mist just above us. My observer hit me on the back and I looked up to see a very big bird of about seven or eight feet wing span flying straight above in the opposite direction. My observer thought it was a heron, but I think it was an eagle. I hadn't time to see if it had long legs and we were too far below to see it very clearly. The wing flap looked like that of a golden eagle and I am sure it was a bird with a very short tail, large rounded wings and greyish brown in colour. It might have been any size from six to sixteen feet across but I put it down at about eight feet.

At 70 mph an RE8 goes past a swallow (all out) as if it was standing still. This happened to me two evenings ago gliding into the aerodrome – I believe it went between the wings.

Friday 17 May, St-André

Just as we were approaching Calais, four cranes sailed over at a comparatively low elevation. We stopped the car and watched them gliding, with an occasional lazy flap or two, towards the sea in a south-westerly direction. In the field of my glasses they were brought so close that I could see, with wonderful distinctness, the details of their huge bodies and could even discern them turning their heads from side to side as they scanned the ground below them as though searching for a landing ground. They could not have been flying at more than 1,000 or 1,200 ft and appeared to be lowering towards the coast. Although their main direction was constant, they did not proceed in the purposeful way of determined migrants and the individual birds swerved slightly, which gave colour to the supposition that they were desirous of coming to the ground.

Whinchats are very common on the grassy places between Boulogne and Calais. I saw a wheatear near an old limestone quarry a few miles out of Marquise. Typical Ray's yellow wagtails occupy the country right up to Calais – I identified one close to

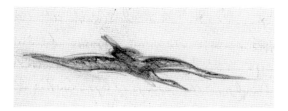

the town. Meadow pipits are common in the coast marshlands – corn buntings numerous between Boulogne and Calais. Saw a stonechat near Montreuil.

For the last week an icterine has been singing loudly in the garden shrubbery, and these birds are now to be met with in their favourite haunts. They cannot have been in full numbers much before 10 May this year. I saw both male and female pied wagtail this morning. Yesterday near Fauquembergues I heard a song thrush singing – a sufficiently individual circumstance to be worth recording.

The willow wrens, chiffchaffs and blackcaps that sang and tarried for a week or more in the château grounds appear to have all passed on and their places are taken by icterine and garden warblers. Possibly these will pass on without nesting too. Spotted flycatchers are now numerous and keep to the higher branches of the tall elms. Their squeaky persistent call-note is repeated constantly and, with very slight variation, is evidently doing duty for a song.

A letter over the initials E.P. in *Country Life* (23.3.18) describes the nest of a 'large brown owl' which 'rises from the ground and flies off to a neighbouring copse'. This is evidently near the front line. 'I now find that she is nesting here. The owl is comfortably installed in the middle of the field and is occupying a nest from which she has evidently evicted the lawful owner, the partridge. I am now watching the nest carefully to see whether she will hatch out all four eggs.'

Sunday 19 May, St-André
The tree-creepers have now flown, so I demolished one of their old nests to examine the materials more carefully. What one might

describe as the original 'scaffolding' – that is to say, the coarser material forming the foundation – was surprisingly large for so small a bird. It was composed chiefly of dead ivy stems, twigs and plant stalks measuring about five or six inches up to eight inches. These were criss-crossed irregularly athwart the crevice, where they jammed and thus effectively supported the mossy superstructure. Pieces of smaller length would have undoubtedly fallen through the open crevice.

Two days ago, I noticed another pair of tree-creepers feeding their young behind the bark of a walnut twenty feet from the ground. The other three nests were as follows: in oak 22 ft, in apple 12 ft, in elm 12 ft. Cuckoos seem to be very scarce hereabouts, and since an occasional cry heard during their passage through the country at the latter end of April, I have had no evidence in the immediate vicinity of the château.

I climbed up to a carrion crow's nest containing young about four days old. The skin on the upper surface was blackish and adorned with tracks of down of a smoky greyish-drab colour. This was fairly short and comparatively dense. Inside the mouth, vivid crimson and carmine (this shows through and tinges the more or less transparent skin of the throat). Gape dull purplish pink and only inconspicuously tipped with yellow at the extreme corner.

Around 20 May, Ingram returned to England on leave.

Wednesday 22 May, London
Went down to see Mervyn[95] at his school near Croydon. Among the beeches that crowned a gravelly hillock I heard a wood warbler singing – the bird was uttering a persistent twittering as it drifted through the green, sun-spotted gloom of the beech forest. A series of clear notes, like the opening of a tree pipit's song, is a variant only uttered once in a while, but the twittering, shivering melody is repeated over and over again. During the song flight, the open wings are thrust forward all a-quiver.

Thursday 23 May, Salisbury
I was rather surprised to find stock doves nesting in the cathedral

27.5.18

Young Jackdaw: about 6 days old showing large
German yellow, wax-like gape.

— two or three pairs had apparently settled there for the summer.
A blue tit also had a home in this edifice and at a very considerable
height from the ground. The bird rose in stages, flying from
buttress to buttress until it disappeared into a little hole, about
200 ft up. Martins, starlings, jackdaws, swifts and sparrows were
also breeding on this building.

Sunday 26 May, Streatley-on-Thames

In a dovecote at Cleeve Court,[96] four or five pairs of jackdaws
are nesting. The nests contained young from six to ten days old.
I examined one of the fledglings and found very little nestling
down adhering to the tips of the sprouting feathers. There were a
few small tufts of grey down on the tips of feathers on the lower
portion of the dorsal tract. Some of the feathers of the scapular
tract possessed filamentous down of a very different character.
Besides this there was a fairly copious growth of grey down
between the feathers on the upper parts of the wings, sides and
centre of back, and sides of breast. This down was also of a pale
grey colour and was in the form of short tufts. These tufts were
still partly in the sheath and were noticeably larger in an older
example.

One naturally asks the question — under what category does
the comparatively short down in the newly hatched carrion crow
come? Does it develop into the body down described in the last

paragraph or not?

Comparing the two nestlings, by far the most striking characteristic is the difference in the gapes. In the young dark-nesting jackdaw, the gape is enlarged and has a conspicuous lemon yellow wax-like appearance. In the carrion crow the gape is inconspicuous and diffused with purplish pink. Although the eggs of the jackdaw are paler than those of the other Corvidae, this wax-like gape is a more eloquent proof of the antiquity of the aberrant[97] practice of this species of nesting in dark places.

Monday 27 May, Streatley

There is a dabchick's nest close to the bridge and it is really pathetic the number of times the poor bird has to 'pack up' and depart, for on each alarm she hastily covers her eggs by turning the trimmings of the nest over them: she then dives smoothly out of sight. Once I surprised her so that she had to leave without properly screening the eggs, and it was very amusing to note her anxiety until this duty was performed. Her head would appear above the surface of the water carrying a shining wet leaf which she would furtively toss on to the nest – by this means quite a lot of material must have been added to the structure. I happen to know that the eggs, even when much incubated, will stand a long exposure but one would think that a sudden enveloping by cold, wet vegetation must be a little disconcerting to the chick on the verge of hatching.

The silvery white patches at the base of the lower mandible are very conspicuous. Do they serve the same purpose as the rabbit's scut? Does this sudden disappearance, as the bird bobs under water, act in the same way as a warning signal to other dabchicks?

There were several blue tits' nests in the boxes in the garden – one with eggs and one with fully fledged young. A great tit had young about three or four days old. The down was tolerably long, loose and of a whitish grey colour. The gape is conspicuous, proportionately thick and pale wax yellow. Inside of mouth, gamboge yellow.

Monday 3 June, St-André
On my return here I found the pied wagtail still about, but it does not appear to be breeding. Found a garden warbler's nest in the shrubbery with young about four days old. No down, lining of the mouth carmine red, gape wax-like, but not very large and conspicuous.

Sunday 9 June
Saw pied wagtail again.

Tuesday 11 June
On my way home this evening, just south of Boisle, I came across a hobby feeding over a sainfoin field and a very interesting and beautiful sight it was. A stiffish breeze was blowing and tossing the pink flowers about, but the powerful-winged little hawk seemed to be in no way inconvenienced by it. Beating up wind and swinging back again, the hobby must have traversed the field at least a hundred times. Every now and then it would give a sudden wrench or flick in the air or it would be seen making a little stoop or quick half turn. These movements denoted the invariable capture of an insect, for they were always followed by the bird's head being bent down to meet the clasped feet holding the prize. Flying leisurely into the breeze, the hobby would immediately proceed to pluck off the wings and inedible parts of its capture

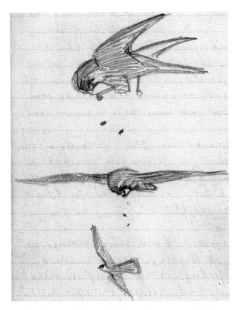

and these discarded pieces could be seen floating down to the ground in quick succession. The body was then transferred to mouth and eaten.

Several butterflies were captured sufficiently close to me to be recognised, but other insects may have been taken as well. The bird must have caught a large quantity as I was watching it hawking for upwards of a quarter of an hour, and it was catching them every half minute or so. The bird's white cheeks and throat marked with a heavy moustachial stripe showed up conspicuously, while its striated, rufous thighs and dark slatey upper-parts were also noticeable features.

I called on Major Ferguson[98] of the 3rd Australian Hospital – Abbeville – a keen naturalist already fairly familiar with many of our European birds. We lunched together at the Officers' Club and afterwards spent half an hour or so in the marshes of the Somme. Common redstarts appeared to be fairly common, and were singing. We saw a marsh warbler but it only uttered a few half-hearted notes. I found a nest which I think unmistakably belonged to this species.[99] It was in some marshy herbage about two and a half feet from the ground and bore all the characteristics of a marsh warbler's nest. It appeared quite fresh but contained no eggs.

Wednesday 12 June, St-André

On the Canche, about three miles below Hesdin, there is a reedy pool encircled by alders and flanked on two sides by tall poplars. Here I found the great reed warbler in comparative abundance, intermingled with the common reed warbler. The smaller species seemed to haunt the reedy fringes of the pool, while the louder-voiced bird croaked and chattered from the middle portions where it could be seen proclaiming from some upstanding spray or dead twig of an alder.

I partly undressed and painfully paddled my way out into the reed bed. I was soon rewarded by discovering a fairly bulky nest slung on to six of the vertical stems. The deep cup contained five youngsters about four days. These were dark-skinned and naked like the young of other acrocephaline warblers and the tongue was ornamented with the usual pair of black spots. Save that they were larger and the bill relatively bigger and blunter these young great reed warblers were very like those of the common British species. The nest too was merely a large edition of the reed warbler's. It was built of reed fibres and contained a certain amount of vegetable down (Bullrush – *Typha*) in the lower portion of the fabric.

The female was greatly vexed at my inspection of her family and boldly came to within a few feet of my head, where she puffed her feathers out and, with a wide open gape, scolded harshly with loud rasping cries. The male was equally annoyed but was scarcely so fearless and only uttered his gruff croaking notes – the notes that usually prelude his song.

Saturday 15 June, St-André

This evening I revisited the marshy pool – this time equipped with gum boots. Although these speedily filled with water, they served to protect the soles of my feet from the spiky stubbles of last year's reeds.

Great Reed Warbler

A second great reed warbler's nest was discovered, containing five much-incubated eggs. This nest was neater than the last in shape, being almost hemispherical in form. The parents were not so agitated and kept somewhat aloof. The male nervously uttered snatches of his croaking song, but the female remained silent. The exterior of the nest contained a dry, felt-like substance, which I took to be desiccated pieces of the slime-like algae formed in stagnant water. The nest was slung about two feet above the surface of the pond.

A dabchick with a full-grown youngster was besporting itself upon the pool. The remains of its striped immature plumage gave the youngster a grizzly appearance on the back of the head. The parent was constantly diving, and each time it reappeared the youngster dashed forward in the hopes of receiving food. A moorhen's nest was found at the root of an alder. Fully fledged independent young were swimming about on the water, so this was obviously a second clutch.

Sunday 16 June, St-André

On the grassy banks of the slopes overlooking the Authie valley, I saw several pairs of tree pipits today. As they were carrying insects in their bills they evidently had young.

Monday 17 June

I explored the level lands near the mouth of the River Authie, hoping to find something of interest in the high hedgerows that separate the large pastures. Near a garden I heard an icterine chattering in a half-hearted sort of way and nearby I also heard a lesser whitethroat, a willow warbler and some common whitethroat – the latter had young on the wing. There can be no doubt that the icterine warbler is partial to the vicinity of human habitation and is more likely to be found in a garden than in a lonely woodland.

Among some conifers in the grounds of the Viscomte d'Applaincourt's château I heard and saw a *Regulus*[100] – no doubt the common goldcrest but I could not get a sufficiently good view of it to be sure. This is the first specimen I have noted about here in summertime.

In the little museum, there is a specimen in down preserved of the corncrake. The down is an almost uniform brownish black in colour, slightly browner on the back. A newly hatched moorhen was a uniform jet black.

Tuesday 18 June

This evening I had a stroll through the Canche valley below Maresquel. In a damp spinney of stubbed alder interspersed with a few lank poplars, I was pleasantly surprised to find the marsh warbler. Half an hour's search revealed a nest of this species placed about 2 ft 4in above the ground among the vertical branches of a bushy alder. Attached to three twigs, it was typical in every respect, and was built of grass-bents kinked round the upright supports, and interwoven into a tolerably substantial structure.[101] The lining was composed of finer material.

The five young were about seven days old and presented a rather curious bristly appearance. This was due to the fact that (with the exception of those on the flanks and dorsal track) all the feathers,

Marsh Warbler's nest in alder bush.

18. 6. 18

although fairly long, were still entirely encased in their sheath. A similar or even more pronounced delay in the unfolding of the vane is observable in the kingfisher, and the young of these birds are notorious at certain stages for their remarkable porcupine-like appearance.

The tongues of these young marsh warblers were ornamented with the usual twin spots, so characteristic of the genus. Although approximately the same in size and distribution these varied slightly in individuals, and one bird was noticeably more heavily marked than its fellows. The skin appeared to be darkish and there was no sign of nestling down.

Cf.
18 6 18

Young Marsh Warbler

The parents were restless but shy and remained hidden for the most part, hopping and gliding through the surrounding herbage in comparative silence. Once or twice the female (?) uttered a distinctive scolding cry and occasionally the male broke into snatches of song. This was imitative, like that of the reed warbler, but it was generally purer and higher in tone. It took me some time to obtain a good view of either bird, but I managed to catch them in the lens of my glasses once or twice and satisfy myself as to their identity, although the nest (thirty yards from the nearest water) and the song had already established this fact. The cold and comparatively greyish tones of their plumage, at the fag-end of the breeding season, is very noticeable. Another point which helped to clinch the bird's identity was that the male flew up into the branches of a high poplar.

I saw the pied wagtail again today.

Wednesday 19 June, St-André
I rode down to the same spinney and re-visited the marsh warbler's nest. Save that the young birds were grown and noticeably more feathered I have nothing to add to my yesterday's notes.

In an adjacent pond, a family of young dabchicks was being fed

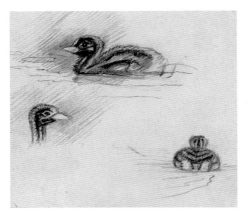

by their parent. As soon as the latter saw me she dived under water with an intentionally loud plopping and splashing, and every time she came up she repeated the performance, obviously with the idea of giving the alarm to her offspring. This sudden noisy plunge is strikingly different to the smooth dive of the bird under normal conditions, and is accompanied with a shrill whistling chirp of alarm. By dint of these demonstrations, repeated many times, she finally persuaded her family to move towards the friendly shelter of the reeds.

The young birds are quaint looking creatures, for besides their unusual zebra-like markings, their bills are of a pale pinkish white colour, slightly whiter towards the tip.

Thursday 20 June, St-André
My tour of duty took me through the three Channel ports – Boulogne, Calais and Dunkerque. Near Marquise I saw several field wagtails, and a pair of *Motacilla flava* were feeding their young which were already strong on the wing. In the same field I saw a yellow wagtail (*Motacilla raii*) so probably the two races overlap hereabouts.[102] If this is the case and they breed true (which seems likely) it is a strong point in favour of giving them specific rank.

A wind sprang up in the afternoon, bringing with it a cold, driving rain. This made bird observation difficult, and although field wagtails are common enough on the flat fertile corn lands between Calais and Dunkerque and the marsh meadows beyond, I was only able to identify one other bird in the limited time at my disposal. This was undoubtedly *Motacilla flava*, near Gravelines. On the Guines side of Calais, I saw a red-backed shrike – a scarce bird in north-east France. Whinchats were seen near Wacquinghen a few miles out of Boulogne.

Major Leather of 88 Squadron says that he has met gulls at 3,500 ft in Scotland and starlings at a similar height over Catterick. Both observations were made in the spring.

Friday 21 June, St-André

I managed to snatch a couple of hours before dinner to explore the Somme valley above Abbeville, having first picked up the Australian naturalist Ferguson. He showed me a marsh warbler's nest containing four eggs (he had taken a fifth). As these were quite fresh this must have been a second laying – probably after an accident to the first clutch.

This nest was about 2 ft 6 in from the ground and was supported on three dead reed stems which were surrounded by the branches of a young, bushy white poplar. The lining was largely composed of black horsehair. Diameter of inside of cup 59mm. Total diameter (to outside edges) 86mm.

Saturday 22 June

On my way back from Alquines I spent half an hour in Hesdin Forest. The wind was roaring overhead and for the most part birds were depressed and silent. A blackcap soliloquised as he hunted through the boughs of a hornbeam, collecting insects for a hungry family cradled somewhere in a nearby brake of brambles and wild raspberries. A casual search for his nest failed to reveal it, but instead I stumbled on a garden warbler's in a young beech, about two feet from the ground. The interesting feature of this nest was that its lining contained the fine stalks of a plant with rust-coloured stems. The five eggs were quite fresh. Chiffchaffs were the only other birds noted. Yellowhammers are very plentiful throughout north-east France.

Sunday 23 June, St-André

For the third time I visited the large marshy woodlands near Petit Ponchel, below Auxi-le-Château. I have always thought this an ideal spot for the marsh warbler and today I was fortunate enough to come across the bird in some numbers, inhabiting withy beds in the middle of the wood. One pair had young just able to fly, but sufficiently alert to escape my inquisitive hand. The parents uttered the same alarm note as the Maresquel bird, which might be described as a jarring, scolding *cherr.**

A nest containing five eggs was subsequently found in the same plantation, suspended on four upright branches of a withy about 2 ft 3 in from the ground. It was composed entirely of grass-bents, finer material being used for the lining – diameter of cup 56mm, depth 54mm. A second nest, evidently abandoned, was similarly placed about two feet from the ground.

The song of the marsh warbler – for I heard one later in the afternoon – is certainly sweeter in tone than a reed warbler's and lacks the jarring banjo notes, which gives the latter something of an unrefined vulgarity.

I was in a lucky vein this afternoon, for a mere fortunate glimpse of a golden oriole – glancing across a ride – prompted me to turn my footsteps towards an ash tree which happened to hold the bird's nest. There was the long-looked-for hammock,[103] slung in a branch some thirty or thirty-five feet from the ground. But what was still more fortunate, the tree seemed climbable and the nest within reach of the trunk.

In a few minutes my coat was off and I was straining and striving up the trunk, which I now found to be rather more sparsely furnished with helpful lateral branches than I had first thought. By the time I reached the level of the nest my strength was pretty well spent and I was glad to entwine my legs about a couple of boughs while I pantingly regained my breath. Four fledglings, about seven or eight days old, were packed together tightly in the nest. Their sprouting feathers carried rather more than the usual amount of nestling down. This was a pale sandy or buffish white colour and was not as long, nor quite so loose in texture, as that of the majority of passerine birds. The chief feature of the down pterylosis[104] was that the two capital and coronel lines curved round and joined the two supra-orbital lines. These latter are usually wanting or else very small. There was also a line of down on the abdominal portion of the ventral tract. The down-tipped secondary coverts formed a slanting line across the secondaries so the proximal ones were almost as long as the secondaries they covered. The bill is purplish or bruised flesh colour. The gape is very small and inconspicuous. Inside of mouth, purplish-red, almost blue on the roof of the mouth.

Perched in the upper branches of the ash, I endeavoured to make a few rough sketches of the bird I was examining, but the position was not an ideal one for free use of both hands. Meanwhile the parents were flying from tree to tree uttering, as their note of alarm and distress, a cry very much like the raucous sound they occasionally produce without provocation – a mewing squawk.

Golden orioles delight in the marshy woods and poplar avenues of the level river valleys such as those of the Somme and Authie, in both of which the species is common.

Added later: This note bears a decided resemblance to the scold of a common whitethroat when its nest is threatened.

Tuesday 25 June, St-André

Went for a ride through Hesdin Forest this afternoon, and very beautiful it was with the sunlight filtering through the over-arching vaults of beech foliage and dappling the gloomy undergrowth with spots of bright light.

Willow warblers and chiffchaffs were heard in about equal numbers, and an occasional robin, garden warbler and blackcap. Several young song thrushes fluttered clumsily away in front of us and later I found a nest of this species in a tangle of honeysuckle. I could see the bird sitting, but the nest was out of reach.

In a more open part of the forest I heard a party of nuthatches – a very local bird hereabouts – discoursing noisily and I spotted a buzzard as it sailed across a patch of blue sky between the over-arching boughs.

Wednesday 26 June, St-André

The clover fields are almost all cut now and it is possible to get a decent canter in a good many directions, which makes riding a much more pleasurable exercise than it was a few weeks ago. Today was especially nice for a cool breeze combined with the sun to make the afternoon perfect.

A number of tree pipits were singing and calling on a chalky slope of waste grass, and I found a youngster squatting under a tuft. A little owl was sitting out on a post in the full sunshine and I think that this was the same bird I had heard calling from a distance.

An icterine warbler was singing in a spinney. I hunted for his nest without success, as has been the case with the bird that has haunted the château grounds all the summer. This latter has been a most industrious songster and has almost unceasingly poured forth its twanging medley of notes. To be honest, after a time these are liable to pall somewhat and especially in the case of this individual, which harps monotonously on a few favourite notes. I suppose he has never wandered more than fifty yards from a small shrubbery since he took up his abode there in the second week of May. I have thoroughly searched all the likely spots for his nest and I now believe he is spending the summer as a bachelor.

Thursday 27 June, St-André
Some peasants, who were cutting a clover field on the uplands above Maresquel, came across a quail's nest yesterday containing eleven eggs, only slightly incubated. These were intact when they left the field at dusk, but this morning not even a fragment of shell was left – presumably the crows had eaten them all. They showed me the scrape that did duty for the nest: this measured about 102 mm (4 inches) in diameter. A few short, shrivelled blades of grass barely covered the naked soil.

Sunday 30 June, St-André
Rode down to Douriez and thence along the valley of the Authie, as far as Argoules and Saulchoy. Between these places there are many marshy pools and alluring swampy woods, but none of these I had time to thoroughly explore.

Great reed warblers croakingly advertised their presence from

Whinchat.
Mouth of the Authie
29/6/18

the swaying reeds that now cover the shallower portions of the *étangs* with a green jungle higher than the tallest man. Moorhens and the ordinary reed warbler were also common denizens of these pools. In or near a little waterlogged spinney, I noted marsh tits and marsh warblers, and I believed I heard the pipe of a bullfinch. Blackbirds, yellowhammers, hedge sparrows, wood-pigeons, turtle doves and whitethroats were also noted, and I have small doubt that a careful search would have revealed grasshopper warblers for in this fenny country suitable localities are not lacking. Major Ferguson has met with this species several times near Abbeville. He also reports seeing a sedge warbler .

Yesterday I was motoring near the mouth of the Authie by Groffliers. On the level cultivated ground near here I obtained a good view of a harrier as it passed close in front of the car. The wing had one, not very conspicuous, bar across the secondaries. I could detect no rufous striations on the thighs although I had a good view of this portion of the body.

Whinchats and meadow pipits were seen on the embankments close to the water's edge. Common reed warblers and, I think, sedge warblers were also encountered. Field wagtails were conspicuous by their absence, although I kept a sharp lookout for them.

209

Monday 1 July, St-André

Being close to the mouth of the Somme, I seized the opportunity to have a bathe, for the day was more than oppressively hot. An immense tract of land had to be traversed first, and then the water was shallow for a greater distance than I cared to wade. Although not deep enough for a swim, the sea was so deliciously warm that the bathe was thoroughly enjoyable.

Northwards, as far as one could see, dazzling white dunes shimmered in the heat, save where their sandy flanks were patched with dark clumps of sea buckthorn. This was the home of innumerable linnets who are always partial to a coastwise country. No doubt wheatears were also here, though I had no time to look for them. Peewits were feeding on the meadowlands behind the sea wall and they had evidently been breeding here, for several young birds, not very strong on the wing, formed part of their number. Ringed plover were also heard on the sandy fields behind the sea wall.

Out on the waste of smooth beach, a vast concourse of seagulls could be seen silhouetted against the sun's sheen, but they were too far distant for identification. A kestrel was stooping at a bird feeding by a creek-side, probably in a playful mood. I rather expected to find redshanks in this country, which appeared to be eminently suited to their requirements, but I was disappointed in this respect.

Mistle thrushes, greenfinches, starlings and meadow pipits were seen, also a whinchat, which was singing very sweetly from the tip of a thorn bush.

Wednesday 3 July, St-André

A beautiful summer's day. Godden and I rode over to a Balloon Wing near Dominois and we both went up for 'joy rides'. The visibility was quite good although a thin layer of grey opalescent mist hung over the country. Compared with the accustomed rush and roar of an aeroplane, the balloon seemed delightfully peaceful as it rose imperceptibly into the sky and the landscape widened beneath. Sounds from the ground reached us with extraordinary clearness and at 2,000 ft the fluting of a blackbird, in an orchard

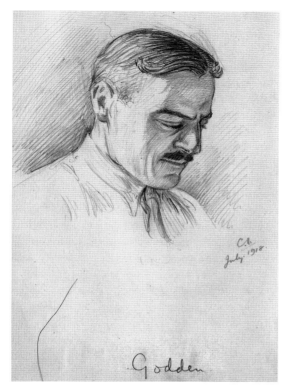

below us, was very distinctly audible.

The pied wagtail is still frequenting the château grounds.

Friday 5 July, St-André

The icterine warbler is truly an ardent singer and its loud shouting voice is as vigorous as ever. I hunted the shrubbery again and am now more than ever convinced that this individual is a solitary, unmated male. Two marsh tits paid us a visit today. Matrimonial duties over, they are doubtless commencing to roam the country as is the way with so many of the titmice.

My friend the pied wagtail is still about. He spends most of the day perched high on the ruins of the gutted château, whence he emits at frequent intervals his cheery *chissick* call. Today he had

211

a battle royal with a white wagtail and, locked together in angry strife, they fluttered down to my very feet.

Sunday 7 July
Today being Sunday, I spent the afternoon by the coast near Quend Plage. On either side, stretching north and south for many miles and with an average depth of a mile or more, is a strange Sahara-like country of sand dunes – range upon range of steep little hillocks whose very existence depends on the binding roots of the marram and the scattered clumps of buckthorn. Seaward, the ebbing of the tide bares a vast level of firm beach. With its kettle nets and long lateral pools, this coastline has a marked resemblance to the coastline just south of Littlestone – the last stronghold of the Kentish plover in England.[105] In short this seemed an ideal terrain for that most charming wader – that dear little bow-legged plover; I would have been more than a little disappointed had I not met with it.

I first heard its twittering call and soft, melodious whistle about a mile south of the half-buried cluster of houses that calls itself Quend Plage. There appeared to be a little colony of them, for I saw seven or eight within the space of a few acres. From their uneasy, fretful behaviour I have no doubt that they were (or had been) breeding here. As I sat, half hidden in a clump of marram, they kept flying round and every time an individual re-discovered my presence it advertised the fact by a fresh outcry of warning notes.

When several settled together on the smooth, sloping shoulder of a dune, I noticed that there was quite a lot of sparring among the males. I observed a similar pugnacity among the Dungeness birds three years ago. Later on, a single Kentish plover was seen on the beach, having a busy time darting after sandhoppers that swarmed there.

At one place, about 100 yards behind the seaward range of dunes, some half dozen common tern were circling high overhead and their harsh vituperations left no doubt in my mind that they had been nesting there. As they were extremely shy, it would have taken a longer time than I could afford to verify this fact by watching them to their eggs or young. The Kentish plovers were more wary than their English representatives.

Monday 8 July, St-André

Between Boulogne and Calais, and particularly near the little fishing village of Wissant, I noted several red-backed shrikes. This eastern corner of France, north-east of Cap Gris-Nez, seems to be the only district hereabouts in which this shrike is not rare. Whinchats and stonechats seen again by the Boulogne–Marquise roadside.

Almost nightly a barn owl flies round in the twilight uttering its unpleasant, strident cry – a grating, creaking screech that jars on the nerves like a discordant note.

Thursday 11 July, St-André

I had feared that my friend, the bachelor icterine warbler, had disappeared. For the last few days I have missed his noisy clamour and the shrubbery has seemed strangely silent in consequence. But during the night a series of thunderstorms, accompanied by drenching showers, has refreshed the air and rejuvenated the waning season to such an extent that he was in full voice again this morning; perched with his lemon breast turned towards the sun and framed by a bower of wet, sparkling leaves he formed a perfectly delightful picture.

Saturday 13 July, St-André

On my way back from Hesdin I was surprised to see a great grey-backed shrike sitting on telegraph wires. As I have passed along this road dozens of times and have never noticed the bird before, I feel sure it must be a newcomer – a wanderer from some other district. Nevertheless it is an interesting observation, and, taken in conjunction with the April-killed specimen in the Applaincourt collection,[106] suggests the possibility of its nesting in this neighbourhood. Migrants are already on the move. Two days ago a chiffchaff was calling in the garden and feeding among the trees – evidently a transient. A grey wagtail was noted in the valley of the Planques, near Fressin.

Sunday 14 July, St-André

A search round about the spot where I saw the great grey-backed shrike was entirely unsuccessful and I am now inclined to think the bird was an immature example on passage. On my way home across the fields a fairly large and bulky bird rose wide in front of me. Against the glitter of the evening sky, I could not give it a name – in general aspect it might have been a little bustard or thick knee,[107] but this was only a general impression and of no identification value. I saw a skylark perched on the wire of a fence – an unusual occurrence. Found a whitethroat's nest with four eggs.

Monday 15 July, St-André

Went north, to Marquise and back, via Alquines and Thiembronne. I saw several *Motacilla raii*[108] midway between Montreuil and Samer and also between Wacquinghen and Marquise. Whitethroats are often met with in the fields at this time of year and I believe they not infrequently nest in the crops.

Six years ago – I think it was six years – I passed along the Montreuil road and pulled up to explore the very quiet valley for birds – a little valley entirely deserted and not a soul to disturb me in my research. Little did I think that within a few short years, this self-same valley would be filled with American troops! Today a battalion of 'Sammys' had 'fallen out' and were resting on either side of the grey bridge that spanned the rivulet, while a few hundred yards further up the road, the shoddy, grey-clad figures of some Portuguese troops could be seen lolling in front of an *estaminet*.

A tree sparrow was carrying food to its nest near Fauquembergues.

Tuesday 16 July, St-André

I visited the shore a few miles north of Le Crotoy. Vast numbers of curlews could be seen on the flats, also gulls. Among the latter, I recognised the greater black-backed, but the majority were probably herring gulls.* Redshanks were heard uttering their unmistakable yelping cries.

214

The absence of field wagtails – at least I have failed to find any – is rather strange on the low-lying cultivation and marsh meadows of this district: one would have thought the country well suited to their requirements.

Added later: I think lesser black-backs were there too.

Thursday 18 July, St-André

Yesterday in the rank herbage of a peaty field in the Authie valley below Douriez, a grasshopper warbler was trilling, while the reeds were also alive with the clamour of their own especial warblers aroused to vocal effort by the splashing of bathers, among whom I must include myself.

A stiff wind was blowing during the early part of this afternoon. A harrier flew over Rang-du-Fliers and, as it headed into the wind, its wings were hooked back in such an unfamiliar manner that I would not have recognised it had I not had a specially good view of it.

Friday 19 July, St-André

I questioned some of the pilots in No. 5 Squadron and the following have, at some time or other, seen birds during their work out here. L.R. Evershed noticed a flock of about forty birds the size of lapwings on about 15 July, at 5,000 ft. These were travelling in a south or south-westerly direction over Arras. F.C. Russell noted six birds about the size of rooks on 10 July. These were also over Arras and flying in a south-westerly direction – height 3,000 ft.

I saw some young sand martins yesterday near Douriez.

Sunday 21 July, St-André

I was at St-Valery on the southern side of the Somme embouchure this evening. Song thrushes were singing quite gaily in the shaded villa gardens. A white wagtail had a nest full of youngsters in an ivy-covered wall and swifts rushed screeching below the old town perched on the cliff's edge.

On the immense, sunlit sands, hundreds of black-headed gulls formed distant clusters of white dots. A great black-backed gull or two were also noted.

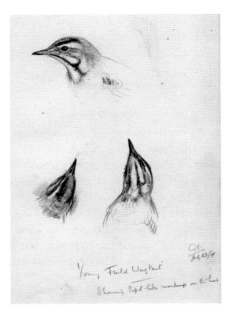

Young Field Wagtail
Showing light-like markings on the head

Wednesday 24 July, St-André

The last two days I have spent in the Calais–Dunkerque region. I had a good look at the field wagtails near Boulogne and Marquise today. They were quite plentiful just south of the latter town and were chiefly frequenting the fields of broad beans. I tried hard to obtain a few specimens for my collection, but had no luck and only gathered one immature example. I am inclined to think *flava* and *raii*[109] interbreed at this point, as I recognised both races and saw several doubtful birds that appeared to be intermediate between the two.

The fields of chicory between Calais and Dunkerque are very beautiful just now and the blue star-like blossoms form a very pleasing sight massed together as a crop, while they diffuse a soft, honey-like perfume. This low-lying soil, intermixed with sand, appears to be eminently suitable to the cultivation of this plant. I believe that the advantage of the light, sandy soil is that it enables the roots to be gathered with comparative ease. Factories for drying and preparing the roots are to be seen in most of the towns

Saltings - St Valery. 28·7·18.

and villages about here.

Crested larks are common hereabouts.

The bean fields I was exploring this afternoon seemed to be very popular with many kinds of birds. I noted an extraordinary number of whinchats, a goodly sprinkling of whitethroats and meadow pipits and a fair number of corn buntings, linnets, greenfinches and reed buntings – the latter obviously on migration. The whinchats were mostly in family parties, as also were the field wagtails. On three occasions I saw a harrier ranging over the country between Wimereux and Marquise and one of these birds dropped into a field of corn, where it remained until I approached to within thirty or forty yards.

Sunday 28 July, St-André
Near Zoteux, about ten miles north of Montreuil, I saw a great grey-backed shrike. It flew out to an isolated thorn bush growing in the open field and then back again to the roadside elms. I think it was possibly a migrant.

Monday 29 July
A hoopoe pitched in a field by some grazing horses, but flew wildly away when approached and I have no doubt it was a transient. This was near Rougefay.

Captain Turner, of No. 57 Squadron, says that in early August

217

last year at 4.45 a.m. when over Ypres at about 9,600 ft, he saw a flock of seven birds 'flying in formation' towards the west.

Friday 2 August, St-André

Garden warblers have been at the currants in the château grounds. At this season they utter a quiet, rather squeaky *cher, cher, cher,* often followed by a harsh, finch-like *tchweet* – a note never heard earlier in the season. The icterine warbler appears to have left the shrubbery.

Saturday 3 August, St-André

On my way to Dunkerque I called on M. Praneuf, M. Meesemaerker's son-in-law, at Bergues and he very obligingly showed his great auk's egg.[110] This was in a very fair condition and the blow holes, although rough and jagged as usual, were not unduly large. On one side there was an indent. Two-thirds of the egg was tolerably well figured with dark-brown irregular marks on a roughish grained white shell: the remaining third was almost devoid of markings. Two eggs were bequeathed to M. Meesemaerker's daughter. The other has been sold to the Paris Muséum d'Histoire Naturelle, the purchase having been negotiated by M. Meesemaerker.*

It was a boisterous day, and a short search failed to reveal any field wagtails. A few cuckoos have been seen in odd places today and yesterday, and these were no doubt migrants, 'held up' by the inclement weather and heavy rain showers. One or two wheatears have also been noted.

*Added later: A footnote in the *Revue Française d'Ornithologie,* 1916, p.314 states that this egg was sold, through the offices of M. Menegaux, to M. Vaucher of Geneva.

Sunday 4 August, St-André

On my way back from the coast, near Le Bahot, I saw a red-backed shrike. A whimbrel passed overhead, unseen in the summer haze, but its rolling trill fell distinctly upon the ear.

Thursday 8 August, St-André

Bird song has nearly ceased. A willow warbler was uttering a thin

Blackbird
adult ♂
Aug. 21st 1918.

old feathers

Primaries.

Secondaries

Primaries, moult outwards.
Secondaries, moult outwards & inwards,

thread of silvery notes – a mere ghost of its former song – from among the scented boughs of the limes. A chaffinch was also vocal, but its weak, tentative attempt at song lacked all the verve and energy of its rollicking spring melody. In Hesdin Forest, a buzzard flapped heavily down the ride in front of us. Gaining a few hundred yards it would settle in a tree, but as we approached it would again fly out and repeat the same tactics.

Sunday 11 August, St-André
I rode before breakfast this morning. The last few days, kestrels have been much commoner than during the previous few months, and I fancy this is accounted for by an influx of migrants.

A few days ago I received an icterine warbler's nest from Sheldon. He had found it in a hedgerow near Hazebrouck and a brood had been successfully reared in it. In most respects it was the typical chaffinch-like structure, but was interesting from the fact that it contained some greenish threads pilfered from a camouflage scrim. I daresay this helped to camouflage the nest more artfully than it did the guns.

On 12 August, Ingram returned to England on leave

Monday 12 August, Stoke Golding
Flew over this morning from Marquise to Lympne. It was rather hazy and somewhat overcast, but we were able to travel at 3,000 or 4,000 ft. The machine was a Bristol Fighter and we did the journey in about 35 minutes.

Thursday 15 August, Stoke Golding
A blackbird I shot today was in heavy moult, the new feathers showing very black by contrast with the weathered brownish old plumage.[111]

Friday 16 August, Stoke Golding
Shot a male sparrowhawk this afternoon – an old bird almost clean moulted. Only the two outermost primaries and the outermost secondary are still in the shaft and also the penultimate pair of tail feathers. The feathers on the head were also in the shaft for the most part, so I think it probable that this region is the last to shed its feathers in the majority of species. Wing of this bird, 7.5 inches.

Monday 19 August, Stoke Golding
In *The Ibis* for July 1918 Major W. Maitland Congreve MC writes an article on the birds of the Somme valley, noted chiefly in the Péronne and St-Valery districts.

Friday 30 August, St-André
That young rooks disperse from their native districts at this time of year seems very probable and I believe the large majority of them pass southwards. This afternoon I took a hasty survey with my glasses and all those I saw were undoubtedly bare-faced adults.[112]

5.
Victory
(2 Sept.–11 Nov. 1918)

BETWEEN THE SPRING AND AUTUMN OF 1918 *the Allies had switched from headlong retreat to rapid advance on a broad front. In September Foch ordered a major offensive. The end of the war was in sight.*

The advance took Ingram once again through a battle-scarred landscape: he described 'a country of weeds and graves, of shell-splintered trees, littered everywhere with the ugly debris of battle.' As dawn broke over the front beyond Longavesnes it seemed to him that even the skylarks were singing half-heartedly. But in the newly liberated city of Lille he was surprised by the warmth of his reception. 'You would feel a little hand being thrust into your own,' he wrote, 'and ... find a tiny child solemnly shaking hands.'

In October the German navy mutinied at Kiel, and the revolt spread to the population at large; and neither the departure of General Ludendorff, nor the hasty introduction of constitutional reforms, sufficed to quell the discontent. On 10 November the Kaiser fled to Holland.

Within twenty-four hours the war was over.

Monday 2 September, St-André

Today I motored through the reconquered territory north-east of Albert, or perhaps I should say north-east of what was formerly Albert, for the town has very much been wiped off the face of the map. Almost as far as the eye can reach, the ravages of war have laid the country waste and now the rolling hills are nothing more than a treeless and lifeless expanse of rank weeds, shell-holes, trenches and graves – with here and there a derelict tank to break the dreary monotony.

I was rather interested to note the number of sparrows that frequent the sites of former villages, places in which every house has lain, for a year or more, a mere heap of rubble and bricks. Their presence exemplifies the tenacity with which many species cling to their old haunts, although they may have completely changed. There was a tolerably large flock at Courcelette and these seemed to have taken up their abode in the splintered trunks of the tree stumps, and I have no doubt many nested there during the past season. Swallows were also plentiful, but apart from these, a magpie or two, and a few starlings that flew over, I saw no other birds.

Tuesday 3 September, St-André
In the spruce trees outside my office window I heard the thin sizzling song of a goldcrest – the first of these tiny migrants to pass.

St-André
I was again in the war area and had evidence that our recent advance on the Amiens front was a victorious one and not the mere occupation of evacuated territory as was the case on the Péronne front some eighteen months ago. The large parks of German guns and the abandoned rifles, ammunition and shells that littered the roadsides were convincing testimony to this fact, but the monstrous fifteen inch gun that lay destroyed in a small hillside spinney was perhaps the most eloquent proof of all.

Bruce's[113] headquarters were near the site of Maurepas and here I visited him in a ramshackle hut and had an hour's chat with him before returning to the more habitable country behind Albert. This war-stricken belt, with its shattered leafless trees, suggested to me a country overrun by some vast horde of devastating insects – a plague of monstrous locusts that had devoured all living things and left behind them nothing but an ugly pock-marked waste. This impression was enhanced by the derelict tanks, that lay like the dead of these devouring creatures scattered over the sombre and uninviting landscape.

On my way home I was asked if I could take a poor fellow, who had had one of his arms blown off, to a Casualty Clearing Station, which of course I consented to do. The cause of the accident was

uncertain, but was probably due to a hand grenade carelessly left behind by some previous unit.

Sunday 8 September, St-André

The last day or two, in the more clement intervals between the showers, a chiffchaff has been singing quite gaily in the old lime trees. Robins have also broken their long silence and sing occasionally. I have scanned several flocks of rooks in a vain search for young birds: they seem to have all gone.

I was walking near Gouy with my walking-stick gun, in the hopes of getting a partridge (of which there are a large number this year), when I flushed a family party of quails. These made away with faint, murmurous cries of alarm and plumped down again after a flight of scarcely more than twenty or thirty yards. Some children guarding cattle succeeded in finding one of these but not without several minutes' search, for although the bird dropped in a fairly open spot, its protective colouration served it remarkably well. So much faith did it place in this natural camouflage, that it allowed itself to be picked up. A few tufts of nestling down were still adhering to the tips of its feathers on the crown and tail, while there was some body down on the interspaces of the under surface.

Wednesday 18 September, St-André

The last two days I have spent in the war-stricken area, which now stretches in an ever-widening belt of desolation, a broadening scar across the fair face of France. This is a country of weeds and graves, of shell-splintered trees, littered everywhere with the ugly debris of battle. Returning to the pleasant valleys and the peaceful cultivated fields was like waking from a horrible nightmare – or the satiating of an aesthetic thirst that had become well-nigh intolerable. And if these were my feelings after two days' sojourn, what of the poor devils who have to stick it out year in year out, fair weather and foul?

This morning the 3rd and 4th Armies made a push on a wide front. Bruce, in his capacity as Staff Captain to the 3rd Corps 'Heavies', had warning of its coming and four of us arranged to go out and watch the opening battle from some commanding eminence. The push was to take place at 'the crack of dawn' and in order to be at the prearranged spot in time, we had to be called at 3.30 a.m. As ill-luck would have it, a heavy rain had set in during the night and this pattered down discouragingly on the canvas walls of our tents. As the other two refused to start, Bruce and I had to set out alone. For half an hour or more we motored through the dripping darkness, when suddenly the desultory flashes, that were momentarily growing nearer, burst into an almost continuous sheet of pulsating light – our barrage had started.

By some curious phenomenon, the rain-soaked, heavy atmosphere muffled the sound and only the nearer guns were loudly audible. These, it is true, made noise enough to frighten the dead, for the crashing ear-splitting roar of a twelve-inch 'How', almost at one's elbow, is always a terrible nerve-wracking sound; but it was the silent bursts of light, brightening the low rain clouds right and left as far as one could see, that passed one's understanding. By and bye, the smoke of the battle mingled with the driving rain and the visibility became so bad in the half light of the grey dawn it was impossible to see more than a few hundred yards.

Later on, as we stood upon the ridge surrounded on all sides by heavy artillery, the roar became almost intolerable and the waves of sound could be felt beating against the body as well as striking violently upon the more sensitive drum of one's ear. The bark

225

of the field guns now also became audible, but still unnaturally muffled.*

This desolate district is poor in bird life save for the swallows, which are tolerably abundant – no doubt the refuse encourages flies and these, in turn, the hirundines, who prey upon them. Near Péronne I noted a flock of tree sparrows, a small assembly of starlings and, most interesting of all, some immature black (?) terns. These latter were hawking insects over a sheet of water or flooded marsh, and kept beating to and fro with graceful flight. Moorhens were calling from the secure depths of the vast reed beds – comfortable croaking sounds. Yellow wagtails were passing through the country in fair numbers, but were restless after the manner of all migrants. A magpie here and there and a number of crested larks were noted near Moislains, while skylarks were singing half-heartedly as dawn broke on the battle front beyond Longavesnes.

The previous night a Hun bombing machine passed over and it was a pretty sight to see it caught in the rays of half a dozen search lights. As it moved across the deep velvety indigo of the sky, it looked like a silvery white cross – a configuration that was certainly not emblematic of its mission to our side of the lines!

*Added later: This attack, launched at 5.30 a.m., proved a great success and resulted in the capture of 11,000 prisoners and an appreciable advance on a front of about 1.5 miles.

Saturday 21 September, St-André
During the last week or ten days I have seen several flocks of magpies – one numbering over 20, another 19 and several of 15 or more. This seems to indicate a genuine tendency to form autumn congregations – that is to say, an awakening of a gregarious instinct that has nothing to do with the so called 'ceremonial gatherings'.

Chiffchaffs are still chanting their song in the château grounds, fitfully and only when the weather brightens, but nevertheless their voice forms a pleasant break in the avian silence. Tree-creepers are becoming slightly more vocal and the little owls occasionally call from the orchard.

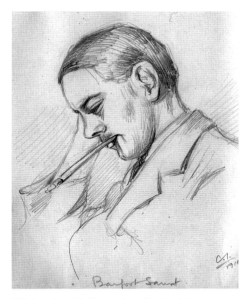

Wednesday 25 September, St-André

A little owl was hunting over a potato field this evening as I came in from a ride. Its flight formed big upward sweeps vaguely suggestive of the wood-pigeons' 'clapping' flight. On the crest of the undulations the bird dwelt as though about to hover and was evidently scrutinising the ground below. A wren was singing in a hedgerow very softly and its voice sounded very far away although the bird was actually not more than a few paces from me.

Monday 7 October, St-André

Together with Colonel Clark, Godden and Saunt, I visited Bourlon Wood[114] and Hill 80. The former has been a very hotly contested spot and has been won and lost on many occasions, but finally fell into our hands a week or so ago. The fresh splintered gashes in the trees, the crumbling brown earth of the shell craters and finally a row of khaki-clad corpses awaiting interment, all bore evidence of very recent strife. And yet this wood was still alive and sufficiently leafy to harbour a jay, and it certainly did not present that gaunt, blighted aspect of the woods of last year's battlefields.

From Hill 80 we looked down upon Cambrai, which was still occupied by the enemy. The city was burning in many places and heavy columns of smoke rolled away from the gushing points of flame. The British were shelling fairly heavily but save at one spot, a canal bridge about three quarters of a mile below us, the enemy was not responding.

During the day I noted: crested larks, magpies, crows, jays, skylarks, partridges, starlings, meadow pipits, white wagtails and sparrows in the battle zone. Some of these were no doubt migrants.

Saturday 12 October, St-André

Despite the inclement weather and the yellowing foliage, which now drifts fluttering to the ground, a chiffchaff still haunts the château garden and sings its pleasant chant – a faltering echo of the ringing notes of spring, but nevertheless a happy little ditty.

Two days ago I borrowed a gun and 25 cartridges and spent a couple of hours among the abandoned trenches and wire entanglements south-west of Albert. Partridges were extraordinarily numerous but somewhat shy. I bagged five and a half brace and lost three other birds through not having a dog, so altogether I had a very pleasant afternoon's sport and the fact that it was strictly against a GRO[115] rather adds spice to the enjoyment.

Starlings have become very plentiful and flocks are now to be seen in the war area behind Albert.

Wednesday 16 October, St-André

I spent a short time this afternoon with a fellow named Orlebar,[116] shooting partridges on the borderland of the late battlefield. Although the birds were as plentiful as before, they were shyer than ever and we only managed to bag three.

There were a lot of song thrushes about, sheltering in the stray bushes and rough herbage. Meadow pipits were also numerous and a few reed buntings were also seen – all migrants no doubt – linnets, yellow buntings, corn buntings and a solitary swallow were observed in the same locality. I heard some bramblings yesterday, near the château.

Thursday 17 October, St-André

This evening I rode for an hour or so in the direction of Douriez and a tiercel[117] passed overhead. The evening was dark and overcast, and against the murky sky the silhouette of the bird looked strangely 'thickset' compared with the long drawn-out form of a hobby or a kestrel. The wings gave one the impression of enormous power combined with a big 'lifting' surface. A magpie uttered strange sounds of displeasure from a neighbouring hedgerow and when the peregrine settled in a tall poplar, he followed him up, angrily vituperating from a safe distance.

Just as we rode abreast of the poplar tree, we flushed a covey of partridge. The peregrine instantly gave chase, but a friendly potato field offered safe shelter. Realising that we might probably disturb other quarry, the peregrine followed our tracks for some time 'waiting on us' – to use a falconer's term – very prettily beating back and forth overhead for about a quarter of an hour. Unluckily we did not put up another covey or else we might have seen a pretty flight. The other evening I heard a lilting song from a tall hedgerow, which I believe to have been that of a lesser whitethroat.

Saturday 19 October

Between Arras and Cambrai a flock of woodlarks passed over with fluty twitterings flying south west.

Beyond Cambrai the Hun has retired without heavy fighting and the cultivated country is practically untouched. When the enemy evacuated this territory he took with him practically all the civilian population, leaving only a few aged or crippled folk. As a result the fields are empty and present a strangely deserted aspect which is not in keeping with the high state of cultivation.

The re-conquered towns and villages – depopulated though they be – are fairly gay with bunting. Heaven knows where all these French flags come from! Could they have been hidden away against this day of victory?

Sunday 20 October

A cirl bunting, perched on a tall tree in the château garden, was

229

singing very merrily this morning.

Friday 25 October, St-André

The last two days I have been visiting the aerodromes in the Lille district. After travelling an odious nightmarish belt of stricken lowlands about La Bassée, I re-entered civilization near Santes. This territory has been so recently re-conquered – about seven days – that the villagers are only now returning to their homes west of Lille. The Germans, it seems, evacuated the civilians from all the villages along the line they intended to defend and it was these folk that I saw trooping back – women, children and old men. Struggling with hand-carts or bent double with ponderous bundles, these people all wore a glad smile and, as often as not, stopped to wave a friendly hand of welcome.

Again the mystery of many flags had to be solved, for the streets were as gay as a carnival day with fluttering tricolor bunting. The enemy had destroyed a large number of private houses of the better class villa type in the suburbs of Seclin, and had shamelessly destroyed the church tower, but otherwise this town was pretty intact.

Lille of course had been abandoned by the Germans without destruction and the only damage visible was probably that of our own bombs or relics of 1914. The citizens thronged the streets as though it was a festival day and their joy at being repatriated was very transparent. Never have I received such courtesy from shop people – it mattered not whether or no they had the goods I required – they were only too happy to chat with their 'liberators', as they called the English, and to help us in any way possible. If one asked to be directed to a certain street or place, the chances were that the individual questioned would volunteer to personally conduct you. Every now and again you would feel a little hand being thrust into your own and on looking down you would find a tiny child solemnly shaking hands with you – this occurred over and over again during the course of the afternoon.

All this atmosphere of whole-hearted, joyous welcome was a very novel and interesting experience, but already it is beginning to wear off. Bruce says that two days ago it was very much more marked and, of course, on our first entry the troops were received with wild and frenzied enthusiasm.

Considering the serious want of brass in Germany, it was surprising to see the number of kitchen utensils of this metal being displayed in the shop windows. It appears that it had been carefully hidden – 'carefully', one may be sure, for the discovery of concealed copper or brass entailed a very heavy fine or even execution. Although the Huns had requisitioned large stocks of goods – giving in exchange apparently worthless documents – the shops had quite a lot to sell. In one case I saw a china pig caricaturing the Kaiser; needless to say this had, like the copper vessels, been very carefully hidden away during the last four years.

Talking of the requisitioning of goods, I heard a story illustrating the shallow pretence of the whole thing. A furrier was making an Astrakhan coat when a German officer came into the shop and calmly appropriated the article. The shopkeeper – the woman who told us the story – followed him down the street remonstrating, demanding payment or at least some documentation to show that it had been requisitioned. The officer however made away without conceding to either request. It so happened that the coat was not quite complete and one sleeve was missing. On the following day the officer had the effrontery to return and demand this other sleeve. I am glad to say he did not get it.

The château I was staying in had its walls decorated with old pictures and was quite nicely furnished, so in this instance at any rate the Huns have not looted the place. The owner's cellar however had been drunk up entirely and the old proprietor had not been invited even to share a bottle of his own wine.

Saturday 26 October, St-André
Large flocks of chaffinches are to be seen in the fields now. Hoodies were noted north of Boulogne today. During the summer the little owls were comparatively or altogether silent – now they have become quite noisy again, and one frequently hears their mewing cries in the orchard.

This afternoon was brilliantly clear and the English cliffs glistened alluringly from across a startling expanse of deep blue sea – bluer than the Channel has any right to be. Altogether it was a delicious afternoon, with an intoxicating air and a landscape bright with the golds, browns and yellows of autumn.

Monday 28 October, St-André

During the course of a ride I saw two peregrines – both old falcons.[118] Both birds were sitting on a clod of earth and had evidently fed fairly recently, for they seemed loath to take wing and flew somewhat ponderously. Flushed by the evening sun, the first falcon made a fine figure as she sat bolt upright overlooking a wide stretch of open country – her creamy-buff breast suffused with the warm level light of the sinking sun. As she rose with outstretched wings and fanned her tail on the turn, I got a good view of her slate-blue back and found myself instinctively listening for the tinkle of a falconer's bell.

Thursday 31 October, Honnechy[119]

Am staying two nights with 22 Wing in order to visit the newly acquired aerodromes in this district. Last night I saw an enemy machine come down in flames at a distance of several miles. Pyrotechnically it was a fine sight, but at the same time one could not help feeling a twinge of sympathy when one thought that a fellow was in the heart of the flames. At first the glowing mass fell slantwise, emitting scattered fragments of fire, but as the speed increased – it never appeared to fall fast – the angle became steeper, the flame increased in volume and the scattered fragments more numerous, and interspersed with occasional green and red lights as the signal cartridges exploded.

The previous night, quite a number of Hun machines had passed over, to the inevitable accompaniment of 'Archie' and machine gun fire – the rat-tat-tat of the latter sounding absurdly futile against an object glistening in the searchlight beams so far overhead, while spitting tracer bullets, quick-firing sparks of ruddy light, seemed to be extinguished before they had travelled a tithe of the distance. Heavy booms, followed by an angry shake of the house, told us that the Hun had dropped his bombs at no great distance.

Rooks are now numerous everywhere – also jackdaws. The former, especially common, appear to flood the country about the third week in October. Song thrushes have also appeared in large numbers and skylarks have increased appreciably. There are likewise quite a lot of goldcrests in the trees surrounding the château at St-André.

Saw three hirundines – swallows, I think, near Cambrai on the 31st.

Sunday 3 November
Noted another peregrine near Wailly this afternoon.

Saturday 9 November, St-André
Today I flew to Estrées-en-Chaussée on the Amiens–St Quentin road in order to visit 54th Wing. The weather was beautifully fine and the air was full of gossamer, especially towards evening. This gossamer clung to the struts pertinaciously, which was rather surprising considering the rush of wind.

Sunday 10 November
Another fine day and, availing myself of the halcyon weather, I ordered the machine again – an RE8 of the Communication Flight – at 10.15 and flew down to an aerodrome near Cambrai. I lunched with the 9th Brigade at Noyelles-sur-Escaut, a half-ruined village a little south of Bourlon. Amos, the Equipment Officer, told me that the place had not been properly cleaned up and that there were several dead Huns still lying in one dug-out and another body behind some sandbags. I had a talk with several pilots of Nos 49, 27 and 62 Squadrons and although two or three patrols had been up, not a single Bosche was to be seen and very little 'Archie' and there was a general feeling that the war was over – as indeed it practically was.

Under the circumstances, therefore, it was more than bad luck that one of 27's machines should have got a direct hit from 'Archie'. These poor devils are almost certainly the last flying men to be killed by the enemy in this war – and by an appalling fluke too!

233

Monday 11 November, St-André

Hostilities have ceased and the flags are flying in the streets. Owing to a steady drizzling rain, not many people were in the streets of Hesdin this afternoon and the majority of those were too merry to mind much what kind of weather it was.[120]

I saw a great grey-backed shrike this afternoon while riding.

THE ARMISTICE LINE
November 1918

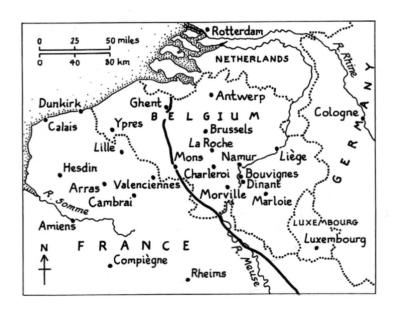

6.
The aftermath
(13 Nov.–31 Dec. 1918)

AFTER THE ARMISTICE, *Ingram was occupied less with birds than with the reawakening world of humankind. Civilians were pouring back into the towns, prisoners-of-war were being released, and the man in the street, if not bruised by defeat, was preparing to celebrate his first peacetime Christmas for five years.*

Ingram too was on the move. From Valenciennes, the site of his new headquarters, he travelled to the war-torn cities near the borders: Mons, Namur, Charleroi, Cologne. Officially his task was to make inventories of the aircraft – the great night-bombers and the Fokker Scouts – that lay in abandoned enemy airfields. In Germany, albeit unofficially, illicit currency speculation could be a source of cash.

Ingram observed a sombre mood on the streets of Cologne. There was little food in the shops: the Allied naval blockade, operative throughout the war and continuing after it, had produced famine conditions, and foreign officers at the fashionable hotels had to supply their own rations. In Brussels, where Ingram found himself on Christmas Eve, the contrast could not have been greater: champagne flowed, there was a pervasive and wild gaiety, and 'every other woman seems to be of doubtful virtue'. It was indeed a different world.

But neither the war nor the birds are forgotten for long. As he drives to the Ardennes, past 'the tawny yellow grasses, the scattered blackthorns' and the abandoned enemy vehicles, Ingram rediscovers his first loves 'in the clearings and among the trees: tree-creeper, goldcrest, blue tit, marsh tit, meadow pipits – two or three, chaffinches, yellowhammers and a party of rooks.'

Wednesday 13 November, St-André
I visited Valenciennes yesterday. On my way home I gave a lift to a French officer and his wife – the two had not met each other for

over four years. The latter told me that French papers smuggled through the lines were in very great demand during the German occupation. An ordinary daily would fetch as much as 300 francs – the owner charging five francs for the privilege of allowing it to be read!

Tuesday 26 November, Valenciennes
We moved into our new HQ in this town yesterday. The population is pouring back, but the place is still depressingly deserted and not a little war-worn in appearance.

Released British, Italian and French prisoners are also arriving in large numbers. One and all agree that they have received every kindness at the hands of the Belgians and without their aid would have been in an even sorrier plight than they are now. The Germans, it appears, merely turned them out without making any kind of provision for their maintenance. Many are without shirts and underwear and a large percentage are wearing German caps, coats, etc. It is hardly to be wondered at that many of these fellows scrounge anything they can lay hands on. At the best of times, 'it is a way they have in the Army' – as the old song goes – and these poor devils are genuinely in want of the ordinary necessities of life. 'They'll steal the blue out of your eyes,' as an Australian once said to me.

Wednesday 27 November, Valenciennes
Visited Mons this afternoon. The town was extraordinarily gay and bright, the streets being heavily draped in bunting. It appears the Belgian King had just passed through and the country folk from all around had thronged to see their popular monarch. On our way home we gave a lift to a man who had travelled 23 kilometres to Mons for this express purpose and, had we not helped him on his way, he would have stood a good chance of having to trudge the whole of this distance back. I am afraid there are not many Englishmen who would walk fifteen miles to get a glimpse of our King!

Friday 29 November, Dinant
General Brooke-Popham has sent me on a round of visits

in connection with the taking over of German machines, in fulfilment of the terms of the Armistice. At Morville I took an inventory of 13 twin-engined night-bombing machines – monstrous things packed away in a gigantic shed. At Bouvignes, on some open fields above the valley of the Meuse, I found another large Friedrichshafener, mothering 24 Fokker Scouts. As the place formed a high bluff, open to the four winds, a gale would have wrecked the whole assembly, the three men forming the guard being ignorant of the necessary precautions in such an event and in any case wholly incapable of carrying them out.

The Belgians – the Walloons inhabiting this district at any rate – are intensely bitter against the Germans and are certainly more vindictive than the average Frenchman. Considering the large numbers of innocent civilians ruthlessly executed during the early days of the war, these sentiments are hardly to be wondered at. A postcard is sold in the shops depicting a house against whose walls 173 civilians – men, women and children alike – were shot.

The prices ruling in Dinant during 1918 were exceptionally high. Tobacco fetched 125 francs a pound, butter 40 francs, a suit of clothes (worth 75 francs in normal times) 900 francs and other commodities in proportion.

Jackdaws were sailing across the rocky escarpment overhanging the town of Dinant – I saw flocks of these birds on other cliffs along the Meuse valley. Breeding sites unquestionably have a considerable influence on the distribution of these birds. Saw what I took to be a dabchick on the Meuse near Profondeville.

Saturday 30 November, Namur

The tawny yellow grasses, the scattered blackthorns and out-cropping of blue-grey rock, betokened a limestone formation which always gives a distinctive character to a landscape. The scenery became wilder and more wooded as we sped eastwards towards the Ardennes. Along the roadside, in ditches or overturned against a hedge or bank, I passed numbers of abandoned German cars, lorries and tenders – I must have seen upwards of 100 or 150 altogether.

As I was approaching Marloie I told my driver to draw up

beside an officer I saw riding ahead of us – the first officer I had seen for thirty or forty miles – in order that I might interrogate him as to the position of the aerodrome. By a strange coincidence the officer turned out to be Timins![121] From my point of view the meeting was a fortunate one and I was glad to accept his pressing invitation to lunch at his Divisional HQ in Marche.

Monday 9 December
Saw two great grey-backed shrikes near Hesdin today.

Tuesday 10 December
I noticed a rookery in the trees surrounding the château at Iwuy (six miles north-east of Cambrai). I met the owner of Plancy, the very large rookery in the Aube department the other day, and he informed me that the number of nests had been sadly reduced, owing to the felling of trees requisitioned by the government.

Sunday 15 December, Spa
Together with Captain Alec Keith, I drove here today on a visit to Cologne, which we hope to reach tomorrow.

Tuesday 17 December, Cologne
Cologne is a fine city and, outwardly at any rate, shows no indication of distress – the shops being brilliantly lighted and filled with Christmas goods. It must be admitted that foodstuffs formed a very small proportion of these displays, but costly jewellery and *objets d'art* were plentiful and made a fine show. The streets were thronged with people who seemed to treat our troops with utter indifference. This attitude of the populace was interesting – they seemed neither curious nor resentful. Although it could not be truthfully said that they were downcast, there was a singular lack of gaiety and there was generally a very sombre tone about this crowd out for their Christmas shopping.

When spoken to, the people are studiously polite before answering, hurriedly raising their felt hats, displaying a close-cropped pate and snatching the inevitable rank cigar from their lips. What bitterness it must be in their cup of pride, to hear the band of the British battalion echoing through their streets! This was a sight I am glad I did not miss, and also the mounting of the guard on the mighty bridge that spans the sacred Rhine!

At the hotel – the Dom – the food was quite good and not extortionately dear, but for the most part, the officers living there supplied their own rations and had them cooked by the hotel staff.

Saw a pheasant near La Roche.

On our way back from Spa we came through Vielsalm, La Roche, Rochefort and Dinant – a route that led over some fine wooded hills and down steep, heavily watered valleys. The trip was marred to a large extent by driving rain which beat coldly in our faces as we breasted the higher ground.

At La Roche we were made very welcome at a little hotel and given an excellent meal which we shared with an old priest. Like all the Walloons these folk were very bitter against the Germans, and the little daughter of the house – a flapper of about fifteen summers – was especially vehement. She told us she had made up her mind to embrace the first officer of the relieving troops that came into the town and curiously enough this proved to be an Englishman who had stayed in the hotel before the War. Upon telling her we had not been received so warmly in Belgium, both Keith and myself came in for a similar salutation!

Wednesday 18 December, Valenciennes[122]
Just back from an interesting adventure – an excursion into Germany to buy 15,000 marks to convert into francs. Owing to the fact that Germany will have to redeem at par, all the marks that she has forced into circulation throughout the occupied territories at the rate of 1 franc 25 centimes per mark, a very safe speculation is offered to anyone purchasing marks in Germany at seventy centimes a piece.

After making enquiries at Mons and Charleroi we got through as far as Verviers, where we slept in a very comfortable hotel. The following day we (Hanson is my companion) passed into Germany and, after purchasing several thousand marks in Jülich, proceeded to Cologne, where, at a number of banks and money changers, we finally succeeded in buying the 15,000 marks with our French money.

Hanson

Loaded with this mass of German notes – a small hand bag well-nigh filled with them – we headed for the frontier at about 4 p.m. As the mark is only redeemable for a certain number of days at the rate of 1.25 francs, time seemed to be an all important factor in the success of our enterprise; moreover we were both anxious to be back as we were both absent, and in Germany, without official sanction. Imagine our chagrin, therefore, when scarcely clear of the suburbs of the city we collided with a peasant's cart with such force that we drove the thing before us for about ten yards on the bonnet of our car! In the darkness, at first we could find neither driver nor horse, but finally they were discovered to be none the worse for their shaking. Having had no light on his cart, the poor devil was in such a fear of the consequences that after scarcely a moment's hesitation he disappeared into the night, leaving his shattered vehicle derelict by the roadside.

It did not require a very careful inspection to discover that our radiator was leaking badly. Here was a pretty kettle of fish! We appeared to be stranded 50 miles into Germany and about 200 miles from Valenciennes where we were officially supposed to be. The driver suggested we might be able to crawl short stages if we constantly replenished the water supply. This we promptly attempted to do. At the first house, we succeeded in exchanging a half loaf of white bread – a rare luxury in Germany – for a few handfuls of meal. This, mixed with water, was put in the radiator and much to our joy we found it was so successful in sealing the leak that we were able to reach Valenciennes on our return journey without further mishap.

The following day was one full of incident and we found it no easy task to dispose of our hoard of marks. Liège was too near the frontier and we soon realised that French francs were very scarce here and only theoretically exchangeable at the rate of 1.25 per mark – truth to tell they were standing at a considerable premium and we had to be satisfied with a much lower rate. We were able to get rid of a few more hundred marks at Huy, several thousand at Namur and five or six hundred at Charleroi, but only by dint of hard work – real hard work. At Namur we sent a runner round the town, offering him a reward if he could negotiate a thousand, and at Charleroi we had to resort to the same expedient. At the end of the day, we found we had made about 60 per cent profit on 6,000 francs, but were still left with about 10,000 marks!

Monday 23 December, Valenciennes
Since arriving in this town I have seen some gruesome sights. Coming back from a ride with Godden about three weeks ago, as we came into the town from the Mons side we found a human skeleton propped up against a lamp-post. Upon the shattered skull some wit had placed a tattered straw hat at a rakish angle. This was gruesome, but not so horrible as the subsequent discovery of a dead German soldier lying in a field just as he had died some three or four weeks before. His boots and socks had been stolen and his pockets rifled.

Thursday 26 December, Valenciennes
Keith and I spent Christmas Eve in Brussels and a very gay spot it is too. Every other woman seems to be of doubtful virtue and one and all are more than pleased to see you. For instance we were partaking of a long and expensive meal at the Palace when our neighbours – an elderly couple from Antwerp – insisted on our drinking champagne with them – no small matter with fizz at 80 francs a bottle! So it is throughout. There is an atmosphere of welcome that makes for enjoyment.

We stayed the night in the hotel and I hear the dancing did not cease until six or seven in the morning – a clearly unconventional gathering of merrymakers bedecked with paper hats and interlaced with multi-coloured paper 'serpentine' (I know not an English word for this paper 'tape' that is so freely used at Carnival time on the Continent).

There are many other dancing halls – equally gay – open every and all night for similar entertainment. About a week ago Keith and I visited Brussels for dinner and returned to Valenciennes in the early hours of the morning, and on that occasion we 'looked in' at several such places. The average *demimondaine* is better looking than her French counterpart – less gaudily made up and more tastefully dressed – they are certainly not so repulsively rouged as English women of a similar profession.

The primary object of our visit was to dispose of another 50,000 marks, a second venture which promises to be more successful than the first. One way or another we expect to make about £1,000 out of the old Bosche.

There were several humorous incidents during this transaction. At the time, when we had about 40,000 marks to dispose of, I asked my hairdresser if he minded me paying him in German money. 'Well sir, I'm afraid it would be no good to me. I had a mark about a week ago and as I couldn't get rid of it I sent it to my wife as a souvenir!' A nice thing if we had been landed with 40,000 such souvenirs.

Tuesday 31 December, Valenciennes
Rode into the Fôret de Raismes. It was a dull afternoon with a

premature twilight which cast a gloom over the landscape. Bird life was not plentiful, but I noted the following in the clearings and among the trees: tree-creeper, goldcrest, blue tit, marsh tit, meadow pipits – two or three, chaffinches, yellowhammers, and a party of rooks flew over.

Postscript

FOLLOWING DEMOBILISATION *Collingwood Ingram and his family left Westgate for Benenden in the Weald of Kent. It was here that he developed the enthusiasm for collecting, breeding and growing plants that dominated the latter part of his long life. As with his love of birds, his passion for gardening stemmed from his delight in the beauty of the living world. His special loves among the plants were the Japanese flowering cherries, and to generations of gardeners he was, and still is, known as 'Cherry Ingram'. He died in 1981, at the age of one hundred.*

If Collingwood Ingram is remembered today chiefly for his gardening achievements, his place among our outstanding field ornithologists is now secure. During the Great War, his ability to identify the songs and calls of every bird had astonished the war correspondent Sir William Beach Thomas, who recorded the phenomenon in his autobiography. Percy Lowe, Curator of Birds at the Natural History Museum, endorsed this. 'I cordially agree,' he wrote to Ingram, 'knowing what an eye and ear you have as a field naturalist – the best in fact which I have ever met.'

Notes

CWGC = Commonwealth War Graves Commission
JC = information provided by John Cantelo

[1]The hooded crow, or 'hoodie', and the carrion crow are once again (as in Ingram's time) regarded as full species rather than races of the same species. The carrion crow breeds in western Europe and is replaced by the hooded crow to the north (including Scotland) and east. The hooded crow is a winter visitor to southern and eastern England and north-east France. It has declined sharply since 1916 and is now very scarce in winter. (JC)

[2]The crested lark has declined in north-eastern France since Ingram's time, no doubt the result of changes in agriculture. The latest bird atlas of the region shows that it still occurs in the St-Omer area, although certainly much reduced. It tends to have fared better in coastal areas. (JC)

[3]Grey wagtail – see Appendix 1 for a summary of wagtail taxonomy.

[4]Only the short-toed tree-creeper is resident in this part of France, while only the common tree-creeper occurs in Britain. Ingram was well aware of the different species (he had written a short paper on the European tree-creepers in 1913), but he usually refers to 'tree-creepers' in the journal, perhaps for brevity. The calls are distinctive, but were only fully described in the 1960s. Identification remained difficult until a paper published in the 1970s. (JC)

[5]Bruce Ingram, brother of Collingwood, became editor of the *Illustrated London News* in 1900 and continued in the post for 63 years. During the Great War he was awarded the MC and OBE (military), was mentioned in dispatches three times, yet somehow remained the active editor of the newspaper.

[6]Allan Maxwell Lowery, Captain, killed aged 27, 24.3.1917. (CWGC)

[7]High explosives.

[8]Samuel Franklyn Leslie (Frank) Cody, 2nd Lieutenant, was killed only three weeks later, 23.1.1917 (CWGC). He was the son of Samuel Cody, the American pioneer aviator, who made the first powered flight in the UK in 1908.

[9]Eric Fox Pitt Lubbock was the son of John Lubbock, the first Lord Avebury,. The family home was at Downe in Kent, Charles Darwin's home village. Lord Avebury, a distinguished scientist, was a friend and supporter of Darwin; his work is mentioned in *The Origin of Species*. Eric Lubbock went to Eton, read Biology at Oxford and enlisted in the ranks before gaining a commission in the RFC, first as an observer and then as a pilot. Although only 23 years old to Ingram's 36,

Eric Lubbock and a letter to Ingram ('Dear Compass')

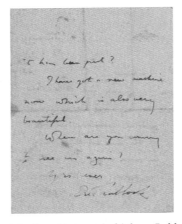

they became friends, perhaps through their shared interest in biology. Lubbock was godfather to Ingram's daughter Certhia, but was killed only two months after she was born. For a full account of his RFC career, see Jefford J (2000) *Cross and Cockade International*, **31**. Two letters from Lubbock to Ingram have survived. They are addressed to 'Dear Compass' and 'Dear Capt. Compass'. One is an acceptance of Ingram's invitation to be godfather to his daughter, promising to 'point out to your daughter the true north of life'. The second, illustrated here, was written only a fortnight before he was killed. It mentions a special compass, probably one designed by Ingram (Appendix 2).

[10]Collingwood and Florence Ingram's daughter Certhia (*Certhia familiaris* is the tree-creeper) was born on 4 January 1917 at Westgate in Kent; she was their fourth and last child, and the only girl. Major William Read of 45 Squadron (whose own diaries are held at the Imperial War Museum) was one of the 'originals' – the first RFC men to go to France in 1914. At the time of this entry, he was having trouble with his commanding officer Webb-Bowen, and in April 1917 left the RFC to return to the Infantry. Later in the War he rejoined the RFC, at first as a training instructor in the UK, but following flights under Tower Bridge (to and fro), was 'punished', as he intended, by being returned to active service. See Barker R (2002) *The Royal Flying Corps in World War I* (Robinson).

[11]Crested larks are certainly no longer common; see note 2.

[12]The slang word Archie was first used for anti-aircraft guns, and later also for the flack produced by the exploding shells. Maurice Baring, in his 1920 book *Flying Corps Headquarters 1914–1918* (Blackwood, p.43), suggests that it was first used for a particular German gun.

[13]John Hay, 2nd Lieutenant, killed aged 28, 23.1.1917. (CWGC)

[14]Marsh tits and willow tits are difficult to distinguish and both are widely distributed in Europe, including this area of France. The willow tit was recognised in Britain only in 1898. In his 1913 draft *Birds of France*, Ingram expresses dissatisfaction with the current state of knowledge of the taxonomy of this group of tits and says 'Personally, we confess at our inability to distinguish the accepted forms of this bird' (the two species and races). It is clear that he was happier with the concept of one species with distinct races. In the journal he makes no attempt at distinctions and refers only to the marsh tit. (JC)

[15]In the autumn of 1915, a failed British attack at Loos resulted in 50,000 British casualties. The battle is especially notorious for an incident in which gas, used by the British, blew back to their own lines when the wind changed direction.

[16]Early 1917 was exceptionally cold. Data from England for the whole 20th century show that February 1917 was the seventh coldest February; March 1917 the third coldest March; and April 1917 the coldest April.

[17]The cirl bunting is no longer found in this area, mirroring its significant decline in the UK. The declines are thought to be associated with changes in farming practices such as autumn sowing of crops, and the consequent shortage of the stubbles, on which they feed in winter, loss of hedgerow nesting sites and loss of unimproved grassland, where they feed in summer. (JC)

[18]M. van Kempen's museum had a collection of stuffed birds. He visited the museum many times subsequently.

[19]Billets of La Gorgue aerodrome were at Filescamp Farm. See O'Connor M (2001) *Airfields and Airmen: Ypres* (Pen and Sword).

[20]This was James McCudden, one of the RFC's greatest pilots.

[21]The white-headed race of the long-tailed tit is generally found no nearer than Denmark, Poland and eastern Germany, although in his draft *Birds of France* Ingram described it as a fairly regular winter migrant to north-eastern France and he was looking out for it on this occasion. He identifies these birds as the race *rosea*, which also occurs in Britain and is now known as *rosaceus*. (JC)

[22]Ingram was Master of the Thanet Harriers at the age of only 17 (see Introduction).

[23]Peewit and green plover are both names for *Vanellus vanellus*, now usually known as the lapwing, a name also used by Ingram.

[24]Edwin Albert Pope, 2nd Lieutenant, killed aged 27; and Hubert Alfred Johnson, 2nd Lieutenant, killed aged 23. (CWGC)

[25]Harold William Tagent, 2nd Lieutenant, killed aged 22, 24.3.1917. (CWGC)

[26]The great auk *Pinguinus impennis* was a flightless seabird of the North Atlantic, hunted to extinction by the mid-19th century. A number of skins and eggs are in museums (see entries for 30.1.18 and 3.8.18).

[27]The brambling is a winter visitor to France, returning to northern latitudes to breed.

[28]The stone curlew (Ingram elsewhere calls it the Norfolk plover), a bird of open countryside, has declined since 1917. A few, perhaps six to twelve pairs, may still breed in this part of France. (JC)

[29]An account of this incident is given in *Bloody April* by Peter Hart (Weidenfeld and Nicolson 2005), including a description of the aerial fight by a German airman who was involved. It seems that the Prince was not killed outright, but was picked up and carried back to an Allied field hospital, where he died a few days later.

[30]The chiffchaff normally reaches Britain in early to mid-March.

[31]The loss of planes and men recorded here heralded the first phase of 'Bloody April'.

[32]The pied wagtail with a black head must have been a melanistic bird, a genetic oddity. (JC)

[33]*Motacilla alba alba*, the white wagtail.

[34]'Yellow-breasted field wagtail', a general term for the species *Motacilla flava*, which has several sub-species; see under wagtails in Appendix 1.

[35]*Motacilla lugubris*, a name then used for the pied wagtail.

[36]Bransby Williams' father was the actor of the same name who lived on into the age of television. The son was the youngest man in Britain to qualify as a pilot and the youngest pilot to be made a captain.

[37]Either yellow or blue-headed wagtails, see Appendix 1.

[38]Bruce Ingram, Collingwood's brother; see note 5.

[39]Tethered kite balloons were used by both sides for observation; information was sent to the ground by telephone. The balloons could be winched down if under attack by aircraft, but were also vulnerable to long distance shelling. If hostile planes were seen too late for winching, the observers (usually two) could parachute to the ground.

William Drury (see note 46) was an unconventional chaplain with left-wing views. He went to France in 1914 and became Deputy Chaplain General. There were many tales about him, including his saying, on meeting a colleague for the first time, that he was relieved to meet a chaplain with other interests beside immediate bloodshed. After the war, he became chaplain at the Royal Hospital Chelsea and finally vicar at the small Sussex village of Binsted, where his love of nature could be indulged. His fertile mind was also engaged by the problems of town planning and transport, including the establishment of the English Linear Cities Association. See Hilda Martindale, Victorian Portraits and Others *(1945).*

[40]Oliver B.W. Wills, Lieutenant, killed aged 27, 10.11.1918. (CWGC)

[41]Interest in the height at which birds fly was a hot topic in the early years of flying. Radar studies gave the subject a sounder scientific basis. (JC)

[42]The genus of warblers which includes icterine and melodious warblers.

[43]The fieldfare, a northern bird which moves south in winter, has increased its breeding range since 1917, when it bred no nearer to this area than Germany. Small numbers now breed here. (JC)

[44]The little bittern (not a British resident) still breeds in the nature reserve there. (JC)

[45]See Appendix 1 for a list of birds recorded on this visit to Clairmarais. The list includes the great reed warbler, which hung on here for many years but now seems to have disappeared. In contrast, the bluethroat and Cetti's warbler, unknown here in 1917, now breed. Another bird that has colonised the region, not specifically the Clairmarais area, is the serin. When Ingram wrote his draft *Birds of France* in 1913 the serin had reached the Paris area. (JC)

[46]Drury was right; Witherby in *British Birds* (1919) recorded a rookery in Dunkirk.

[47]A scops owl would have been an exceptional record. (JC)

[48]This would be an exceptional record, and it is a pity he did not give details. (JC)

[49]The great reed warbler may still be here in low numbers. (JC)

[50]The yellow wagtail, which occurs in Britain and the near continent.

[51]Ingram was a member for 80 years, a record. Harry Witherby was a major figure in British ornithology and a publisher of bird books: with others, he wrote the standard *Handbook of British Birds* (five volumes, 1938–41).

[52]Ingram knew that the bird was either *Hippolais icterina*, the icterine warbler, or *Hippolais polyglotta*, the melodious warbler. His identification is probably correct, based on the known distribution at the time. The melodious warbler has since become the more common of the two in the area, having spread from the south-

west. Field identification is tricky and was not fully sorted out until long after the Great War. (JC)

[53]Recent DNA studies confirm Ingram's feeling that the *Hippolais* warblers (icterine, melodious and other warblers) are closely related to the *Acrocephalus* warblers (marsh, reed and other warblers). (JC)

[54]He also spent a short time in Clairmarais Forest; the birds he recorded are listed in Appendix 1.

[55]Field wagtail – either yellow or blue-headed wagtail, see Appendix 1.

[56]Here he contrasts the blue-headed (*flava*) and yellow (*raii*) wagtails (both field wagtails) – see Appendix 1.

[57]*The Merchant of Venice*, V.i.104–6.

[58]There were five accredited official war correspondents, two permanent – Philip Gibbs and Percival Phillips – the others changing from time to time. They were heavily censored and the censors travelled around with them. Curiously, several were naturalists. Philip Gibbs (1946, *The Pageant of the Years*, Heinemann) describes Beach Thomas of the *Daily Mail*: 'As I knew him in those days, was the sweetest natured man – a scholar, once an athlete, and a lover of nature and the game of life. ... He hated the war and bled at the heart over the sacrifice of youth.' Beach Thomas's memories of his meeting with Ingram are quoted in the Postscript.

[59]Ingram later added '*Boarmia consortaria? crepuscularia*, pale oak beauty.' It is probably the closely related mottled beauty *Alcis repandata*, a common moth over much of Europe, including the UK.

[60]Telephone communication was possible only when wires could be set up; radio was in its infancy, so carrier pigeons were still important for carrying messages from the front line to HQ. Agents who landed behind the lines by plane also took pigeons with them.

[61]There is a description of this experiment in the *Illustrated London News*, April 1919.

[62]Ingram shows his acute observational skills here and his description of the distinctive shape of the honey buzzard could scarcely be bettered today, despite our wealth of field guides and superior optics. He mentions honey buzzards several times in the Journal. Since his time it seems to have increased both in north-east France and the UK. This may be a real increase, due to a decline in persecution, or an apparent increase, due to greater observer awareness (they are not easy to distinguish from common buzzard). Almost certainly there has been a genuine increase in both countries. The honey buzzard still occurs near St-Omer. (JC)

[63]The name in common use today is corncrake.

[64]Ingram was almost certainly right to be sceptical, as the location does suggest reed warbler rather than marsh warbler. The marsh warbler is a fairly common, if easily missed, inhabitant of northern France today. They are very fickle in their habits, frequently deserting colonies and moving on. (JC)

Gerard Manby-Colegrave, photographed by Ingram in 1904. See note 71

[65]The lesser ringed plover (or little ringed plover) spread north to be common in this area only in the 1920s and 1930s so this is an interesting record – confirmed by Ingram on 30 July. (JC)

[66]Gordon Sheldon, aged 25, the son of a Norfolk vicar.

[67]*Calidris minuta*, little stint, as opposed to *Calidris temminckii*, Temmincks stint. Ingram's instinctive identification is probably correct, in the light of modern knowledge. (JC)

[68]*Poilu* – the hairy or unshaven one – was an informal name for the French infantry soldier.

[69]The RFC headquarters were now in the Château of St-André near Hesdin. Ingram sometimes refers to it by its full name of St-André-aux-Bois (we have used St-André for consistency) and sometimes by the name of the nearby town, Hesdin.

[70]Adult rooks have a bare facial patch at the base of the bill; this area is feathered in the young rook and in the carrion crow.

[71]Gerard Manby-Colegrave had been a friend of Ingram since at least 1904, when they travelled in France together. His family had a house in Westgate where the Ingrams lived. He was 31 when he was killed in April 1917, a Lieutenant in the Army Service Corps.

[72]Genus *Phylloscopus*: chiffchaff, willow warbler, wood warbler and others.

[73]Ingram had used his walking-stick gun in France before the War when shooting birds for his collection, to avoid detection by *gendarmes*.

[74]Benjamin James Silly, MC, DFC, became an Air Commodore in the Second World War, was captured by the Japanese and died in captivity. (CWGC)

[75]Louis Noël was a famous pre-war French aviator.

[76]The common buzzard is *Buteo buteo*, the honey buzzard *Pernis apivorus*.

[77]In October 1917, 41 Wing, the first dedicated bombing wing, was established to attack strategic targets within Germany. Its first squadrons were Nos 100, 55 (both visited by Ingram) and 16 (RNAS).

[78]When the nestling sparrows reached a good size they were cooked. Sparrow pots are also mentioned in a list of birds made on 1 November 1918, see Appendix 1.

[79]A boar's bristle is threaded through a page of the journal here.

Peter Portal. See note 85

[80]Wild boar.

[81]About 20 kilometres south of Nancy.

[82]If not a meadow pipit, this is likely to have been a water pipit, until recently regarded as a race of the rock pipit but now considered a separate species. The water pipit breeds in mountainous areas but moves to lowland wetlands in winter. (JC)

[83]Grey crow was another name for the hooded crow or hoodie.

[84]See note 27.

[85]The officer severely cross-examined by Ingram on 16 February 1918 was Charles (known as Peter) Portal (1892–1971). Portal began his army career as a dispatch rider, cutting short his undergraduate life at Oxford. He transferred to the RFC as an observer, soon becoming a pilot and a Flight Commander, and was promoted to Major in June 1917. In the Second World War he was Head of Bomber Command and then Chief of Air Staff; Eisenhower described him as 'the greatest British war leader, greater even than Churchill'. After the Second World War he was created Viscount Portal of Hungerford. His knowledge of birds was based on a keen interest in hawking, beginning when he was a schoolboy. Both Portal and Ingram had been members, at different periods, of the Hawking Club. His articles in The Field, mentioned here, were on hawking. Although when he met Ingram he had the rank of Major, in command of Squadron 16, he was still only 24 years old.

[86]After the Zeppelin raids of the early part of the Great War, England was visited by German bombers from mid-1917 until October 1918.

[87]This appears to be the same Taylor who was described as an observer in the entry for 23 September 1917. He was killed on 24 August 1918. (CWGC).

[88]J.H. Gurney (1848–1922) was a wealthy Norfolk banker and ornithologist, whose father of the same name was also a notable ornithologist. He had a collection of 5,000 birds of prey. See Mearns B, Mearns R (1998) *The Bird Collectors* (Academic

Press).

[89]The Delacour collection of living birds from all over the world was destroyed in the German advance, which began on 21 March, only a few days after Ingram made his sketches. Jean Delacour, a lieutenant in the French army, visited the house on the 25 March as the first shells were falling. He was only 28 years old, but had assembled the collection himself, starting before he was 10. In his autobiography, Delacour wrote: 'I learnt that the number of shells that Villers received varied between 3,000 and 30,000 daily. Naturally all my birds were killed and plants destroyed and all the buildings wrecked.' After the War, Delacour began a second collection of birds, which was destroyed by fire in 1939. In 1940 Delacour fled to America, where he began a new collection (subsequently left to the state) and became a major figure in ornithological research.

[90]Probably Frank Lewis, 2nd Lieutenant, aged 23, who died the following day. (CWGC)

[91]Pied wagtails occur mainly in Britain; the presumption here is that this bird was likely to have been moving north to its breeding area in Britain.

[92]The birds collected by Dr Marmottan are at the Muséum d'Histoire Naturelle de Paris.

[93]The slaughter of birds was for Parisian milliners, but the use of feathers in fashionable ladies' hats was in decline by 1914.

[94]Portal was a reliable observer; see 16 February 1918. When, after the War, Ingram published a paper in *The Ibis* on the height at which birds fly, based on the information provided by pilots in response to his persistent questioning, Portal's observations took pride of place.

[95]Collingwood's son; see entry for 10 October 1917.

[96]Cleeve Court, see 9 June 1917.

[97]That is, different from others of the crow family, which nest in the open. The lemon yellow gape is conspicuous and so, in a dark hole, a useful aid to feeding by the adults.

Cleeve Court, Streatley-on-Thames, was built by the river in the late 19th century by Sir William Ingram, Collingwood's father. It has since been demolished.

[98]Ingram was impressed by the Australian naturalist, Major Eustace Ferguson. His knowledge of European birds had been gained in a very short time. He was a gifted naturalist and, although primarily a medical entomologist, had wide knowledge of ornithology, botany and archaeology. On his return to Australia he soon made his mark in the scientific world, but died young before he could realise his potential. Information from the *Australian Dictionary of Biography*, online edition, author Peter Vallee.

[99]In 1908, Ingram had recorded the first nest of the marsh warbler to be found in Kent, in the Isle of Thanet; *British Birds*, **1**, 387 'Nesting of the marsh warbler in Kent'.

[100]The genus *Regulus*, goldcrest or firecrest.

[101]Ingram's drawing shows the 'handles', structures characteristic of the marsh warbler's nest. (JC)

[102]On the next page of the journal Ingram mapped the distributions of the yellow wagtail (*flavissima* or *raii*) and the blue-headed wagtail (*flava*), two subspecies of *Motacilla flava* – see Appendix 1.

[103]The golden oriole's nest is slung like a hammock between branches, often very high up. Evidently this was the first that Ingram had found.

[104]The arrangement of the feathers.

[105]Here Ingram harks back to his period with the Kent Cyclist Battalion in 1915, when he made many sketches of Kentish plover on Dungeness (see Introduction). The area was indeed their last stronghold in England and they bred there for another fifty years.

[106]See 9 May 1918 and Appendix 1.

[107]Now usually known as the stone curlew.

[108]Yellow wagtail.

[109]Blue-headed and yellow wagtails, Appendix 1.

[110]For the earlier story of these eggs, see entry for 30 January 1918.

[111] Detailed description of plumage omitted.

[112]Adult rooks, unlike juveniles, have a bare patch at the base of the bill.

[113]Bruce Ingram, brother of Collingwood, see entry for 28 December 1916.

[114]Bourlon Wood was the focus of the Battle of Cambrai in November 1917. Only ten days before this entry in 1918, the wood was taken by the Canadians as part of the wide Allied advance. Cambrai was captured the next day.

[115]General Routine Order.

[116]There were several of the Orlebar family in the RFC, including Augustus Orlebar, later a distinguished pilot, sometime holder of the air speed record and a senior RAF officer in the Second World War.

[117]Male peregrine falcon.

[118]In falconry, the falcon is the female peregrine and the tiercel (see 17 October 1918) the male, although in common usage 'falcon' includes both. Ingram had for a short time been a member of the Hawking Club, which met on Salisbury Plain;

hence no doubt his strict use of the words.

[119]About 20 kilometres south-east of Cambrai.

[120]These celebrations were of victory, not liberation. Hesdin, well behind the lines, was not occupied by the Germans.

[121]Timins was an old friend from pre-war hunting days.

[122]The dates for the two trips into Germany are confusing. This account of the second trip (with Hanson), which occupied at least three days, is dated 18 December. This is only one day after Ingram was in Cologne on the first trip (with Captain Keith). It seems likely that the second trip *began* on 18 December.

[123]William Beach Thomas (1944) *The Way of a Countryman* (Michael Joseph). See the journal entry for 8 July 1917 for Collingwood's account of a walk, perhaps this one, with Beach Thomas.

We believe that 'Moonyang' Ffrench (left) was the remarkable Australian stockman Evelyn Alexander Wilson Ffrench. He was an exceptional horseman, fought in the Boer War, and was severely injured in the second battle of Ypres, yet joined the RFC and became its oldest pilot at the (estimated) age of 44. He was killed on 23 December 1918, while serving as a flying instructor.

Appendix 1
Birds

Bird lists

THE LONGER LISTS OF BIRDS in the journals are not included in the main text, but are gathered together here. Collingwood Ingram was studying the distribution of birds in France for his proposed book, and his lists provide an important record of that study. They are also of wider importance, as rare historical records of bird assemblages from specific localities in a countryside before the modern revolution in farming methods. Their value will increase over time. Most ornithologists of his day were interested primarily in the rarer species, but Ingram was interested in all. No list has been omitted, and, together with the main text, they provide a full record of his field observations.

Considerable fieldcraft is needed to compile such lists. Some birds hide away, perhaps in dense scrub or reeds, and their songs or calls are the only guide to their presence. In other cases, a quick glimpse of a silhouette or a characteristic manner of flight is enough for identification. Sometimes it is difficult or impossible to distinguish between two or more species in flight, and a clear view of a settled bird is needed. Often both sight and sound come into play and the whole depends enormously on the skill and experience of the recorder. On a few occasions during the War (but more frequently before it), Ingram shot a bird to check an identification or examine the plumage.

Ingram used plus signs to give a rough indication of abundance. He did not provide a key, and quite possibly did not even define the symbols himself; however, they clearly indicate something like 'not uncommon' (+), 'moderately common' (++), and 'very common' (+++). Actual numbers are given for rarer species.

The words of the lists are Ingram's own; the format has been changed and made consistent, partly to make them easier for the reader to scan for birds of particular interest. In general, the localities given are those in the heading of the journal entry of that day. Localities in brackets are provided by us when we feel greater precision would be helpful or when no locality was given in the heading. A few of the lists are of collections of stuffed birds or skins that he examined.

1916

15/16 December, St-Omer (collection of stuffed birds, thought to be killed locally). Long-tailed tit – four, none with white heads/short-toed tree-creeper/yellow wagtail – three specimens of *raii* only/grey wagtail – one/white wagtail – no pied/cirl bunting – three/robins – fairly dark breasts, but it is doubtful at what season they were killed/tree sparrows/siskin – three/great grey shrikes – three/quail – one/barn owls – one with a white breast, others with under surface suffused with a fairly pronounced tawny wash/Montagu's harrier/hobbies – two/honey buzzard/garganey/shoveller/wild swan – whooper/black redshank/dabchick.

17 December, St-Omer. The following is a complete list of birds observed on this day: blackbird +/mistle thrush – one/redwing – one/hoodie +/carrion crow +/ jackdaw +/rook ++/jay – two or three/magpie ++/starling ++/grey wagtail – one/meadow pipit – three/wren – three or four/house sparrow +++/chaffinch ++/linnet ++/siskin – eight or nine/goldfinch – four or five/yellowhammer ++/blue tit/great tit ++/robin – a few/hedge sparrow – attempting to sing in a half-hearted way, three or four/skylark ++/crested lark – near aerodrome only, six or eight/kestrel – two/little owl – one/moorhen – six or seven/partridge (grey) ++/tree-creeper – two or three/wood-pigeon.

1917

15 January, Auchel. The following is a list: jay – two or three/yellowhammer +/ great tit +/blue tit/blackbird +/mistle thrush/magpie/moorhen/rooks – several/hoodies/grey wagtails – two/robins – a few/chaffinches +/tree sparrow/ sparrows/starlings.

20 January, Aire. Among the other birds noted were the following: starlings +/ blackbird +/robin +/meadow pipits – a very fair number/yellowhammer – large flocks, 20 to 30 individuals among which were chaffinches/great tit/common sparrows/grey partridges.

26 January, Hesdigneul. Among other birds were the following: grey wagtail – one/ white wagtail – two/meadow pipit – one/great tit – two/blue tit/hedge sparrow – one (?)/blackbird/starling +/magpie +/fieldfare – one/wren – one/tree sparrow +/common sparrow +/rook ++/jackdaw +/hoodie/yellowhammer +/robin +/chaffinch +/crested lark. Yesterday a solitary peewit flew over calling.

4 February, St-Omer. The following is a list of birds seen during the last two days: cirl buntings – two, a pair, seen on same hedge as when first noted/yellowhammer – many, country round farmyards etc./grey wagtail – two/wren – several/marsh tit – three or four/great tit +/chaffinch ++/common sparrow ++/robin ++/ blackbird ++/song thrush – one or two/hoodie +/rook ++/jackdaw ++/ jay – five or six/carrion crow +++/skylark ++/crested lark +/tree-creeper/ partridge +/greenfinch +/bullfinch – two/starling ++/mistle thrush – one or two/sparrowhawk one/wood-pigeon ++/woodcock – two/meadow pipit – one or two/goldcrest – one or two only.

1 March, Sombrin. During a short walk the following birds were noticed: rook +++/jackdaw ++/carrion crow ++/magpie ++/jay – two/(no hoodies were seen)/blackbird/fieldfare – two or three flying east (song and mistle thrushes not seen)/sparrow, house +++/chaffinch +++/goldfinch – two/yellowhammer ++/cirl bunting – eight or nine/kestrel – two/grey partridge +/wood-pigeon – twenty or more/robin/meadow pipit – a few passed overhead/skylark +/ woodlark – ten or eleven/blue tit ++/marsh tit ++/great tit ++.

6 March, Candas. Wrens – three/robins +/tree-creepers – two/white wagtails – four/tree sparrows ++/common sparrows +++/blackbirds/mistle thrush – two or three/grey partridges/magpies +++/rooks +++/jackdaws +++/jays ++/ wood-pigeons ++/skylarks +++/kestrel – two or three/marsh, great and blue tits and two parties of woodlarks have been noticed (nine & twelve in number respectively). Meadow pipits have also been recorded.

4 April, Candas. During the course of a short stroll I noticed the following birds: rooks – a fair number – but these birds keep more to the vicinity of their rookeries now/carrion crows ++/jackdaws – a few seen/magpies ++/jays – a pair, I surprised them, evidently basking on a sunny woodland bank, from within a few feet/starlings – a large flock, these flocks visit the grass fields in which cattle are grazing, in preference to others. A flock settles in the high trees in the centre of Candas village every evening and sets up a chattering confusion of whistling sounds. Presumably these retire to the eaves of the church or houses for the night/redstart – a light sandy-coloured male, I think it was almost certainly a black redstart, it was feeding on the sunny side of a hedgerow, constantly dropping to the ground to pick up an insect and returning to a post with quivering tail/

greenfinches – in small parties, rather wild and keeping much to the high tree-tops/linnets – same as above, occasional burst of song, yellowhammer ++/ blackbirds – along the hedgerows or in the wooded dingle bottoms/robins – a few near the village/hedge sparrow – more common, also on outskirts of village/ wren – ditto, only fewer in numbers/sparrow (house) ++ in village/chaffinch ++ everywhere/skylark +/wood-pigeon – one very large flock, a hundred or more. Feeding on newly sprouted luzerne/great tit – two or three seen.

8 April, Candas. A white wagtail with a clean grey back was seen on a plough. Tree sparrow ++/tree-creeper – one/crested larks – near Candas only/magpies ++/marsh tits – three/great tits +/robins +/hedge sparrow +/rooks ++/ jackdaws +/jays – two/carrion crows +/partridge +/skylark ++/blackbirds +/ greenfinches ++/linnets +/yellowhammer +++/house sparrows +++/starlings +. I heard a little owl. No thrushes, goldfinches or woodlarks have been noted for some time now.

23 April, Vert Galant. Among the other species noted today and yesterday are the following – carrion crows ++/magpies ++/blackbird +/robin – a few/black redstart – a couple always near the farm/starlings – still in small flocks, of an evening a male or two come in from the fields and perch on the tree over-looking the farmyard where they whistle, chatter and clap their wings/white wagtail – two/tree-creeper – one/chaffinch ++/house sparrow ++/wood-pigeons – a fair number/grey partridge ++/skylarks ++/hedge sparrows +/yellowhammer ++/ cirl bunting, linnets, greenfinches – a few/meadow pipit – two or three/kestrel – one/mistle thrush – one or two/garden warbler?, heard singing in the distance/ goldfinches – three.

28 April, Candas. Among the other birds seen and heard are the following; wren/ tree-creeper/crow/jackdaw/magpie/chiffchaff/skylarks/starlings (some still in small flocks)/wood-pigeons/kestrel/crested lark/black redstart.

1 May, Estrées-en-Chaussée. Birds noted round Estrées-en-Chaussée 1 May to 3 May, swifts – one on 1/5/17, a small party flying NE 2/5/17/skylarks ++/crested larks – a few, although a fairly stiff clayish soil/chaffinches ++/house sparrows ++/wren/grey partridge +/yellow wagtail (race?)/grey wagtail – one/swallows ++/house martins +/meadow pipits – a party of 8 seen in an old luzerne field, evidently on passage/great grey-backed shrike – one on 3rd May/wood-pigeons – several, had the appearance of being rather small/linnets +/carrion crows +/ magpies ++/yellowhammer/blackbird/hedge sparrow/willow wren – in wood near river/corn bunting – one/Montagu's (?) harrier – one, on dry upland.

5 May, Le Roisel. Black redstart – several seen and heard on the house-tops in

Péronne/swallows and martins – both busily building among the ruins of the town/swifts – plentiful over the town and are probably in their full numerical strength/spotted flycatcher – one seen in Péronne/wrens ++/tree pipit – a few/ blue and great tits/cuckoo.

7 May, Estrées-en-Chaussée. Among other birds seen in this wood were: wrens ++/ marsh and blue tits – a few/starling – one or two/reed warbler?/magpie/jays – six or seven/little owl – one heard/garden warbler/tree-creeper/carrion crow – six or seven.

8 May, Nurlu. During the course of a short evening walk, I noted the following species: grasshopper warbler – two or three singing and skulking among the tangled undergrowth of brambles that have spread over the felled trees/hedge sparrow ++/mistle thrush – five or six/song thrush – two or three, singing beautifully/blackbirds – a few, also singing/garden warbler and blackcap – a fair number/chiffchaff – one/willow warbler – several/whitethroat +++/ wrens +/yellowhammer +/linnets/magpies/kestrel – two, evidently breeding/ wood-pigeon – several, some indulged in their aerial display, rising with half a dozen clapping wing–beats and then floating downwards with outstretched and depressed wing tips/nightingale – one or two singing splendidly/cuckoo.

9 May, Nurlu. All the species mentioned under yesterday's date were encountered.

10 May, Nurlu. The following species have been noted near Nurlu: song thrush – a few pairs evidently nest in the most humid woods/mistle thrush – a fair number, rather commoner than the last/blackbird – common, one was seen heckling a jay/nightingale – plentiful/robin – a few pairs in the shady woodlands/garden warbler – heard commonly/blackcap – common woodland species/whitethroat – very plentiful, woods, spinneys and roadside bushes/grasshopper warbler – one or two pairs presumably have taken up their summer quarters among the tangled growth of the woodland clearings/chiffchaff and willow warbler (see above)/ starling – fairly common, though not obtrusively so as in England, mostly nesting in the woods etc., although houses are also freely used for the purpose/golden oriole (see above)/skylarks – abundant/crested lark – a few only, near village/ great-spotted woodpecker – one seen and heard in the wood/green woodpecker – several heard/wood-pigeon – common/turtle dove – common/jay – common in woods/magpie – abundant/carrion crow – common (no rooks have been observed)/jackdaw – one flew over, but evidently this species is not nesting in the immediate vicinity/linnet – fairly common, nesting/goldfinch – a few seen/ greenfinch – heard only, does not seem to be common/chaffinch – nesting/house sparrow – in village/black redstart – one (pair?) has taken up its abode among the ruins of the village/spotted flycatcher (see above)/wheatear (see above)/field wagtail (species?) – one or two have been heard flying over/blue tit – a few/great tit – ditto, not very typical 'tit' country/tree pipit – one, singing in a woodland glade/yellowhammer – common/cirl and corn buntings not noted.

16 May, St-Omer. The following is a fairly complete list of the birds noticed today near Clairmarais: magpie ++/jay – one or two/carrion crow – a few/blackcap ++/garden warbler ++/willow warbler ++/chiffchaff – only one singing: judging by the song, the willow warbler greatly predominated/robin – one or two/great reed warbler – one only, reeds not high or thick enough/grasshopper warbler – common in rank undergrowth of rushes etc in forest/blackbird + (no song thrushes heard, doubtless on account of cold overcast weather)/starlings – a few/golden oriole +++/tree pipit +++*/yellowhammer ++/spotted flycatcher +/little bittern – five or six/common heron – twelve or more/pheasant – before war many used to be reared and turned out/tree-creeper/hawfinch – one or two/chaffinch +++/common sparrows +++ (no tree sparrows seen)/cuckoo +/blue tit – several, one pair building in old fruit tree/great tit – a few/white wagtail – one/house martins ++/swallows +++, Drury says that last year he found nightjars nesting in the forest glades/nightingale – one heard/green woodpecker +/sparrowhawk – one. Apart from the above – jackdaws, swifts and black redstarts were seen in St-Omer itself.

   *Added later: meadow pipits were singing round the edge of the aerodrome where they apparently feed, Drury says he has found them nesting here.

21 June, Candas. I saw a song thrush and among others noted the following species: starlings ++, including young birds not long from the nest/spotted flycatchers – several/wrens/great tits – young birds flying about an orchard/yellow and cirl bunting/black redstart – still in full song, especially in the early morning when they may be heard from the housetops; youngsters on the wing/tree-creepers/ greenfinches/linnets/garden warblers/robins +/house martins/swallows and swifts.

24 June, Treizennes. The following species were noted: swallows ++, – some just on the wing/whitethroat +, – young fledgling met with/blackcap – one heard/ willow warbler – one heard/martins and swifts/common and tree sparrows/tree-creepers – very shabby and worn plumage, several seen/linnets/greenfinches +/ great tit/meadow pipit +/tree pipit – one heard/cuckoo/common redstart – one/ magpies/crested and skylarks/blackbirds/wrens/white wagtail – one/yellow ++ and cirl bunting/partridges – heard/chaffinch ++/spotted flycatcher – a few/ turtle dove. The following were conspicuous by their absence: song thrush, corn bunting, goldfinch, rook, hawks, jackdaws.

26 June, Aire. Other birds seen or noted and not included in my previous list are: lesser whitethroat – one singing softly in a willow/mistle thrush – one or two/ (blue) grey-headed wagtail – several/hedge sparrow – a few.

27 June, Lealvillers. Young willow warblers were on the wing but despite this fact a few males were still singing, as were chiffchaffs – indeed judging by their notes, the latter was the commoner species. Whitethroats were plentiful in the clearings. A well-grown family party of marsh tits were seen and the following species were also noted: carrion crows – six or more/magpies – several/wrens, blackbirds and yellowhammers were singing.

28 June, Lealvillers. Other birds noted are: rooks – one or two largish flocks, evidently a rookery in the neighbourhood/grey partridge – common/corn bunting – common/cirl bunting – a few seen/carrion crow – a few seen/magpie – common/nightingale – one heard croaking in the wooded dingle behind our huts/garden warbler – in dingle, nestlings on the wing/icterine warbler – one heard/yellowhammer/mistle thrush – one or two seen about/wood-pigeon – a few seen/turtle dove – apparently fairly common/little owl – heard calling in a tall belt of trees in the middle of the afternoon – a muffled, halting, long-drawn *hue*/robin – in dingle, one has a nest containing *six* eggs among some pendant tree roots on the side of a chalk pit/quail – quite a number heard calling among the crops/swallows/swifts/martins/blackbird +/kestrel – one. I understand there is a large rookery at Toutencourt and a smaller one at Achieux.

29 June, Lealvillers. Wood-pigeons were common and crashed out of the beech trees in front of me. In this wood I heard or saw in addition the following species: blackbird/song thrush – one heard in full song/robin/nightingale/tree pipit/willow wren/chiffchaff? Round about the village: cirl bunting – common/ yellowhammer – plentiful/linnet +/house sparrow – very abundant/starlings/ wrens – young on the wing/great tit – two or three family parties/whitethroat – in hedgerows/crested larks/rooks/carrion crow/chaffinch/greenfinch?

2 July, St-Omer. On going to the forest, the following birds were observed during the half hour I spent there: wood-pigeon – common/turtle dove – two or three/ blackcap – heard/whitethroat ++, – with fully fledged young/garden warbler – heard/willow wren/swallows and house martins ++, the latter were hawking over the tree-tops/mistle thrush/blackbird ++/tree-creeper/great-spotted woodpecker/green woodpecker/kestrel/blue tit.

4 July, St-Omer. Between Longuenesse (where I am billeted) and the aerodrome the following were noted: marsh, great and blue tits, robin, chiffchaff, chaffinch, carrion crow, magpie, cirl bunting, wren, song thrush, blackbird, spotted flycatcher, wood-pigeon, hedge sparrow, willow warbler, blackcap, garden warbler, starling, white wagtail, greenfinch.

8 July, St-Omer. Besides the above-mentioned there were noted: marsh tit, great tit, tree-creeper, moorhen, carrion crow +/reed warbler (these could only be induced to sing with difficulty)/white wagtails – one had commenced a nest earlier in the season under the tiles of an old boat house/magpies/spotted flycatchers.

13 July, St-Omer, Clairmarais Forest. These species were recorded: blackbird/green woodpecker/nightingale – uttering their croaking alarm note and sundry other sounds expressive of resentment/robin/wren/whitethroat/garden warbler/ chiffchaff/willow wren/blackcap?/spotted flycatcher – one was building its second nest in the knotted folds of an old ivy on the monastery wall/chaffinch/ house sparrow/moorhen/swallows, martins and swifts/yellowhammer/meadow and tree pipit/song thrush/blue, great and marsh tit – the latter is well named in this part of France in as much as they always prefer the swampy parts of the woods/greenfinch.

30 July, St-Omer (coastal birds at Dunkirk). Field wagtails were also much in evidence, but very restless – I think they were all *flava*/skylarks and crested larks common/ flocks of starlings seen/a small colony of sand martins were nesting in the face of a cliff of hard sand/swallows – common, wheatears two/peewits – a flock feeding in a meadow near Bergues.

21 August, Izel-lez-Hameau. Birds noted today: wood-pigeon +/rooks +/carrion crows +/magpies ++/sparrows ++/swallows ++/martins +/greenfinches +/ linnets/yellowhammers +/cirl bunting – a few (no corn buntings about)*/kestrel – two or three/blackbird/great tit – one or two/willow wren – one/skylarks +, – singing/crested larks +/icterine warbler – one in the orchard. These were all noted during the course of my day's work.

    **Added later.* Some of these birds were noted four days later.

25 August, Izel-lez-Hameau. Besides the species mentioned on the previous pages I encountered the following species: wood-pigeon +/corn bunting – half a dozen or so together: they uttered the usual 'ticking' call-note one hears at this time of year/cirl bunting – a few/robin – a few/wren/partridge – several big coveys, one of about 18. I thought I heard a goldcrest in the orchard.

19 September, Chocques. Without search, the following birds have forced themselves on my notice: wrens – singing sporadically/blackbirds/house sparrows – one pair are still feeding young in one of the hangars/crested and skylarks – a few in the neighbourhood/wood-pigeons/starlings – a fair number, but not plentiful/

robins – singing/green woodpeckers – one was shot by the owner of the chateau/ sparrowhawk – one seen/field wagtail – two or three seen flying over/great tit – two were singing quite loudly early this morning/house martins – a number are nesting round the chateau, both on the north and south aspect, fledged young are in several of the nests/swallows – a fair number still about.

31 October, Ochey. By the roadside I noted the following species: skylark ++/ sparrows +++/starlings +/yellowhammer ++/chaffinches +++/carrion crow +/corn bunting – two/kestrel – two/green woodpecker – one/black redstart – this latter I am not quite sure about, but as we whisked by I am pretty sure I recognised the quiver of the tail and upright carriage of a bird I saw perched on the ledge of a limestone quarry.

1 November, Ochey (while boar-hunting). The following is a list of birds seen: black redstart – two seen near the village, one (a full-plumaged male) kept flitting in front of us along the road from tree to tree, apparently they leave towns and villages at this season and repair to the country/meadow pipit – several heard, also a (white?) wagtail/common buzzard – one sat in a solitary tree about 80 yards away as we passed; in the white fog he looked a bird of imposing size/ jay – very common in the forest/carrion crow – common in the surrounding fields/nuthatch – common in the forest/great tit and marsh tit – common in the forest/long-tailed tit – one or two heard/bullfinch – constantly heard piping in the forest/chaffinches – very numerous/brambling – the unmistakable twanging note was heard many times/goldfinch – flocks near the village feeding on the weeds of a neglected field/linnet – same as above only more numerous/skylarks – numerous in open fields, evidently on the move as they fairly often passed over the forest/yellowhammer – very common/robin – one or two in the forest/ blackbird – one or two in the forest/pheasant – one cock flushed by hounds, the *chasseurs* all declared that gélinotte – hazel hen – were also to be found in small numbers/wood-pigeon – a fair number seen at intervals, though not abundant/great-spotted woodpecker – heard in several parts of the wood/green woodpecker – one heard/peewits – a small flock feeding round a flooded pool/ great grey-backed shrike – one perched on the tip of a young pine where it looked exceedingly handsome in the bright sunlight/kestrel – one flew over/sparrow – very common about villages – earthenware pots are placed on the walls of many of the houses to induce them to breed, so that their young may be eaten/tree sparrow – in flocks/magpie – several/starlings – a small flock.

18 November, Ochey (while boar-hunting). Among the birds noted I might mention: hawfinches – several seen, on one occasion four or five together – their call note was a small shrill cheeping sound/blackbird/song thrush – one or two/marsh tits – common/common buzzard – one seen and heard/nuthatch – a number heard/great-spotted woodpecker – several heard, this bird seems commoner than the green woodpecker hereabouts/bullfinches – seen and heard fairly frequently/ linnets – a flock near Ochey/sparrows, chaffinches and etc. also noted. A pheasant and a woodcock were seen by members of the party, gélinottes (hazel hens) are apparently scarce but undoubtedly exist/starlings – one was plausibly reproducing the mellow notes of an oriole, so truthfully that I took some trouble to trace the utterer.

23 November, Tantonville. I saw quite a number of hoodies today: also rooks, carrion crows, magpies and jays are common, especially the latter. Other birds noted: yellowhammer, great tit, goldcrest, greater-spotted woodpecker, goldfinch, grey partridge, marsh tit – common, long-tailed tit, starlings etc.

25 November, Tantonville. The following is a complete list of the birds noted during the short walk: house sparrows – common, but only near the village/ yellowhammer – several/skylark – a few – it is interesting to note that crested larks have not been seen for the last three weeks; the limestone slopes and dry vineyards would appear to have been suitable territory for this species/grey partridge – two coveys seen/meadow pipit – one seen on a wet marshy meadow/ redwing – one flew over at dusk/carrion crow – several/rooks – large flocks passed down wind at dusk, evidently making for their roosting grounds/magpie – a large assembly, I counted 45 feeding in one of the riverside meadows/goldfinch – a party of four or five flew down the valley/buzzard – one, sweeping and manoeuvring gracefully over the valley. The light patches on the wing were rather noticeable.

26 December, St-Omer, Clairmarais. The day was too cold and inclement to yield good ornithological results and my list of birds observed is small: heron – two or three seen/kestrel – two/black-headed gulls – a flock flew across the face of one of the meres/greenfinches – one small party/starlings – a few flocks/grey wagtail – one seen at a distance/hoodies – a fair number/rooks and jackdaws – seen flying over/chaffinch – a few/sparrows. Drury tells me he has seen one or two snipe about during the recent cold snap.

1918

3 February, Poperinge. List of birds seen near here the last two or three days: jay – a few/jackdaw +++/rook +++/hoodie +++, hoodies are extraordinarily abundant in this part of Flanders/chaffinch ++/house sparrows +++/ greenfinch +/blackbird +/song thrush – one/starling +++/green woodpecker – one/great tit +/robins – a few/moorhen – a few on La Lovie lake/blue tit/ magpie – a few/skylark +/crested lark +/grey wagtail – one/white wagtail –

one(?)/wood-pigeon ++.

9 March, Hesdin. Wrens/wood-pigeons/jackdaws/rooks/crows/starlings/ magpies/chaffinches/blackbirds/mistle thrushes (but no song thrushes) and a white wagtail were among the birds that forced themselves on my notice this morning.

12 March, Champien. The following is a list of birds I have noted round Champien, Noyon and Faillouel: rook ++/carrion crow +/hooded crow – one or two near Faillouel, these birds are greater scavengers than their black relatives and come to the refuse heaps of the camps in search for food/jackdaw +/magpie ++/ starling – not very plentiful, a small flock seen near Champien/blackbird – a few/ wren – I heard one at Champien with a slightly aberrant song, very sweet in tone and not so hurried and blatant as the usual outpouring of notes/robin – a few/ yellowhammer ++/cirl bunting ++/chaffinch +++/house sparrow/skylark ++ – singing well/crested lark – a fair number, but not abundant/great tit and blue tits – both common/grey partridge – two small flocks passed in the fields and a third flying north-east about 500 ft from the ground.

21 March, Fienvillers. The following is a list of the species heard and seen: carrion crow ++/rook +++/magpie ++/jackdaw ++/jay – a few/redwings – flock of 100 or more/fieldfare – a small flock/blackbird +++/song thrush – one heard singing in a wooded glen: these birds are not numerous and probably do not occur more frequently than about one pair to every square mile; another one can often be heard in the woodlands below the aerodrome/mistle thrush – two/ linnets – still in flocks that perch in twittering companies towards the evening among the upper branches of the trees/chaffinches +++/brambling – heard/ kestrel – one or two/wood-pigeon +/grey partridge – one or two pairs/starling +/wrens ++/hedge sparrow ++/robin +/cirl bunting +/yellow bunting ++/ tree-creeper/blue tit +/great tit +/long-tailed tit – two/marsh tit – two or three/ house sparrow +++/skylark ++/crested lark – a few only.

2 April, St-André. I noted also: robin +/song thrush – one/mistle thrush/blackbird +/green woodpecker/blue tit/marsh tit/white wagtail/starling/sparrowhawk – one/tree-creeper +/carrion crow/greenfinch – two or three/goldfinch – two or three/magpie +/jay/yellow bunting/house sparrow +.

6 May, St-André, Clairmarais Forest. Other birds seen and heard: yellowhammer, blackbird, mistle thrush, great, blue and marsh tits, jackdaw, carrion crow, blackcap, hedge sparrow, nightingale, wren, greater spotted woodpecker, swallow, greenfinch, magpie, wood-pigeon, skylark, swift.

8 May, Le Crotoy, bird-stuffer's specimens. The following species were noted in his shop: two tawny owls (one grey, one brown) – this bird is uncommon near Le Crotoy/one nutcracker – apparently long-billed form/one waxwing/two stormy petrels/sheldrake/garganey/smew – male/scaup/common scooter/eider/ goldeneye – winter/tufted duck/dotterel – 'very rare'/one reeve/three spoonbills – killed about first fortnight of April this year, the usual time of their passage/ one little gull – in full breeding plumage (i.e. a black hood), this was regarded as a rarity, on the four or five occasions this species has passed through Yaune's hands it has always been in May (Yaune has practised taxidermy at le Crotoy for fifteen years)/one 'bridled' guillemot/two puffins/Montagu's (?) harrier/three black-necked grebes (April)/red-throated diver (winter)/whimbrel.

9 May (collection of stuffed birds at the Château de la Triquerie, all obtained at the mouth of the Somme). Norfolk plover – d'Applaincourt believes this species breed near Le Crotoy/black throated diver – female in breeding plumage (14.5.13)/three little gulls – not in breeding plumage but killed in spring – May? – in one example head splashed with dark – le Crotoy/purple heron – immature 1913 – rare/little bittern – nests in the marshes near Cambrai/two nutcrackers – these specimens are apparently of the Siberian race/male and female Montagu's harrier – killed in the marshes – emarginated to the fourth primary – thighs streaked/roseate tern – very rare/lesser tern/sandwich tern/great grey-backed shrike – female 10.4.08 – killed locally/red-crested pochard – male and female, valley of the Maye 10.12.06 – these birds were killed by a friend of the Viscomte's who considers them great rarities/scaup – Cambrai marshes – 10.11.08 – rare/long-tailed duck – Noyelles-sur-Mer – autumn 1912/white-eyed duck – same locality 8.9.11/gadwall – fairly rare – November/sheldrake – immature – Noyelles, September 1917/ three hobbies – 25.9 & 30.11.1905 – all locally killed/three great snipe – Sailly Bray – 19 August, 13 September, 14 September/four jack snipe – Sailly Bray, 10 April/garganey – male and female, 19.3.07/pintail – male and female, 30.3.11/ golden-eyed duck – Feb. 29 December/brent geese – 10.3.07, February 13/little crake, baillon crake, water rail – all nesting, second rarish/black-necked grebe, red-necked grebe – males 4.10.1913 & 24.3.1913, female 19.3.13.

9 June, mostly Abbeville area and Crécy Forest. Other species seen: crested and common larks/black redstart – in Abbeville/turtle doves/jackdaws +, round Abbeville/*garden warblers +/*blackcaps,/cirl bunting – one or two only/ swifts – near Abbeville only/corn bunting +/whitethroat/nightingale/*willow wren/*chiffchaff/*cuckoo/those marked with an asterisk chiefly in Crécy Forest. Although this is the first entry of turtle doves, they have been noted fairly commonly.

17 June, near the mouth of the Authie. Other birds noted: starling – many/skylarks/

crows/magpie/rook/swallow/swift/housemartin/sparrows/blackbird/ yellowhammer/corn bunting/hedge sparrow/crested lark on the higher ground/ jackdaw near Verton only, there is a colony here in the church belfry/chaffinch.

21 June, Somme valley above Abbeville. In a marshy copse we saw the following species: great, blue, marsh and long-tailed tits, garden warblers, wrens, robins, willow warbler, chiffchaff. Two or three pairs of yellow wagtails were encountered in a large meadow. These were feeding young on the wing. Meadow pipits were also inhabiting this pasture. Great reed warblers heard, also a golden oriole. Linnets fairly common.

7 July, coast near Quend Plage. Besides these, the following birds were seen among the dunes: wheatear – one or two only/meadow pipits – several/linnets – common/ harriers – a single male, probably a hen harrier/herring? gulls – on the beach.

25 October, around Lille. The following is a list of birds noted in the environs of Lille: starling – common/hoodie – common, the one seen on the 23rd is the first I have noted this year/rooks ++/jay ++/jackdaw +/common sparrow +++/ tree sparrow +/white (?) wagtail – one seen/song thrushes – a few on migration/ yellow buntings ++/chaffinch ++/crested lark – fairly common, some were seen in the low clayey country near la Bassée/skylarks +/partridges – one or two coveys/meadow pipits – common, on migration/goldcrests – a fair number in the conifers of the château garden/wood-pigeon – one seen/tree-creeper – several in château grounds/brambling – common/kestrels – common/sparrowhawk – one seen/great grey-backed shrike – one was observed. This bird had just captured a full-sized field mouse and was considerably hampered with it when disturbed. It carried the mouse in its claws during flight, transferring it thence soon after 'taking off' from its perch on a telegraph wire.

Wagtails

Taxonomically, the wagtails are a complex group and the changes in names since Ingram's time could cause confusion. He recorded five species or subspecies, listed with their modern English and scientific names, as follows:

White wagtail, Motacilla alba alba
Pied wagtail, Motacilla alba yarrellii
Grey wagtail, Motacilla cinerea
Blue-headed wagtail, Motacilla flava flava
Yellow wagtail, Motacilla flava flavissima.

Other scientific names used by Ingram (usually only the last element) were:

Pied wagtail, Motacilla alba lugubris
Grey wagtail, Motacilla baorula
Yellow wagtail, Motacilla flava raii; once (p.193) he referred to this as Ray's yellow wagtail.

He also used the names 'yellow wagtail', 'yellow-breasted field wagtail' and 'field wagtail' to cover both subspecies of Motacilla flava.
Thus he used 'yellow wagtail' in two ways – for the subspecies (Motacilla flava raii) and for the pair of subspecies of Motacilla flava. He usually added '(raii)' when referring to the single species.

Scientific names

Names of birds observed in the field by Ingram and recorded in the main text of the diary. A few uncertain identifications are included.

barn owl, Tyto alba
black redstart, Phoenicurus ochruros
blackbird, Turdus merula
blackcap, Sylvia atricapilla
black-headed gull, Larus ridibundus
blue tit, Parus caeruleus
blue-headed wagtail, Motacilla flava flava
brambling, Fringilla montifringilla
bullfinch, Pyrrhula pyrrhula
buzzard, Buteo buteo
carrion crow, Corvus corone corone
chaffinch, Fringilla coelebs
chiffchaff, Phylloscopus collybita
cirl bunting, Emberiza cirlus
common bunting – see yellowhammer
common gull, Larus canus
common sandpiper, Actitis hypoleucos
common tern, Sterna hirundo
coot, Fulica atra
corn bunting, Miliaria calandra
corncrake, Crex crex
crane, Grus grus
crested lark, Galerida cristata
cuckoo, Cuculus canorus
curlew, Numenius arquata
curlew sandpiper, Calidris ferruginea
dabchick, Tachybaptus ruficollis
daw – see jackdaw
dunlin, Calidris alpina
dunnock – see hedge sparrow
dusky redshank, Tringa erythropus
eider, Somateria mollissima
fieldfare, Turdus pilaris
firecrest, Regulus ignicapillus
garden warbler, Sylvia borin

270

goldcrest, Regulus regulus
golden eagle, Aquila chrysaetos
golden oriole, Oriolus oriolus
golden plover, Pluvialis apricaria
goldeneye, Bucephala clangula
goldfinch, Carduelis carduelis
goshawk, Accipiter gentilis
grasshopper warbler, Locustella naevia
great grey-backed shrike, Lanius excubitor
great reed warbler, Acrocephalus arundinaceus
great tit, Parus major
greater black-backed gull, Larus marinus
greater spotted woodpecker, Dendrocopus major
green sandpiper, Tringa ochropus
green woodpecker, Picus viridis
greenfinch, Carduelis chloris
greenshank, Tringa nebularia
grey crow – see hooded crow
grey partridge, Perdix perdix
grey plover, Pluvialis squatarola
grey wagtail, Motacilla cinerea
guillemot, Uria aalge
hawfinch, Coccothraustes coccothraustes
hazelhen (mentioned but not seen), Bonasa bonasia
hedge sparrow, Prunella modularis
hen harrier, Circus cyaneus
heron, Ardea cinerea
herring gull, Larus argentatus
hobby, Falco subbuteo
honey buzzard, Pernis apivorus
hooded crow, Corvus corone cornix
hoopoe, Upupa epops
house martin, Delichon urbica
house sparrow, Passer domesticus
icterine warbler, Hippolais icterina
jack snipe, Lymnocryptes minimus
jackdaw, Corvus monedula
jay, Garrulus glandarius
Kentish plover, Charadrius alexandrinus
kestrel, Falco tinnunculus
kingfisher, Alcedo atthis
landrail – see corncrake

lapwing, Vanellus vanellus
lesser black-backed gull, Larus fuscus
lesser grey shrike, Lanius minor
lesser whitethroat, Sylvia curruca
linnet, Carduelis cannabina
little bittern, Ixobrychus minutus
little bustard, Tetrax tetrax
little grebe – see dabchick
little owl, Athene noctua
little ringed plover, Charadrius dubius
Little stint, Calidris minuta
long-tailed tit, Aegithalos caudatus
magpie, Pica pica
mallard, Anas platyrhynchos
marsh harrier, Circus aeruginosus
marsh tit, Parus palustris
marsh warbler, Acrocephalus palustris
meadow pipit, Anthus pratensis
mistle thrush, Turdus viscivorus
Montagu's harrier, Circus pygargus
moorhen, Gallinula chloropus
nightingale, Luscinia megarhynchos
nightjar, Caprimulgus europaeus
Norfolk plover – see stone curlew
nuthatch, Sitta europaea
partridge – see grey partridge
peewit – see lapwing
peregrine falcon, Falco peregrinus
pheasant, Phaseanus colchicus
pied flycatcher, Ficedula hypoleuca
pied wagtail, Motacilla alba yarrellii
pochard, Aythya ferina
quail, Coturnix coturnix
red-backed shrike, Lanius collurio
red-legged partridge, Alectorix rufa
redshank, Tringa totanus
redstart, Phoenicurus phoenicurus
redwing, Turdus iliacus
reed bunting, Emberiza schoeniclus
reed warbler, Acrocephalus scirpaceus
reeve (and ruff), Philomachus pugnax
ring ouzel, Turdus torquatus

ringed plover, Charadrius hiaticula
robin, Erithacus rubecula
rock pipit, Anthus petrosus
rook, Corvus frugilegus
sand martin, Riparia riparia
sanderling, Calidris alba
scops owl, Otus scops
sedge warbler, Acrocephalus schoenobaenus
short-toed tree-creeper, Certhia brachydactyla
shoveler (or shoveller), Anas clypeata
siskin, Carduelis spinus
skylark, Alauda arvensis
snipe, Gallinago gallinago
song thrush, Turdus philomelos
sparrowhawk, Accipiter nisus
spoonbill, Platalea leucorodia
spotted flycatcher, Muscicapa striata
starling, Sturnus vulgaris
stock dove, Columba oenas
stone curlew, Burhinus oedicnemus
stonechat, Saxicola torquata
swallow, Hirundo rustica
swift, Apus apus
tawny owl, Strix aluco
tawny pipit, Anthus campestris
thick knee – see stone curlew
tree creeper, see short-toed tree-creeper
tree pipit, Anthus trivialis
tree sparrow, Passer montanus
tufted duck, Aythya fuligula
turtle dove, Streptopelia turtur
water rail, Rallus aquaticus
wheatear, Oenanthe oenanthe
whimbrel, Numenius phaeopus
whinchat, Saxicola rubetra
white wagtail, Motacilla alba alba
whitethroat, Sylvia communis
wigeon, Anas penelope
wild duck – see mallard
willow warbler, Phylloscopus trochilus
willow wren – see willow warbler
wood warbler, Phylloscopus sibilatrix

woodcock, Scolopax rusticola
woodlark, Lullula arborea
wood-pigeon, Columba palumbus
wren, Troglodytes troglodytes
wryneck, Jynx torquilla
yaffle – see green woodpecker
yellow bunting – see yellowhammer
yellow wagtail, Motacilla flava flavissima
yellowhammer, Emberiza citrinella

Disturbance of nesting birds

The modern ornithologist may be surprised, perhaps even alarmed, by Collingwood Ingram taking young birds from the nest for study and sketching. It would not have occurred to him, or to other ornithologists of his time, that this might be a questionable practice. His motivation was scientific curiosity and the subsequent publication of his researches added significantly to knowledge of the biology of young birds. Readers in Britain who wish to find nests should join the British Trust for Ornithology's nest record scheme and follow the code of conduct.

Appendix 2

Aero compasses in the Great War

THE MAGNETIC COMPASS, as used in planes in the Great War, consists of a pivot assembly, carrying a magnet and a compass card, inside a sealed case filled with liquid. The magnet and card rotate on the pivot and the compass direction is read through the glass front, using a fixed 'lubber' line.

Ingram wrote an official booklet, 'Notes on aero compasses and their adjustment', printed by the army in September 1918. We can use his words to describe the type 5/17 compass which is illustrated below. 'The card is carried on an inverted pivot, without the support of a float, and is in the form of a ring sloping inwards

Compass (Type 5/17), and its placement in the cockpit of an RE8, a type of aircraft in which Ingram had several flights. The photograph was taken at the Imperial War Museum at Duxford.

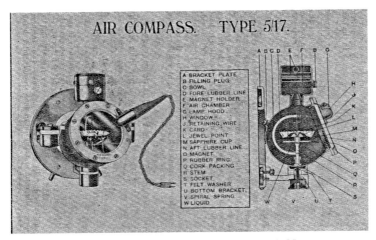

AIR COMPASS. TYPE 5/17.

A BRACKET PLATE
B FILLING PLUG
C BOWL
D FORE LUBBER LINE
E MAGNET HOLDER
F AIR CHAMBER
G LAMP HOOD
H WINDOW
J RETAINING WIRE
K CARD
L JEWEL POINT
M SAPPHIRE CUP
N AFT LUBBER LINE
O MAGNET
P RUBBER RING
Q CORK PACKING
R STEM
S SOCKET
T FELT WASHER
U BOTTOM BRACKET
V SPIRAL SPRING
W LIQUID

Illustration of the Type 5/17 from Collingwood Ingram's *Notes on aero compasses and their adjustment*, September 1918

at the upper edge at an angle of 30°. It is marked on both inner and outer surfaces, the forward, or direct, readings being obtained against the inside graduations. These graduations indicate every 10° and are numbered every 30°. It should be noted that the final cipher of these numbers is always omitted to avoid overcrowding, thus 6 represents 60, 15 represents 150, and so on. The outer surface of the card is black with the eight principal points painted on it in radium compound for use in night navigation'.

'Notes on aero compasses and their adjustment', written by Ingram. It comprised forty pages of detailed descriptions and instructions, including worked examples, on compass work and other aspects of navigation. As an official handbook, it was anonymous, but he wrote 'by C. Ingram' on his own copy.

The major problem was to adjust for the errors caused by the various iron objects in the planes, including magneto, guns and the disintegrating belt carrying the ammunition. Adjustment, with compensating magnets in the compass, formed a major part of Ingram's work, but there was no permanent solution to the problem, because the amount of iron changed when the guns were fired.

There were other difficulties associated with using a compass in a plane, notably a phenomenon known as the 'Northerly Turning Error'. The effect was a substantial, short-lived, compass error when a plane, heading north, banked in a turn away from north.

The compass was placed in the cockpit so that it was easily visible to the pilot, but also in a position selected to reduce the effects of iron in the plane. The card had to remain as steady as possible, and return to the true position as quickly as possible in highly unstable conditions. Such problems were a matter of compass design, and there were many variations. Ingram himself designed two: the Airman's Compass and the Raider's Compass, drawings for which have survived. On 20 March 1917, Ingram received a favourable report from Lt W.R Bruce Clark, stating that 'the compass is neat and compact, and, considering the difficulty of fitting a compass in a good position on the Sopwith, is in the best possible position. ... It is clear and easy to read. ... Compared with the No. 259 pattern with the hooped shaped card it is an improvement. ... It is also an improvement on the Chetwynd 200. ... This is a good compass for a Sopwith 2/Seater.'

Even the best-designed compass had to be adjusted frequently, if possible after every flight. Adjustments were made with the plane on the ground with the tail propped up, in a position similar to that in flight, and with all its necessary iron objects on board. Ideally, the plane was placed on a 'swinging base' with the cardinal points marked at the edge. The plane was aligned to each of these points in turn while adjustments were made to the compensating magnets; further adjustments might require re-adjustment of earlier changes, so the exercise could be lengthy and complex.

Ingram says almost nothing about compasses in his Journal, although clearly his work occupied most of his time. Perhaps this was from considerations of security. All there is in the sketchbooks is a single set of very brief notes, made while he was adjusting a compass.

Appendix 3
Selected publications on birds by Collingwood Ingram

BELOW ARE LISTED some of the more notable of Collingwood Ingram's publications on birds, selected from a total of over eighty. He also wrote many popular articles on birds for *Country Life* and *The Field* and published even more on plants than he did on birds.

(1901) On a Scops owl from Kent. *Bulletin of the British Ornithologists' Club* **12**: 39.

(1905) On the nesting of the marsh warbler in Kent. *Bulletin of the British Ornithologists' Club* **15**: 96.

(1907) On the birds of the Alexandria district. Northern Territory of South Australia. *Ibis* **49**: 387–415.

— On tongue marks in young birds. *Ibis* **49**: 574–8.

— Egg of the greater birds of paradise. *Avicultural Magazine* **5**: 364.

(1908) Ornithological notes from Japan, *Ibis* **50**: 129–69.

— On the birds of the Inkermann Station, North Queensland, *Ibis* **50**: 458–81.

(1909) The birds of Manchuria. *Ibis* **51**: 422–69.

(1912) The birds of Yunnan, *Novitates Zoologicae*. **19**: 269–310.

(1913) Birds of paradise in the West Indies, *Avicultural Magazine* **5**: 35–41.

— A few remarks on European Certhiidae, *Ibis* **55**: 545–50.

(1919) Notes on the heights at which birds migrate. *Ibis*, **61**: 321–5.

(1920) A contribution to the study of nestling birds. *Ibis* **62**: 856–80.

(1926) *Birds of the Riviera*. Witherby, London.

— Ouessant ornithology and other notes on French birds. *Ibis* **68**: 247–69

(1942) Field notes on the birds of Iceland. *Ibis* **84**: 485–98.

(1955) The order in which the remiges and rectrices are moulted in certain birds. *International Ornithological Congress*, **11**: 270–4.

(1959) The importance of juvenile cannibalism in the breeding biology of certain birds of prey. *Auk*, **76**: 218–26.

(1960) Camouflage in nestling birds. *International Ornithological Congress*, **12**: 332–42.

(1966) *In Search of Birds*. Witherby, London.

(1974) *The Migration of the Swallow*. Witherby, London.

(1978) *Random Thoughts on Bird Life*. Privately printed.

Appendix 4
The journals and sketchbooks

COLLINGWOOD INGRAM'S WARTIME JOURNALS were written in five leather-bound books, measuring about 5 × 8 inches (130 × 210 mm), supplied by Harrods. During the Great War he also used six sketchbooks; three measured 4 × 5½ inches, two were about 5 × 8 inches, while the sixth, which was used only in England for family portraits, measured 7 × 10 inches. They were manufactured by Geo. Rowney & Co., London, and styled *The Sketcher's Notebook*.

A few sketches were drawn directly in the journals, some were taken out of sketchbooks and pasted into journals, and others remain in the sketchbooks. A very few sketches were redrawn in the journal from originals in sketchbooks. Often the sketches were dated, and – of those used in the transcript – we are confident of the dates in all but three or four cases.

The journal was written in pencil, and there were no problems with legibility. In preparing the transcript, we have made only minor changes: we have corrected spelling errors, inserted occasional missing words, and brought consistency to the spellings of place-names (largely basing them on modern maps), dates and measurements. As the paragraphs in the original tend to be short, frequently consisting of only one sentence, we have often combined two or more. Punctuation was minimal and we have inserted commas, in particular, quite freely. Most English names of birds are unchanged or have changed only slightly since this period, but a few names may be unfamiliar to naturalists today and these are identified in endnotes and in the index. Ingram's additional notes are marked with an asterisk and placed at the bottom of the entry. Some of these are dated, others seem to have been made very soon after the date of the entry, perhaps even on the same day, others are of unknown date.

The journals include many lists of birds. These are important records, but not material for easy reading and we have gathered them together in Appendix 1.

Acknowledgements

We are grateful to John Cantelo of Canterbury who provided ornithological notes based on his extensive knowledge of the birds of north-east France. We thank Edward Fenton of Day Books, who has guided us throughout, and also the readers and designers at Day Books. Others who have helped us, in a variety of ways, include the late Certhia Harden, daughter of Collingwood Ingram, the late Geoffrey Harden, Richard Harden and the extended Harden and Ingram families, Jude Skurray, Philip Eagles, Philip Hood, Tony Iveson, Jeff Jefford, Barbara and Richard Mearns, Charles Trollope, Geoff Blackburn, Tony Statham, Sarah Thomson, John and Tessa Pollard, Nick Greatorex Davies and Beatrice Winny. We also thank Brian Riddle and Christine Woodward of the Royal Aeronautical Society Library (now the National Aerospace Library), Peter Murton of the Imperial War Museum at Duxford, and Andy Presland of the Shuttleworth Aircraft Collection. Any errors are our own responsibility. EP thanks his wife Veryan, a granddaughter of Collingwood Ingram, for her support throughout the preparation of the book.

Index of birds

Index to the birds recorded by Ingram, excluding the bird lists in Appendix 1. For abbreviations, see General Index

avocet, museum specimen, 125 (illus.)
barn owl, 55, 167, 170–1; escaped squadron pet, 45; often present at St-André, 213
black redstart, 178; museum specimen, 125 (illus.); near hangars 139; singing from Amiens cathedral, 71–2; singing from house roofs, 71–2 (illus.),113, 127, 168–9
black tern, tentative identification, 226
blackbird, 16, 17, 18, 34, 40, 42, 54, 57, 64 (illus.), 75, 79, 97, 99, 102, 107, 119, 149, 171, 209; about the aerodrome, 24, 156; alarm rattle, 81; article in The Field, 179; feeding on ivy berries,173; heard from balloon, 210–11; imitated by blackcap, 177–8; nest with eggs, 175; shot by Ingram, 219 (illus.), 220; singing from chimney pots in St-Omer, 102–3, 120; song perhaps a redwing, 163;

trapped by gardener for stew, 36; weak and tame from cold, 35
blackcap, 79, 107, 120, 170, 173, 176, 207; first of spring heard by Ingram in bed, 167–8; habitat compared with garden warbler, 189; imitating other birds, 81, 177–8; Ingram searches for nest, 205; moving through château grounds, 193; song compared with garden warbler, 93–4; undisturbed by shell-fire, 182
black-headed gull, 117, 147, 148, 157, 176, 215; captured for the feather trade, 186; in Folkestone and Boulogne harbours, 16, 128, 156; sign of bad weather, 146; stuffed bird, 29
black-tailed godwit, shot by RFC officer, 113
blue tit, 17, 23, 34, 57, 149, 170, 178 (illus.), 195, 243; feeding on willow buds, 48; imitated by icterine warbler, 112; in nest boxes, 197; singing in January, 149
blue-headed wagtail (see Appendix 1, p. 269), 97, 205; about the aerodrome, 70 (illus.); flying about aimlessly, 126(x2); meeting

General index

A page with a sketch or sketches is indicated by 'illus.' or 'illusts'; 'ph.' or 'phs' indicates a page with one or more photographs. 'x2' means that there are two references on a page, and editors' notes are indicated by 'n' following the page number. Aerodromes visited by Ingram nearly all take their names from towns or villages and can be found on modern maps. Latitude and longitude are given for two which are difficult to find.

Abbeville, 147, 205; Australian Hospital at, 198

Abeele aerodrome, 20–3, 27–8, 30

AD, see Royal Flying Corps, Aircraft Depots

aerial combat, 21–2, 23, 24–5, 32, 59

Aerodromes visited by Ingram (for page references see individual aerodromes). West of Ypres: Abeele, Bailleul, Droglandt, Poperinge, Ste-Marie Cappel; around St-Omer and west towards the coast: Boisdinghem, Claimarais, Marquise, St-Omer; west of Lille: Aire, Auchel, Bruay, Chocques, Hesdigneul,

La Gorgue, Treizennes; west of Arras: Avesnes le Comte, Camblaine l'Abbé, Filescamp, Izel-lez-Hameau, Savy, Sombrin; much further west than this group but on the same latitude is St-André, near Hesdin; east of Péronne, Estrées-en-Chaussée, Longavesnes, Nurlu; west and northwest of Albert to the coast: Candas, Fienvillers, Le Crotoy, Lealvillers, Vert Galant, Warloy; south and east of Amiens: Cachy, Champien, Villers-Bretonneux; south and west of Nancy: Ochey, Tantonville

aircraft, Allied: BE2d, 46; BE2e, 54, 84, 86; Bristol Fighter, 220; FE2B, 39, 121; FE2d, 68; FE8, 22; Maurice Farman, 116; RE8, 86, 110, 116, 192, 233, 275 (illusts); SE5, 160; Sopwith, 24, 26, 31, 71, 277

aircraft, German: Ago, 120; Albatross Scout, 59; Fokker Scout, 237; Friedrichshafener, 237

Aire aerodrome, 29, 98

Airmen, killed in action, 21, 24, 32, 47, 68–9, 71, 146, 167, 245n, 249n, 252n, 255n (illus.)

Albert, 87, 120; 'what was formerly